D0847891

NEITHER ANGEL NOR BEAST

Neither
ANGEL nor BEAST

The Life and Work of
Blaise Pascal

FRANCIS X.J. COLEMAN
DEPARTMENT OF PHILOSOPHY
BOSTON UNIVERSITY

Routledge & Kegan Paul
New York and London

First published in 1986
by Routledge & Kegan Paul Inc.
in association with Methuen Inc.
29 West 35th Street, New York, NY 10001

Published in Great Britain by
Routledge & Kegan Paul plc
11 New Fetter Lane, London EC4P 4EE

Set in 10 on 12½ pt Linotron Garamond
by Inforum Ltd, Portsmouth
and printed in Great Britain
by T J Press (Padstow) Ltd
Padstow, Cornwall

Library of Congress Cataloging in Publication Data
Coleman, Francis X. J.
   Neither angel nor beast.

   Bibliography: p.
   Includes index.
   1. Pascal, Blaise, 1623–1662.   2. Philosophers—
France—Biography.   I. Title.
B1903.C65   1986   230'.2'0924 [B]   85–28271

British Library CIP data available

ISBN 0–7102–0693–3

Man is neither angel nor beast; and the misfortune is that he who would act the angel acts the beast.

L'homme n'est ni ange ni bête; et le malheur veut que qui veut faire l'ange fait le bête.

Pascal, Pensées (329)

For Mary Arms Edmonds
1881–1966
scholar, linguist and bibliophile

CONTENTS

CONTENTS

PLATES

between pages 84 and 85

Plates 1–11 Photo: Musées Nationaux, Paris

PREFACE

The research materials on which the present work is based are largely drawn from the collection of Mary Arms Edmonds, who was fascinated by the writings and historical milieu of Blaise Pascal. During her frequent trips abroad, Mrs Edmonds collected books and manuscripts connected with the history of Port-Royal and Jansenism, with the ultimate goal of writing a detailed analysis of Pascal's life and writing. Unfortunately, her untimely death prevented her from fulfilling her goal. Although I have examined Mrs Edmonds's notebooks concerning her project on Pascal, and read the marginalia in her own hand in her collection, I can make no claim that the present work is similar to the one that she had in mind, or even that it would have pleased her. I can only hope that it would have done so, since I am greatly indebted to her ardor for Pascal. Mrs Edmonds's collection of works by and pertaining to Pascal is the best and most comprehensive in the United States, and second only to the holdings of the Bibliothèque Nationale in Paris.

The collection is now in the archives of Special Collections of Boston University. I am also greatly indebted to Dr Howard B. Gotlieb, Director of Special Collections, for his vast support and patience in seeing the present work to its completion. Dr Gotlieb, the foremost curator of twentieth-century collections and memorabilia, has directed me to parts of the Pascal collection that I would otherwise have missed, and has encouraged the kind support of his own staff.

I must also thank Dr Dean S. Edmonds, Professor of Physics at Boston University, for his generous support of the present work. I have therefore dedicated it to the memory of his mother, Mary Arms Edmonds.

I should like to thank Mr John Pearson for his conscientious preparation of the manuscript.

All references to the *Pensées* are numbered following the Bibliothèque de la Pléiade edition, *Pascal: Oeuvres Complètes*, edited and annotated by Jacques Chevalier (Paris, Gallimard, 1954). The numbering of the Pléiade edition can readily be correlated with the earlier and less accurate edition by Léon Brunschvicg. E.g., *pensée* 329 is 358 in Brunschvicg's edition. (Cf. 'Table de Concordance' in the Pléiade edition.) Louis Lafuma has another system of numbering Pascal's *Pensées*. The difficulties surrounding the manuscript are discussed in the present study in 'The Supreme Apologist', below, pp. 137ff. All translations are by the author.

INTRODUCTION

I

Pascal was a mathematician, a physicist, an inventor, a theologian, a philosopher, and the greatest prose stylist in the French language. The son of a minor nobleman, Pascal was born at Clermont-Ferrand, in the Auvergne, in 1623. He began as a mathematical prodigy, developed into a student of physics, and completed his brief life in 1662 as a profound religious thinker. Pascal never attempted to base his theology on any particular philosophical system; indeed, he found skepticism to be the most convincing of all philosophies. To Pascal the long skeptical tradition beginning with the ancient Greeks provided the best arguments not only for the impossibility of constructing a philosophy, but also for subduing man's natural arrogance and for 'man's misery without God' – a theme that pervades all of Pascal's philosophical and theological works.

Although both Pascal and Descartes were Catholics, and philosophers, Descartes cannot be called a 'Catholic philosopher' in the sense that Pascal can. Descartes was not concerned with defending the tenets of the Christian faith: he simply accepted them, and proceeded to do his work in mathematics and physics. Pascal strove to show how the Christian revelation explained and justified the human condition. Descartes held that the mathematical method alone had universal applicability. As we shall see, Pascal argued that the method was limited, and that the human heart required other forms of discourse to come to terms with the basic questions of man: his nature, his purpose, and his relationship with God.

When a thinker centers so much of his thought on the primacy of God, it might be doubted whether he really is a philosopher. Without attempting to define what 'philosopher' means – and surely the shades of meaning are vast – it might be helpful to notice what some other French philosophers have said of Pascal. Henri Bergson placed Pascal on the same plane as Descartes. Jacques Chevalier called Pascal a great philosopher because he was concerned with 'the questions that a man puts to himself face to face with death.'[1] On the other hand, Emile Bréhier, the historian of philosophy, states flatly that 'Pascal is not a philosopher, but a scientist and an apologist of the Catholic religion.'[2]

Pascal was certainly not a systematic philosopher in the style of St Thomas Aquinas or Descartes. Pascal was suspicious of philosophic system-building. Nor was he a philosophical analyst, in the style of St Augustine, a philosopher who often posed questions of meaning: What do we mean by 'time'? What do we mean by 'evil'? and so on. It is fair to call Pascal an 'existential' philosopher if this term is construed in a careful way. Pascal begins with the brute existence of man in the world, his anxieties and miseries, and his yearnings for peace and love. He then proceeds to ask questions about the relationship between such a fallible creature and a God who is at least a logical possibility, and who, according to faith, has spoken through the prophets. What must put a halt to the question whether Pascal was a philosopher is an examination of the central events in his life, and of the profundity and lucidity of his writings: such an examination is the goal of the present study.

Long before the possibility of the nuclear destruction of human life was envisioned, Pascal realized the fragility of human existence more keenly than anyone since the prophet Isaiah:

> Man is but a reed, the weakest thing in nature; but he is a thinking reed. It is not required that the entire universe arm itself to crush him: a vapour, a drop of water suffices to kill him. But if the universe crushed him, man would still be more noble than that which kills him, because he knows that he is dying, and the advantage that the universe has over him, of which the universe knows nothing. (*Pensées*, 264)

Following Professor James Collins I find it helpful to describe Pascal as a 'paraphilosopher.' Although no one could deny Pascal's genius, his role in the history of modern philosophy is not central, compared, for example, to that of Descartes or Kant. Yet no one could fairly describe Pascal as 'a minor philosopher.' By a 'paraphilosopher' Collins means to point to 'a methodological term having a threefold signification. .... (1) that the source thinker has notably reshaped some methods and questions, concepts and living springs of evidence, in modern philosophy; (2) that his chief orientation and activities lead him toward some other sphere of creativity; and (3) that nevertheless a responsible historical judgment must recognize his philosophical influence and try to determine more precisely its basis and manifestations.'[3]

Like music, mathematics can be the most elegant and concise expression of the human mind. Pascal's mathematical genius found its perfect expression in the aphorism, the finely honed '*pensée.*' The maxim or aphorism is the perfect surgical instrument for piercing the pretensions of society, for lancing ponderous philosophical systems. It must be remembered that Pascal was also a social critic and '*moraliste*' – a highly reflective observer of the follies, miseries, and deceptions of mankind. When Pascal was 'in society' he quickly learned that the fashionable world was not interested in philosophical systems or elaborate arguments. Indeed, such things reeked of pedantry or provincialism. What the '*beau monde*' instinctively responded to was the sharp aphorism, the cutting '*aperçu.*' Such maxims or '*pensées*' would be remembered long after the social occasion had been forgotten. A departing guest, still searching for a witty reply, might think of some mordant response, too late, while going down the stairs: this is called '*l'esprit d'escalier.*' From Pascal's sister Gilberte we learn that her brother cut a figure at Court as if he had been brought up there. However, Pascal's love of antithesis, his verbal brilliance, transcended the clever talk of the Court and the salons. He turned his gift for the maxim to the service of God.

From the twentieth-century point of view, it might seem surprising, even wasteful, that a man of Pascal's genius in mathematics and physics should channel most of his mature energies into justifying the Christian religion. Yet in the seventeenth century, still in the throes of religious controversy, many of the finest minds devoted as much of their intellectual strength to theology and Christian apologetics as they did to physics or mathematics. After finishing his *Principia*, Sir Isaac Newton devoted most of the rest of his life to writing on theology. Again, Leibniz, who had discovered the infinitesimal calculus independently of Newton, wrote an elaborate defense of God's goodness in the face of evil, the *Theodicée.* But to explain why

Pascal felt it incumbent on himself to write the *Pensées*, the *Provincial Letters*, and other quasi-religious works, a broad account of the religious and political temper of France in the seventeenth century should provide some background.

Although describing such a broad period in history is always hazardous, it might be of help to begin with a date when many things both came together and began to fall apart. The Peace of Westphalia, concluded in 1648 between the Emperor of Germany, France, and Sweden, put an end to the Thirty Years War. The peace treaty, terminating one of the most catastrophic wars that Europe had ever known, gave the German princes of northern Europe, whose territories were also expanded by the treaty, the freedom to practise their own religion and the right to make their own foreign alliances. It also blocked the aspirations of the Habsburgs to unite Germany with the Austro-Hungarian Empire. The peace of Westphalia marked the termination of the Reformation and the Counter-Reformation, yet it could not disentangle the warp and woof of politics and religion; indeed, it is difficult to do so without unravelling the fabric of human society.

In France, and to a lesser degree in Austria, controversies still raged between Catholics and Protestants, between defenders of what Pascal and many others believed to be the 'true faith,' and what they considered to be the Protestant-inspired heresies. Pascal found himself caught in the middle. Some thinkers, such as Leibniz, were contemplating a synthesis of the divergent Christian religions under the aegis of rationalism, in the hope that a new tolerance would thereby be effected. Although Pascal could never be charged with religious intolerance, he believed that any such rationalistic synthesis of Catholicism, Lutheranism, and Calvinism was impossible, for two basic reasons: first, the premises of Catholicism and of the new Protestant sects were logically incompatible with each other; and second, reason is itself a weak and limited instrument and consequently should never engage in theological system-building or theodicy. As we shall see, Pascal relied far more heavily on 'the heart' to find his way through the forest of religious controversy. When Pascal writes of '*le coeur*' he means a number of different but related concepts, such as instinct, will, feeling, and intuition. When Pascal limits the powers of '*la raison*' – 'reason' – he should not be interpreted as being against the use of reason in the broad sense, but rather against the mean and presumptive use of *a priori* and metaphysical reasoning.

Pascal also found himself inevitably caught between the power of the Church and the power of the State. The Peace of Westphalia, instead of bringing about peace between Catholics and Protestants, simply intensified their religious and institutional differences. In both Catholic and Protestant nations tensions between Church and State had become exacerbated because the dramatic rise in nationalism had rejected, or at least weakened, loyalty to any external religious authority, such as the papacy. Tension between Church and State can be healthy; for when religion has absolute dominance over the State, a stifling rigidity sets in, as was the case in Byzantium and ancient Egypt. Conversely, when the Church is simply a puppet of the State totalitarianism knows no bounds: such has been the history of various Latin American régimes. But in seventeenth-century France the tensions between Church and State were heightened by unique factors. Louis XIV, basing his own authority on divine right, was the most resourceful and ambitious monarch of his time. The Anglican Church had already separated from Rome; although the Gallican Church would never separate, the fear of that possibility strengthened Louis XIV's hand in confrontation with Rome.

With her clerical immunities and vast land-holdings, the Catholic Church in France was immensely wealthy. The Church became a natural object of envy for a monarch trying to finance his wars. Nonetheless, Louis XIV's predilection for Catholic orthodoxy made the Church into one of his chief supports. His staunch Catholicism also made him intolerant of the Protestants in his realm, and also of the new Catholic sect that came to be called the Jansenists. Pascal was strongly attracted to the teachings of Jansenism – a topic that will be treated at length later in the book. France was a deeply Catholic nation in the seventeenth century, with the teachings of the Church permeating all classes of society. Yet the respect, and it is not an exaggeration to say love, for Louis XIV was also extraordinary. Inevitably, when the pope and the '*Roi Soleil*' had differences, those who maintained both loyalties would be caught in the middle. And differences did occur, for example over the status accorded to the papal nuncio, and again over the Jansenists.

It is difficult to imagine the unequalled awe with which Louis XIV's subjects regarded their monarch. He considered kings, queens, and royal princes as beings of a higher order than other humans; nonetheless he treated persons of all ranks with impeccable politeness, and would address a chambermaid as '*Madame*.' The king often spoke of God as a sort of higher king, but still a fellow ruler. On hearing the news of the French defeat at Malplaquet, in 1709, Louis XIV asked: 'How could God do this to me, after all I have done for Him?' Many such comments are recorded by the great memorialist, the duc de Saint-Simon.

Pascal was twenty years of age when Louis XIV became king of France. It was to be the longest reign that Europe has ever known, from 1643 to 1715. As a young man Pascal had experienced the civil war known as the Fronde (1648–53) when the lords and the Princes of the Blood had revolted against the crown. The nobility had primarily wanted to strengthen their power against the monarchy, and went so far as to appeal to the enemy Spain for help. Louis XIV neither forgave nor forgot the dissidence of the nobility; indeed, he constructed the château of Versailles to keep the nobility under his own roof for constant surveillance. Instead he turned to the minor nobility, who had remained faithful to the crown, and to the bougeoisie, for the management of his vast bureaucracy. Among these civil servants was Pascal's father, Etienne Pascal.

Louis XIV presented the brief for the State in characteristically olympian terms: 'Kings are absolute *seigneurs*, and from their nature have full and free disposal of all property both secular and ecclesiastical, to use it as wise dispensers, that is to say, in accordance with the requirements of their State . . . those mysterious names, the Franchises and Liberties of the Church . . . have equal reference to all the faithful whether they be laymen or tonsured, who are equally sons of this common Mother; but . . . they exempt neither the one nor the other from subjection to the Sovereign, to whom the Gospel itself precisely enjoins that they should submit themselves.'[4] Louis XIV is obviously referring to St Matthew 22:21: 'Render therefore unto Caesar the things which are Caesar's; and unto God the things that are God's.' The pope – the '*servitus servitorum*' or 'servant of servants' – and the 'Sun King' both posited their authority on the same God and on the same scriptural tradition. Although the papacy and the monarchy needed each other, their aims sometimes diverged. In France Gallicanism marked the major source of divergence.

Gallicanism may be described as an expression of French nationalism within the peripheries of Catholic teaching and tradition, and as a challenge to ultramontanism. The latter term also needs defining in the seventeenth-century context: literally, 'ultramontanism' means 'beyond the mountains,' i.e., the Alps, and implies support of papal authority and even infallibility. 'Gallicanism,' a word which was not used before 1648, could serve a number of causes. The king could invoke it to argue that, because his power was given directly from God, he was in charge of all property in the State, including that of the Church. The Faculty of Theology at Paris appealed to Gallicanism to stress the priority of councils over papal pronouncements. And the *Parlements* tried to present historical arguments for Gallicanism by citing the supremacy of such emperors as Constantine and Charlemagne over the Bishop of Rome.

Many French Catholics were not, however, Gallican in their learning, but were strong supporters of the papacy, for example the families of the old aristocracy who wished to offset the power of the monarch. The Franciscans, and other mendicant orders, were also ultramontanists. More important, the Jesuits – whose views on morality and theological argument would be the target of Pascal's *Provincial Letters* – supported papal infallibility in matters of faith and morals, with papal politics trailing not far behind.

Nothing is more important in assessing the character of an age than an understanding of the modes of education prevalent at the time. In seventeenth-century France the boys from the leading French families – from the Dauphin to Descartes – were taught by the Jesuits. The Jesuits, who have from the inception of their order taken a special vow of loyalty to the pope, were also the confessors to many of the leading families of the kingdom, including Louis XIV himself.[5] In time, and especially at the Court of Versailles, Jansenism too would be associated with ultramontane causes.

As the conflict between Church and State progressed in France, Pope Innocent X began to show that the papacy was less in need of Louis XIV's support than conversely. By 1681 Louis expressed fears of being excommunicated, in part because of the fiscal demands that he had placed on the Church, and in part because of his attempt to manipulate ultramontane bishops and religious. With the support of

Spain and Austria behind him, Innocent X felt confident that he could allow the factions in the French Church to fight it out among themselves, and then intervene and reestablish order without appealing to Louis XIV for support.

By 1681 the French Assembly had decided formally to delimit papal authority, and drafted what are called the Four Articles. Briefly stated, these recapitulated the tensions between Church and State as Pascal would have felt them, although he was himself an ultramontanist:[6] (1) kings are not subject to ecclesiastical authority in matters concerning the State; (2) decisions of the councils of the Church are more binding than the authority of the pope; (3) traditions of the Gallican Church must be respected and conformed to by the pope; and (4) although the pope's authority is preponderant, his authority is not binding without the assent of the universal Church. Innocent X denounced the Four Articles. Division grew among the clergy of France and in the College of Cardinals.

Although Louis XIV's religious convictions may be described as in part a matter of decorum and style, rather than of strong devotion, he was convinced that national cohesion and royal authority demanded allegiance to one confession: and he believed, in spite of the many tensions, that it must be Roman Catholic. The king believed that pluralism in religious matters would lead to nothing but disruption. He therefore embarked upon a policy of suppressing Protestantism thoughout his realm. To show himself more Catholic than the pope in his suppression of heresy, Louis acted with consummate consistency in his self-conceived role of 'Sun King' and his passion for '*gloire*' and grandeur.

Louis's efforts to extinguish heresy did not meet with the success he had hoped for. The persecution and subsequent emigration of the Huguenots – there were perhaps as many as 200,000 – hurt the economy and jeopardized the future of France. In an attempt to root out Jansenism, Port-Royal was destroyed, but Jansenism was to return in various guises in the eighteenth century. Louis's religious zeal failed to impress the pope, and Innocent X frowned on the king's violent methods.

Jansenist thought and writings will be covered in detail later, in the section on the *Provincial Letters*, but it may be useful to sketch in here the history of Port-Royal and to mention some of the most

INTRODUCTION

prominent Jansenists connected with it.

Notable among them were the numerous and gifted Arnauld family. Antoine Arnauld the elder (1560–1619) was a lawyer and leader of the Paris bar who in 1594 accused the Jesuits of disloyalty to Henry IV. Of his twenty children several were to fight the Jesuits. Only two, the eldest son and daughter, married. Of the others, a number joined the Church, some becoming leading Jansenists.

The family became linked with Port-Royal des Champs, a Cistercian convent founded in 1204 near Versailles, southwest of Paris, when the gifted and precocious second daughter, Angélique (1591–1661), became abbess in 1602, at the age of eleven (her father having falsified her date of birth). In 1609 Angélique decided to reform the somewhat lax discipline according to the strict rule of St Bernard, which included sequestration (never leaving the convent), long periods of silence, extensive meditation, and rigorous asceticism. These reforms were part of a general Catholic reformation of religious life that swept through France in the seventeenth century. Port-Royal now attracted so many young women wishing to make religious vows that new buildings had to be constructed. Angélique's sister Agnès and her mother soon joined the convent. Penitents, among them the duchesse de Longueville (sister of the Prince de Condé and the guiding Spirit of the Fronde), made retreats there, and many noble families subsidized the convent. The marshy surroundings proved unhealthy, and in 1625 Angélique's mother had constructed at her own expense a convent in the Faubourg Saint-Jacques in Paris. The nuns moved to Port-Royal de Paris in 1626. In 1630 Agnès Arnauld succeeded her sister as abbess, but Mère Angélique remained extremely influential at Port-Royal, and was abbess again in 1642–54.

Mère Angélique was the spiritual director of various important lay persons, including the queen of Poland, with whom she corresponded. Mère Angélique herself was first directed by St Francis de Sales, and then in 1633 she came under the influence of Jean Duvergier de Hauranne, abbot of Saint-Cyran. Saint-Cyran was a friend of Cornelius Jansen, whose tenets he popularized, and he introduced Jansenism to Port-Royal, where he became spiritual director in 1634. Spiritual directors had always been part of Catholic religious life, but under Jansenism, with its emphasis on spiritual interiority and strict examination of one's conscience, the spiritual director assumed even greater importance.

Saint-Cyran was a close friend of Cardinal de Bérulle and an early critic of the Jesuits. As a leading Jansenist he became an object of calumny to the Jesuits. On the death of Cardinal de Bérulle, Saint-Cyran became the head of the *'parti dévôt'* – fundamentalist Catholics with Jansenist leanings, who also opposed the political policies of the chief minister, Cardinal Richelieu. At Port-Royal Saint-Cyran became the spiritual director of many members of the French aristocracy, who were also opposed to Richelieu's increasingly successful attempt to centralize all power in the monarchy. Saint-Cyran's *Lettres chrétiennes et spirituelles* ('Christian and Spiritual Letters') gained him an enormous following, and made him the first leading spokesman for Jansenism. Richelieu had Saint-Cyran imprisoned in the donjon of Vincennes in 1638, and he was only released on Richelieu's death in 1643. Regarded as a saint by many, Saint-Cyran emerged from prison an exhausted man, and died two months later.

After Saint Cyran's death Antoine Arnauld (1612–92) became the leader of the Jansenist cause. The younger brother of Mère Angélique, he was the twentieth and youngest child of Antoine Arnauld the elder, and the most distinguished member of that gifted family. He was ordained priest and earned a doctorate in theology in 1643. One of the most brilliant thinkers of his time, known as *'le grand Arnauld,'* he was active in philosophical controversies with Descartes and Malebranche. His *De la fréquente communion* (1642), which made the ideas of Jansen accessible to a wide public, was so controversial that he was forced to go into hiding and was unable to appear in public in Paris for twenty years. With Pierre Nicole he wrote *La logique, ou l'art de penser* (1662), known as the *Port-Royal Logic*, a handbook on how to think clearly and consecutively, following Cartesian rather than Aristotelian principles, and one of the best expressions of Jansenist thought. In 1656 Pascal wrote the first of the *Provincial Letters* in defense of Arnauld, who was nevertheless stripped of his doctorate by the Sorbonne. An ardent opponent of the Jesuits, he was ultimately obliged to flee the country, and died in exile.

Very different from the fiery Arnauld were the *'Solitaires'*, gentlemen scholars and teachers who espoused the tenets of Jansenism and lived celibate and quasi-hermitical lives in the Granges, or outbuildings, of Port-Royal des Champs without, however, having to belong to a religious order. Between 1651 and 1652 the Petites Ecoles were constructed for teaching the young sons of the nobility, or boys who were exceptionally gifted. Pascal was to write for the pupils. Jean Racine received his early education at Port-Royal.

The earliest of the 'Solitaires' was Antoine Le Maître (the son of the older Arnauld daughter), who gave up a brilliant career in the law. He was later joined by other hermits, including his younger brother, Louis-Isaac Le Maître de Saci (or Sacy), who took holy orders and later became Pascal's spiritual director. In 1646 they were joined by their uncle, Robert Arnauld d'Andilly (the oldest son of Arnauld the elder), who had held various important offices at Court where he had been an especial favourite of the queen regent, Anne of Austria. His five daughters took the veil at Port-Royal and one later became abbess, and one of his sons also joined the 'Solitaires'.

Pascal had died some twenty-four years before the publication of Fontenelle's influential work, *Entretiens sur la pluralité des mondes* (1686), but the ideas which it contained would have been familiar to him, even if some of the conclusions would have appeared extreme. Certainly the salon exposition of philosophical theses would have been part of Pascal's own milieu:

> 'I perceive,' said the Countess, 'that philosophy is now become very mechanical.' 'So mechanical,' I replied, 'that I fear we shall quickly be ashamed of it. The philosophers will have the world to be in great, what a watch is in little; and that means that it is very regular and depends solely upon the just disposition of the various parts of the movement. But I beg of you, Madam, had you not previously held a more sublime conception of the Universe?'

The purely naturalistic and mechanical interpretation of the cosmos, and the supernatural and providential conception, were magnetic forces between which Pascal found himself pulled. He knew the sheer delight in performing scientific experiments – such as his confirmation of Torricelli's work on the vacuum – but he also felt the attractions of prayer and the mysteries of the Christian religion. Never a compartmentalist, Pascal hoped to wed both the scientific and the religious into some form of higher marriage.

The model of explanation to which Fontenelle was referring, the 'mechanical' explanation, was based solely upon atoms in collision with each other, their cohesions and their eddying, and their subsequent description by mathematical law. Such was 'philosophical explanation,' held to be the true and accurate account of events. All other explanations were either metaphorical, literary, or superstitious; however, if they had acquired sufficient academic weight, they were 'Aristotelian' or 'scholastic.' The disdain with which Aristotelianism and scholasticism were commonly regarded by intellectuals of Pascal's era might be compared to the disdain of early chemists for alchemists, or of astronomers for astrologers. Pascal politely disclaims knowing 'scholastic philosophy,' or having read Aristotle. In England in the seventeenth century, writers as diverse as Bacon, Hobbes, Milton, and Browne charged that scholastic philosophy only set up barriers to new and experimental thought. In France, Montaigne and Descartes complained of the aridity of the last phases of scholasticism, although acknowledging the brilliance of the synthesis of St Thomas Aquinas in the thirteenth century. The seventeenth-century mind had begun to look at the great architectural masterpieces of the Gothic period as structures which they could still enter, but to which they could add nothing. The human mind tends to prefer destruction to stiflement. The discoveries and theories of Galileo, Copernicus, and later of Newton, left seventeenth-century intellectuals in a mood for destroying the vestiges of the Middle Ages. But with the new independence and emphasis upon science went the apprehension, shared by both the Catholic Church and the Protestants, that the gates were being opened to deism or atheism.

Pascal was again caught between opposing forces. Many of his friends were *'libertins'* – people who held unusual if not pointedly opposing views about God, the immortality of the soul, and the purpose of human life.[7] Pascal felt that the rising secularism would force him to make a decision between Church and State, for he knew that the two were no longer pillars supporting the vault of the same social edifice. Pascal did not want to leave his laboratory, so to speak, nor did he want to leave his chapel. His attempt to bring together these two attitudes of mind, these two methods, is basically the theme of the present study of Pascal.

Throughout this introduction to the life and thought of Pascal, I have referred to the recurrent use of antithesis in Pascal's literary style and philosophical thought. The same structural analysis may be used to understand Pascal's life.

To understand one's own life is difficult: to understand the life of someone else might be less difficult, for fewer temptations to misrepresentation usually arise. But on balance, both biography and autobiography present the same difficulties: the temptation to gloss over the unpleasantnesses, or to dramatize them; to plead a special cause; or to impose a narrative line when there is none. Understanding and describing are difficult activities, for one may understand without being able to describe, and describe – as one knows from the popular press – without understanding. What often helps in both description and understanding is reliance on a structure. Throughout this study I have implicitly, sometimes explicitly, relied on the structure of the oxymoron.

Claims concerning uniqueness are fraught with danger, for they are either so general as to be irrefutable, or so particular as to be readily falsified. Uniqueness, by definition, admits of no degrees: it is either present or not. The thesis behind this study of Blaise Pascal is that he was unique: his life, literary style, and philosophical thought are based on one rhetorical figure, oxymoron.

'Oxymoron' is a composite of two Greek words, the one meaning 'sharp' and the other meaning 'dull, or 'foolish.' An oxymoron is a figure by which contradictory or startling terms are brought together in the hope of giving point to a statement, and to launch the reader, or listener, into a transcendent realm that alters the superficial meaning of the terms. It is a daring figure, sometimes a dazzling one, yet it can fall, like an acrobat, quite flat.

The oxymoron is but one of dozens of tropes, or rhetorical devices, that constituted the Greco-Roman rhetoric, now largely fallen into neglect, and others have only an antiquarian interest; their names are sonorous and awesome: anaphora, epanalepsis, epanastrophe, prolepsis, and so forth. Aristotle gives an exhaustive inventory in his *Rhetoric* and *Poetics*. These figures abound in classical Greek and Roman writers. In English the most seriously afflicted author was John Lyly, who used at least one such trope in every sentence he wrote; Lyly was especially fond of combining oxymoron with alliteration. But while today Lyly can be read only for his giddy quaintness, Bacon's *Essays*, which abound in rhetorical figures, remain serious reading. Almost every trope can be found somewhere in Shakespeare, whose best-known oxymorons occur in *Romeo and Juliet*. Romeo says:

> Here's much to do with hate, but more with love.
> Why, then, O brawling love! O loving hate!
> O any thing, of nothing first create!
> O heavy lightness! serious vanity!
> Mis-shapen chaos of well-seeming forms!
> Feather of lead, bright smoke, cold fire, sick health!
> Still-waking sleep, that is not what it is!
> This love feel I, that no love in this.
> Dost thou not laugh?
>
> (Act I, Sc. I, 169–77)

Benvolio replies: 'No, coz, I rather weep.'

These lines contain some fifteen oxymorons, some highly compressed, such as 'O loving hate!' 'cold fire, sick health!' and others loosely conjoined, such as the last exchange – 'Dost thou not laugh?' 'No, coz, I rather weep.'

In French literature, rhetorical devices permeate the works of Rabelais, Montaigne, and Corneille; they become far less frequent in the pure and olympian Racine. Descartes, the first master of classical French prose, allows himself only an occasional nip of simile, and always of the lowest proof. In the *Discours de la méthode*, for example, Descartes compares holding to a single moral course to following a sole direction when lost in the woods. Descartes will have none of the heady rhetorical brew of earlier French writers. As for Pascal, other than oxymoron, the only rhetorical devices that he employs are ellipsis, litotes or understatement, an occasional metaphor, and a few others. Pascal's metaphors are always as lucid and traditional as those of Descartes:

> Some vices belong to us only by means of others, and these, like branches, fall on removal of the trunk.[8]

> Man is but a reed, the weakest thing in nature; but he is a thinking reed.[9]

> One believes one is playing on an ordinary organ when playing on man. It is true that men are organs, but odd, changeable, variable (with pipes

not arranged in proper order. Those who know how to play solely on ordinary organs) will not produce harmonies on these. One must know where [the keys] are.[10]

The last metaphor is among the most elaborate to be found in Pascal, and certainly the most original. From the inventor of the computer – his *'machine d'arithmétique'* – it is also the most far-seeing. Elsewhere in the *Pensées* Pascal draws a comparison between the human mind and the *'automate'*:

> For we must not misconceive ourselves: we are as much automatic as intellectual; hence it follows that the instrument by which conviction is attained is not made by demonstration alone. So few things are demonstrated! Proofs convince only the mind.[11]

Just as a computer can print out all the permutations and commutations of a given model, so Pascal translated almost all of his experience through the oxymoron. It is therefore appropriate to look more closely at the grammar of this figure. It is essentially a form of rhetorical antithesis, an instance of which is called antitheton. An oxymoron brings together a thesis and an antithesis, something positive and something negative: what is meant and what is not meant. Superficially a rhetorical antithesis appears contradictory, a flagrant denial of the supreme principle of thought, the law of non-contradiction. But on scrutiny, in the union of opposites – called antisyzgy – a new balance, a greater insight is attained. Behind the figure lies a philosophy: out of the conflict of opposites a new transcendence is generated.

Oxymoron has always dwelled in poetry, and so long as poetry endures, oxymoron will have a place to dwell. Among twentieth-century poets making occasional use of the figure is T.S. Eliot. In 'Burnt Norton,' from *Four Quartets*, for example, he gives a graphic oxymoron:

> Garlic and sapphires in the mud
> Clot the bedded axle-tree.

Oxymoron was employed by the earliest apologists of Christianity. Quintus Septimius Tertullian (*c.* 155–225), who was converted at the age of thirty-three, was the first Christian theologian to write in

Latin. Both his literary style and his thought are rhapsodies on the figure. In *De Carne Christi* (*Concerning the Flesh of Christ*) Tertullian writes:

> It is to be believed because it is absurd.[12]

and,

> It is certain because it is impossible.[13]

This statement is sometimes called 'Tertullian's rule of faith' and is sometimes rendered as *Credo quia Impossibile* – I believe because it is impossible. It is an angular proposition, based on an argument from Aristotle's *Rhetoric*.[14] After a general discussion of the varieties of the possible and the impossible, and the grounds for belief and disbelief, Aristotle turns to particular modes of obtaining someone's assent. An example of what one wants to show is the readiest method, but parable, fable, and maxim can also be useful. Aristotle is especially interested in the force of enthymene as a mode of persuasion. An enthymene is an argument, especially a syllogism, in which one of the propositions, usually a premise, is not explicitly stated. Enthymene works when the reader or hearer can fill in the gap and supply the missing proposition, which is occasionally the conclusion itself. Aristotle develops an argument that it is likely that unlikely things should happen.

> All the more reason for believing more strongly; in effect one admits only what exists truly or what is likely; the fact in question, being neither believable nor likely, has chances of being true, for it is not by its true or possible character that it so appears.[15]

Tertullian's belief in the Incarnation is in part based on the sheer unlikelihood that it happened. It could be argued that Christianity itself is rooted in a theological oxymoron: Jesus was both man and God, fully human and fully divine. Years of heresies were spent in trying to resolve the oxymoron, some emphasizing the divine element at the price of the human, others construing the divine allegorically and the human element literally. Mystical theology often revelled in the grand antithesis of the contradiction. By the seventeenth century, when Pascal became an apologist for the Christian religion, most of the logically possible variations on the Incarnation had been composed. As a deeply religious man, and a sincere Catholic, Pascal centered his apologetics on the central 'folly' of Christianity.

II

T.S. Eliot wrote an admirable introduction to an edition of Pascal's *Pensées*.[16] To place the present study in better perspective, the first paragraph should be quoted in full:

> It might seem that about Blaise Pascal, and about two works on which his fame is founded, everything that there is to say has been said. The details of his life are as fully known as we can expect to know them; his mathematical and physical discoveries have been treated many times; his religious sentiment and his theological views have been discussed again and again; and his prose style has been analyzed by French critics down to the finest particular. But Pascal is one of those writers who will be and who must be studied afresh by men in every generation. It is not he who changes, but we who change. It is not our knowledge of him that increases, but our world that alters and our attitudes towards it. The history of human opinions of Pascal and of men of his stature is a part of the history of humanity. That indicates his permanent importance.

Eliot's statement echoes two of Pascal's *'pensées'* in the section entitled 'Misère de l'homme':

> Le temps guérit les douleurs et les querelles, parce qu'on change, on n'est plus la même personne. Ni l'offensant, ni l'offensé, ne sont plus eux-mêmes. C'est comme un peuple qu'on a irrité, et qu'on reverrait après deux générations. Ce sont encore les Français, mais non les mêmes. (112)

> Il n'aime plus cette personne qu'il aimait il y a dix ans. Je crois bien: elle n'est plus la même, ni lui non plus. Il était jeune et elle aussi; elle est tout autre. Il l'aimerait peut-être encore telle qu'elle était alors. (113)

Had Proust chosen a quotation to introduce *A la recherche du temps perdu*, he could not have chosen anything more appropriate:

Time heals pains and quarrels, because one changes and is no longer the same person. Neither the offender nor the offended are any longer the same. It is like people that one has irritated and that one sees again after two generations. They are still Frenchmen, but not the same.

He no longer loves this person whom he loved ten years ago. I quite understand: she is no longer the same, nor is he. Once he was young, and so was she, though now quite different. He might love her still if she were as she used to be.

The present study of Pascal therefore makes no claim to being definitive, for that would either imply the paucity of its subject or betoken the pretensions of its author. The thesis of the study is simple: Pascal's life, style, and thought may be best interpreted as variations on a figure of rhetoric. The details and ramifications of the thesis form the body of this work. What follows are brief illustrations of the thesis, for the most part presented as preliminary documents of the case.

1 LIFE

In 1624, a year after his birth, Blaise Pascal fell desperately ill. A witch was believed to have cast a spell on him. Blaise could not bear to see his mother and father approach him together, though he ceased crying when they came to him separately. He also went into convulsions when he saw water being poured from one container into another. In 1626 his mother died. Blaise was to be educated solely by his father. The family moved to Paris in 1631.

While working on his *machine arithmétique*, or calculator, Pascal was introduced to disciples of the new religious movement which would later be known as Jansenism. What is called Pascal's 'first conversion' occurred in 1646. Pascal's mind was occupied equally with his mathematical research and his religious meditations. While attempting to perfect his calculating machine, Pascal read the spiritual works of Saint-Cyran and Arnauld, the two leading exponents of Jansenism. In 1646, assisted by his father and others, Pascal repeated Torricelli's experiments on the vacuum. Orthodoxy had held that nature abhors a vacuum; Pascal showed again that nature does not at all mind a vacuum. A year later Pascal engaged in his first religious controversy, championing the cause of faith against a new rationalist tendency in the Church.

In 1647 Descartes twice visited Pascal in Paris. Although Pascal was flattered by the visit, he would comment later, according to his sister Gilberte: 'I cannot forgive Descartes: in his entire philosophy he would like to do without God; but he could not help allowing him a flick of the fingers to set the world in motion; after that Descartes had no more use for God.' In 1649, during the troubles of the Fronde, the Pascal family returned to Clermont-Ferrand. Pascal's younger sister wanted to enter the austere convent of Port-Royal. Both Pascal and his father vigorously opposed it. In 1651 Pascal's father died. Pascal's life took a new turn: he continued his scientific research but began consorting with the *beau monde*. 1652 marks the beginning of Pascal's so-called 'worldly period.'

By 1652 Pascal's physical health had badly deteriorated, though his mental life showed signs of even greater brilliance. Queen Christina of Sweden asked to see a copy of the calculating machine. Pascal had a model sent to her with a letter in which he sketched out his thesis concerning the orders of reality. Pascal wrote that the intellectual order outstrips the physical order. Later he would write that the order of charity infinitely surpasses the intellectual order.

In 1653 Pascal took a trip through Poitou with some of his elegant friends, all of them atheists or agnostics. By September of the following year Pascal conceived a violent aversion to the so-called '*libertins*.' Pascal journeyed to Port-Royal des Champs, and confessed to his sister that his life was undergoing a radical change. In November 1654 he experienced a mystical conversion. His account, the 'Mémorial,' written on parchment, Pascal sewed inside the lining of his doublet. Whenever he bought a new doublet, he would sew the parchment into the lining. The 'Mémorial' begins with 'God of Abraham, God of Isaac, God of Jacob, not the God of philosophers or of scientists.'

In October 1654, while out for a drive in his four-horse carriage, near the bridge of Neuilly, Pascal was almost killed. Near a place without a barrier along the Seine, the first two horses took fright and plunged into the river, but the carriage remained on the bank. Years later, Voltaire, the greatest scoffer of all time, would comment to Condorcet: 'Mon ami, ne vous lassez point de répéter que, depuis l'accident du Pont de Neuilly, le cerveau de Pascal était dérangé' ('My friend, never weary saying that since the accident on the Neuilly Bridge, Pascal's brain was damaged!').

In 1656 Pascal published the first of his *Provincial Letters*; the theme throughout is the antithesis between the old Augustinian morality and the new, relaxed morality of the casuists. In the same year the miracle of the Holy Thorn occurred. 'Holy Thorn' is oxymoronic, like 'Crown of Thorns.' Pascal's niece (not his sister, as T. S. Eliot mistakenly states in his Introduction) had been suffering from an eye infection that not even the best doctors of Paris could cure. Pascal was impressed by the cure effected by the relic, as was Louis XIV and his Court, enemies of Port-Royal and the Jansenists. In 1657 Pascal composed 'Ecrits sur la grâce' and 'Eléments de géométrie,' both intended for the pupils of Port-Royal. In the same year he began his project for a defense of Christianity, the notes for which have come to us as the *Pensées*. Nonetheless, his mathematical interests remained as intense as ever; he published a challenge to the mathematicians of Europe to solve the problem of the cycloid. Characteristically, Pascal believed that he already had the answer.

By 1659 Pascal's health had become very much worse. He had given away most of his fortune to the poor, and had ordered his tapestries and library to be sold. The stables had long since been empty. During his brief worldly period, Pascal had enjoyed dashing about Paris and the countryside in his carriage. In 1659, when he could walk at all, he went on foot. Even his table abruptly altered from gourmet to ascetic. In 1660 Pascal wrote 'Prière pour le bon usage des maladies.'

By 1661 the power of the monarchy and of Rome had united against Port-Royal and the Jansenists. It had become increasingly clear that the political and religious tensions between the two opposing forces could no longer be sustained. Having withdrawn from the controversy, Pascal died in 1662.

In 1709 Louis XIV ordered the total destruction of Port-Royal des Champs, from chapel to convent. Even the cemetery was dug up. All that stands today is the dovecot.

2 THOUGHT

Pascal looked profoundly into being: his own being, the being of others, the being of God. Pascal found the self *'haïssible'* – 'odious' –

and the being of others '*misérable.*' Only God's being was lovable. Already convinced of a radical antithesis between the transcendent and the secular, Pascal divided his method of exposition into two diametrically opposed routes, the one based on reason and geometry, and the other based on will and rhetoric. Pascal's aesthetics is an intricate orchestration of both sources of awareness.

Pascal held that reason is discursive and meretricious, simply because it can be bent to any purpose. The heart, which he sometimes calls '*intelligence,*' is a source of certainty, in the sense that one 'just knows' that space is three-dimensional or that numbers are infinite. Pascal contrasts the faith of the simple, who 'know in their heart' that God exists, with the abstruse and labyrinthian arguments of the philosophers, who employ reason.

Pascal's thought is ultimately based on the oxymoron of the infinite and the finite, with man as the epitome of the two extremes: limited in the brevity of his life, yet possessed of eternal longings; a speck in a vast cosmos; caught between misery and grandeur.

> What a chimera then is man! What a novelty! What a monster, what a chaos, what a contradiction, what a prodigy! Judge of all things, imbecile worm of the earth; depository of truth, a sink of uncertainty and error; the pride and the rubbish of the universe!
> Who will unravel this tangled mess?[17]

This study makes no pretension of unravelling the tangle of contradictions that is man, but is only an invitation to interpret the tangled life of Pascal, and the entanglement of his style and thought, in the light of a single rhetorical figure. I have no religious or ideological axe to grind, nor any 'literary theory' to champion, for literary theory is as illusory as pure literature. A broader thesis may perhaps emerge from this study, namely, whether literature and much of philosophy should be studied as modes of rhetoric. Rhetoric is the most ancient of man's arts and sciences, encompassing all forms of persuasive discourse. Man could be defined as the persuading animal: Pascal may be described as one of the most original persuaders in human thought.

Part One
Scenes from the Life of Pascal

1
A SISTER'S BIOGRAPHY

There is no reason to suppose that a member of one's own family should record a more accurate or benevolent account of one's life than some impartial spectator of the same period or in some following century. Some of the most rancorous and warped biographies have been written by members of the same family, from the royal houses of Europe to the would-be royal houses of Hollywood. Yet the reasons for turning first to the biography of Pascal written by his sister Gilberte Périer militate against any predisposition against families writing about families. First, Gilberte, who was born in 1620, and was therefore the oldest of Pascal's three sisters, had never been separated from him for any length of time. Surely such first-hand observation cannot be called into doubt. Second, Gilberte had none of the intellectual ambitions of her brother and, it seems evident, none of his high religious aspirations. Gilberte was married on 15 April, 1641, to her cousin Florian Périer, counsellor of the king at Clermont-Ferrand; together they had produced many children by the time that she wrote her brief biography. There are no grounds for rivalry or resentment in Gilberte's account. There is even a touch of pride when she recounts how her brother was so impatient while their father was trying to explain some deduction in Euclid's *Geometry*. Gilberte even implies that her brother Blaise had discovered the first principles of geometry by the age of twelve. Given the many examples of mathematical precocity, her account is not to be dismissed out of hand. Third, there is the incontestable fact that posterity would have had none of the manuscripts of the *Pensées*, or others of Pascal's works, if the piety of the Périer family had not considered his writings in some sense sacred, and had kept every scrap. Although many French seventeenth-century manuscripts have vanished, the holographs of Pascal's *Pensées*, the 'Mémorial,' the 'Mystère de Jésus,' and other fragments are preserved in the Bibliothèque Nationale in Paris, thanks to the devotion of his sister Gilberte and her family. Finally, there is the evidence of style: Gilberte writes with a simplicity, a frankness, an aloof lovingness that brings to mind Céleste Albaret's memoir of Marcel Proust. Styles can be elaborate and involuted, like Proust's, or stark and unadorned, like Madame de La Fayette's. But a style should never break down under scrutiny: and Gilberte Périer's does not.

Biography in the seventeenth century had not been established as a distinct or important literary genre. To be sure, the tradition established by Plutarch's *Lives* continued, but these lives were almost without exception those of kings, exalted nobility, or princes of the Church. The other tradition of biography, beginning in the earliest years of Christianity, was hagiography, and this was actively sustained, and even subsidized, by the Catholic Church in the seventeenth century. Pascal's life obviously falls into none of these categories: lives of philosophers and scientists, or *savants*, were not deemed important enough to be written about. And with a few exceptions, notably Franz Hals's portrait of Descartes, scientists were not thought worthy of having their portrait painted. Although it was a considerable expense to commission a portrait, the nobility and the Church always found it within their means to have one of their own represented in oils or in an engraving. We possess no authentic portrait of Blaise Pascal, for none was made in his lifetime; even the so-called portrait by Philippe de Champaigne is highly dubious. The reason for this absence is not hard to find: Pascal and his family, and those of the same theological and spiritual inclinations, would have considered it a grave fault, an extreme form of vanity, perhaps even a mortal sin, to sit for their portrait. It would be a violation of the fundamental Christian virtue of humility to presume that one's own physiognomy should be worthy of being objectified onto a canvas and transmitted to posterity. Biography is nonetheless a form of portraiture, and the mere fact that Gilberte Périer painted it, albeit in words, makes her portrait of her brother all the more remarkable. Brief by modern standards (only thirty-two pages in the Pléiade edition) the biography is a milestone for its time.

Entitled 'La Vie de Monsieur Pascal,' with the authorship given as 'écrite par Madame Périer, sa soeur,' the work begins with a few facts that none but the rarest biographies can pass over without notice: when, where, and from whom their subject was born. 'My brother was born in Clermont' (now called Clermont-Ferrand), 'the nineteenth day of June, in the year 1623. My father's name was Etienne Pascal, president of tax levies, and my mother's name was Antoinette Bégon.' In French, Etienne Pascal's title was *'président à la Cour des Aides'*; under the old monarchy *aides* would have meant the subsidies or benevolences levied for state purposes. Pascal's father was therefore part of the vast bureaucracy of Louis XIV's financial system, ensuring that taxes, or in the case of the Church voluntary 'benevolences,' were forthcoming. The city of Clermont-Ferrand (382 kilometers south of Paris) had once been the capital of the Auvergne. With both Gothic and Renaissance buildings, it was the city in which Pope Urban II convoked a council at which Peter the Hermit preached, and during which the First Crusade was decided upon. Blaise Pascal was born in the virtual womb of the Crusades, those wars against the Muslims to recover the Holy Land. In Pascal's mind, Crusades became wars against the atheist, the skeptic, the materialist, the pyrrhonist, the unconverted, and finally against anyone who believed that science was or would ever be capable of giving the answer to the meaning of man's existence.

The details of Gilberte Pascal's biography might be better understood with some background details. In the seventeenth century Clermont-Ferrand was an unimportant town, both culturally and economically, of about 9,000 inhabitants. The Pascal family lived in a house in the rue des Grads (from the Latin *gradus*, or 'degrees') close to the cathedral. It was an old medieval townhouse, with thick walls and only a few windows. A week after his birth, Pascal was baptized in his parish church, Saint-Pierre, and given the first name of Blaise, which was common in his family. The Pascal family can be traced to a nearby village, Cournon. The family had included some rich merchants. The Pascals had risen on the social scale around 1580 when Martin Pascal married Marguerite Pascal de Mons, who belonged to a family ennobled by Louis XI in 1480. Martin Pascal became secretary to the wife of Henry III, Queen Louise of Lorraine, and was finally in charge of the king's finances for the region of Riom, once the capital of the dukes of Auvergne. Martin Pascal had seven children, the eldest being Blaise Pascal's father, Etienne (1588–1651). Etienne studied law in Paris, returned to Clermont in 1610, and in 1624 became second president of the Cour des Aides, thereby becoming a member of the lower nobility, the '*noblesse de la Robe*.' Although he had had to pay some 30,000 old francs (or livres as they were then called) Etienne's title of *chevalier* could be transmitted to his descendants, and he himself was entitled to be called president.

Etienne Pascal was not only an excellent lawyer and Latinist, but a considerable mathematician, and also greatly interested in the physical sciences. Although a devout Catholic, it was not until the mid-point of his life that his religion was transformed from a formal and social dimension to an interior and personal one. Etienne also experienced a religious conversion, of which more will be said later. Gilberte, in her biography of her brother, attests that her father held that 'whatever is the object of faith cannot be the object of reason.'

Etienne Pascal was married in either 1616 or 1617 to Antoinette Bégon (1596–1626), a daughter of a merchant bourgeois of Clermont-Ferrand. They had four children: Antonia, born in 1617, who died very young; next came Gilberte, born in 1620; then Blaise; and finally Jacqueline, who was born one year before their mother died. Unlike most widowers in the seventeenth century, Etienne never remarried, (at that time remarriage could almost have been considered a moral counsel of the Church). Instead, Etienne resolved to rear and educate his three children himself, which he did with great affection and intelligence. If progeny bear witness to the strength of their parents, then Etienne Pascal must be recorded as one of the best of fathers and teachers, in light of the remarkable lives of both Blaise and Jacqueline. Let us follow the life of Blaise, as viewed through the mind of his 'big sister' Gilberte.

> From the time that my brother was old enough that one could talk to him, he gave signs of an extraordinary mind by the little responses that he gave, but even more so by the questions that he asked about the nature of the world, which surprised everyone. This beginning, which gave great hope, was never proved false, for, the more he grew in age, the more he grew in powers of reasoning, in such a way that he was above his natural age.
>
> Meanwhile, my mother died in 1626, when my brother was only three years of age. My father, finding himself quite alone, took complete charge of our family. Because he had no other son than my brother, the fact of his uniqueness and other extraordinary qualities

perceived in this young child, gave my father such a great affection for him, that my father could not bear the thought of consigning my brother's education to anyone but himself, and resolved to instruct my brother himself, as he in fact did: my brother having never been to college, and having never had another teacher than my own father.

This was a brave step for a father of Etienne Pascal's social class, when sons were regularly sent if deemed sufficiently gifted to college. The typical college in seventeenth-century France was under the administration of, and staffed by, the Jesuits. To such a college, La Flèche, Descartes's own parents, or father, had chosen to send him, as we know from the *Discours de la Méthode*. Pascal's father took a unique pedagogical route, not only for his own time, but for most times, including our own. A great father such as Johann Sebastian Bach tutored his lesser sons in musical composition and performance. A lesser father such as Leopold Mozart gave similar instruction to a far greater son. Even a pedestrian father-philosopher like James Mill took charge of his more than pedestrian offspring – John Stuart Mill. But typically, from the aristocratic sons of Athens, who studied with Socrates, Plato, or the Sophists, to the scions of the great families of the Middle Ages, such as St Thomas Aquinas, who studied first with masters in Naples, then in Paris and Cologne, gifted offspring have been sent away from home to learn. It was not so with Blaise Pascal: he learned the bulk of what he knew at his father's knee. What Blaise deduced, or imagined, or prayed for was the natural result of the son's own genius.

In 1632 Etienne Pascal took his family to Paris, apparently to assume new administrative duties. Records show that the family moved several times within the city, first to the rue des Juifs, close to the aristocratic section of the Marais, later to the Left Bank, rue Neuve-Saint-Lambert, then close to the Luxembourg Palace.

My brother, who was only eight at this time, received a great advantage in moving to Paris, given the plan that my father had in educating him; for there is no doubt that my father could not have given him the same care in the provinces, where constant work overcame him. But in Paris he was at complete liberty, and he gave himself entirely to the education of his son, and he had the total success that only a father so intelligent and affectionate could have.

The chief maxim of this education was to keep the child on top of his work; it was for this reason that my father did not want to teach him Latin until he was twelve years old, so that he could teach it with greater facility. During this interval my father did not let him remain idle, for he instructed him in all things of which he found him capable. My father made him understand in general what languages are; he showed him how languages have been reduced in grammars to certain rules; he showed him how these rules have certain exceptions which one has taken care to note; and how by this means all languages are communicable from one country to another. This general idea clarified my brother's mind, and permitted him to see the rationale behind the rules of grammar, so that when he came to learn another language, he knew how he did it, and he applied himself precisely to those matters that required his application.

After this instruction, my father moved to other subjects. He often talked to him about the extraordinary effects of nature, like gunpowder and other such things that are surprising when one considers them. My brother took great delight in all this information, but wanted to know the reasons behind everything; and as they are not all known, when my father could not explain them to him . . . he was not at all content . . . Thus from his infancy my brother could commit himself only to what appeared to him evidently true, so that if one did not give him good reasons, he searched for them himself . . .

Gilberte illustrates her little brother's insatiable curiosity by the following event which occurred when he was about eleven. One day when the Pascal family were at table, someone accidentally struck a faience plate with a knife. He noticed that it made a big noise, but that it stopped immediately when one put one's hand on the plate. He wanted to know the cause, and began experimenting with other forms of sound. At the age of eleven he wrote a treatise on sound which his father and others found entirely well-reasoned.

In sum, Pascal's father taught Blaise a logical method and the art of reasoning that could be applied to any subject. Etienne Pascal also imparted a great sense of curiosity about both the physical and human sciences. The father made the son realize the equal importance of general theories and of individual cases. Pascal's youthful mind emerged with a great distrust of verbalism and of theories that have no relationship to the complexities of the world.

Pascal's sister tells us that his genius for geometry began to appear when her brother was twelve. Gilberte finds the event so extraordinary that she insists on describing it in detail. Pascal's father, himself an excellent mathematician, often invited some of his mathematician friends to visit him at home. But because Etienne wanted to teach his son languages first, and because 'he knew that mathematics is something that can completely fill and satisfy the mind, he did not want my brother to have any knowledge of it, for fear that he might neglect his Latin and the other languages that he wanted him to perfect.' So Etienne locked up all the books on mathematics. He even refused to speak about mathematics in front of little Blaise. This only served to excite the boy's curiosity further, and he begged his father to teach him mathematics. Etienne promised him that he would begin instruction as soon as Blaise mastered Greek and Latin. One day Blaise asked his father what mathematics was and of what it treated. 'My father replied in general that it was the way of making accurate figures, and to find the proportions among them. At the same time he forbade him to say anything more about it, and to think any more about it.' This was enough to set Blaise's mind dreaming, and he began to draw geometrical figures on the walls, trying to find out how to draw a perfect circle or a triangle with perfectly equal sides. He proceeded to figure out the relationships between various geometrical figures, then devised a basic language for his geometry. Expressing her awe, Gilberte writes: 'After devising these terms, he made himself some axioms, and finally some perfect demonstrations. And as one goes from one thing to another in these sort of things, he extended his research so far that he got as far as the thirty-second proposition of the first book of Euclid.' Obviously Gilberte means the theorem: The sum of the angles of a triangle is equal to two straight angles.

Pascal's father came into the room in which his son was discovering geometry out of the powers of his own mind. 'One cannot say who was the more surprised – the son to see his father when he had been expressly forbidden to do mathematics, or the father to see his son in the middle of such things.' Blaise proceeded to explain his discoveries to his astonished father, who finally burst into tears. One of the father's intimate friends, Monsieur Le Pailleur, whom he had asked to come and witness the remarkable event, begged Etienne not to be so displeased. 'My father replied: "I am not weeping for sorrow but for joy. You know the care I took to keep my son from having any knowledge of geometry, so as not to keep him from his other studies. Nonetheless you see what he has done." ' Gilberte rightly concludes that her little brother had in a certain sense 'discovered' mathematics.

The boy was promptly given the *Elements* of Euclid and on his own quickly mastered the entire system. His father took him to various convocations of learned mathematicians at which Blaise not only held his own but astounded everyone. At the age of sixteen Blaise wrote his first work, the 'Traité des Coniques.' 'People said that not since Archimedes had anyone seen anything of such power.' Many mathematicians urged him to publish it, 'but as my brother had never had a passion for reputation, he was not excited about it, and so this work has never been published.'

Blaise continued to perfect his Greek and Latin, and Gilberte tells us that both during and after meals, his father would instruct him in logic, physics, 'and other parts of philosophy.' Although Etienne Pascal was vastly pleased by the progress that his son was making in the sciences, he failed to be aware that such steady and arduous study was beginning to take its toll on his son's health, which began to be seriously affected by the age of eighteen: Gilberte does not give any medical details, and is so vague that speculative diagnosis is impossible: 'But as the discomforts ['*incommodités*'] that he was undergoing were not so severe, they did not keep him from continuing all his usual occupations . . .'

Gilberte immediately mentions, as if to prove that her brother was in no way failing, that he invented, at the age of nineteen, what she calls a '*machine d'arithmétique*,' which in effect is the precursor of all mechanical calculating devices. Gilberte adds that with it one can make all sorts of mathematical operations 'without knowing any rule of arithmetic, and with infallible certainty.' She waxes lyrical about the powers of the new machine, which 'turns what had always been a science of the mind into a mere machine,' the implication being that even the least intelligent can use it with entire certainty. Returning to how much fatigue this invention caused her brother, who had been working on it for two years (1640–42), Gilberte adds that 'it was not so much the idea of the calculator, or of figuring out all the requisite movements, but instructing the workmen how to make it that cost him so much tiring work.'

Although Gilberte does not mention why her brother invented the machine, all the evidence suggests that Blaise primarily wanted to help his father with his financial accounts, or anyone who was placed under his father's authority either in Paris or in the provinces. In the following years Blaise ironed out all the imperfections in the calculator – the progenitor of the modern-day computer. He dedicated the machine to the Chancelier de Séguier, after first giving a demonstration of it, in February 1644, at the palace of the duc de Bourbon, father of the Prince de Condé. After all, Pierre de Séguier was one of the most powerful men in the kingdom, chancellor under both Louis XIII and Louis XIV, and one of the founders of the Académie Française. Pascal received a patent from the king for the machine in 1649, and on the invitation of the Abbé Bourdelot, had a copy of the machine sent to Queen Christina of Sweden.

Gilberte's main concern was how seriously the invention of the 'machine d'arithmétique' had affected her brother's health. 'He sometimes told us that since the age of eighteen he has not passed a single day without pain. These discomforts' – still the same vague term 'incommodités' – 'were not always of equal violence; as soon as he had some rest and relaxation, his mind immediately began searching for something new.'

At the age of twenty-three, Gilberte tells us, her brother's interests turned to physics, in particular to Torricelli's experiments on the vacuum. Gilberte does not mention that these experiments were first done by Torricelli in Florence, and had sufficiently proved his theory; or that Pierre Petit, who was in charge of ports and fortifications of France, had performed the experiments with both Etienne and Blaise Pascal. But in 1647 Blaise Pascal published a pamphlet entitled 'Expériences nouvelles touchant la vide . . . Dedié à Monsieur Pascal, conseiller du Roi . . . par le sieur B. P. son fils.' The title implies that the son is paying homage to the father, who was his sole teacher and preceptor.

After mentioning how her brother's experiments proved 'so clearly that all the effects that one had previously attributed to the void are caused by the weight of air' – reminding one of the charmingly airy dialogue amongst the bas bleus in Molière's play Les Femmes Savantes – Gilberte's tone dramatically changes. It is like moving from a sidewalk café, after a heady meal and conversation, into the majestic gloom of a great cathedral like Chartres. The passage must be quoted in full.

Immediately afterwards, and when he was only twenty-four, God's

Providence having made an event occur which obliged him to read books of piety, God illuminated him in such a way by his reading, that he understood perfectly that the Christian religion requires us to live only for God, and to have no other object than Himself. And this truth seemed so evident to him, both so necessary and so useful, that he stopped all his research, in such a way that from then on he renounced all other enquiries in order to apply himself to the unique thing that Jesus Christ calls necessary.

What event or events occurred that brought about this dramatic change in Blaise Pascal's interests? It is as if his entire family had been converted – father, son, older sister, and Jacqueline. Jacqueline had shown a remarkable and precocious talent for poetry, having at the age of fourteen recited her verses at an audience with the queen, Anne of Austria, at the château of Saint-Germain-en-Laye, and had even been embraced by Cardinal Richelieu. It was not of course a conversion from Catholicism to another religion or sect, but a movement from a formalistic and traditionalist conception of their own church to a sense of greater interiority. Gilberte, to be sure, says no such thing in her biography of her brother, but begins by ambage, by implication, by hyperbole – strangely parallel to the music of Marc-Antoine Charpentier and his rival Jean-Baptiste Lully. 'By a particular protection of Providence my brother had always been protected from all the vices of youth . . . he was never attracted to libertinism in regard to religion, having always restricted his curiosity to things of the natural world, and he often told me that he joined this obligation to all the others that he owed to his father, who always had great respect for religion . . . ' As for the '*libertins*' who scoffed at religion, Gilberte writes that 'even as a very young man, he regarded them as persons with the false principle that human reason is above all things, and who did not understand the nature of faith.' Gilberte proceeds to speak of her brother's great intelligence, his insatiable curiosity, his incredibly elegant powers of reasoning, his natural simplicity, only to conclude that all these talents were suddenly consecrated to 'knowing and practicing the perfection of Christian morality.' She adds that although her brother had made no particular study of scholasticism, he knew about the heresies that the Church had condemned. 'And God gave him at that time an opportunity to show his zeal for religion.' Gilberte writes that 'he was then in Rouen, where my father was employed in the service of the king . . . ' In 1639 Etienne Pascal had received a new appointment, from Cardinal Richelieu, to aid in the supervision of taxation in the province of Normandy. At this time Rouen, the capital of the province, was the second most important city in France, both commercially and intellectually. Gilberte tells us of a man at that time teaching what she calls 'a new philosophy which attracted all the curious.' Pascal and two of his friends listened and talked to the man, and were startled to discover that they could derive propositions contrary to the teachings of the Church. Gilberte gives one example, that Jesus Christ was not formed from the blood of the Virgin Mary.[1] Pascal and his friends decided that the man, who was a former Capuchin named Jacques Forton de Saint-Ange, should not be allowed to teach the young. First Pascal and his friends decided to warn him, then to denounce him. Forton ignoring their warning, Pascal and his friends denounced him to the adjunct bishop of Rouen, Monsignor de Belley. After listening to the charges, de Belley summoned the Capuchin, who gave 'a confession of equivocal faith' that nonetheless satisfied the monsignor of his orthodoxy. Infuriated, Pascal went several times to the château de Gaillon, residence of the archbishop of Rouen, François de Harlay. Pascal quickly received a condemnation of the Capuchin, who was forbidden to teach until he toed the theological line. Pascal's sometimes violent, always antithetical nature emerged for the first time in a theological context.

Although the event sounds like a storm in a teacup, Gilberte points out some of the consequences of her brother's first engagement in theological disputation. First, their father was won over to his son's more exact and interior conception of Christianity, which spread throughout the household. Second, their younger sister, Jacqueline, who has been recorded as a woman of extraordinary intelligence, had decided to become a nun, and entered the austere convent of Port-Royal des Champs. Jacqueline Pascal chose to enter Port-Royal because she knew that the rigorous spirituality associated with Jansenism flourished there. Although Jacqueline never took part in the theological or philosophical controversies of the Jansenists, she strictly followed the religious life associated with the movement.

The controversy with the Capuchin is also related to the Pascals' first encounter with Jansenism. In 1646, a year before Pascal won his condemnation from the archbishop, Etienne Pascal had slipped on the ice and broken his hip. He was taken care of by two lay brothers who were under the direction of the pastor of Rouville, who was himself a disciple of the abbot of Saint-Cyran, and also of the bishop of Ypres, Cornelius Jansen – from whose name 'Jansenism' is derived. In the controversy of 1647 we can perceive the rudiments of the *Provincial Letters*, not only Pascal's penchant for Jansenisms's interiority and transcendence, but also his love of theological disputation and even vituperation. Throughout his life Pascal was intellectually combative, obsessed with what must lie behind the veil of appearances. Throughout his life he never doubted that much must lie behind appearances: in mathematics, physics, or the simple fact of being conscious in a world of moving objects.

Although Gilberte's biography is sometimes doting, sometimes vague, it has the patina of portraits painted by first-class amateurs of their own kin. When she tells us that at the age of twenty-four her brother's physical discomfort became so severe that he could swallow nothing but liquids, and those only if they were hot, and drop by drop; and that he had terrible pains in his head and his gastric system, one can imagine Gilberte watching over her brother. 'But my brother no longer complained. He regarded all that like a gain for himself . . . he made his sufferings with joy for penance . . . ' Now both sister and brother interpret physical suffering as a form of appearance: it cannot be mere events, mere physiology, any more than reality could be simply atoms and the void, as Lucretius had argued in *De Rerum Natura*.

His doctors advised Pascal to give up his strenuous intellectual endeavours at least temporarily, and to make more time for relaxation. Gilberte writes: 'Le voilà donc dans la monde' – 'And so he appeared in society.' She records that he was also seen at Court, 'where he immediately assumed the manners with such aplomb that people thought he had been born there.' Instant mathematician, instant courtier! But Gilberte laments that this period of his life was the most badly spent, although we are assured that Blaise avoided the vices of the Court. By Gilberte's account, it was their younger sister, Jacqueline, who rescued him.

Ever since Jacqueline had entered Port-Royal, her religiosity had grown more intense, and all her feelings 'breathed an unreserved holiness.' Blaise had at first tried to persuade her not to enter the convent, and had even gone so far as to threaten not to have her dowry deposited with the mother superior if she did so. But following the example of other brave women, such as St Teresa of Avila,

Jacqueline had entered the convent secretly. Blaise visited her often at Port-Royal. Repeatedly Jacqueline preached to her brother – apparently from behind the convent screen, since the nuns of Port-Royal were entirely sequestered. Jacqueline urged him to give up society and return to his studies, even if it meant that his health would again deteriorate. For 'it was false reasoning to stop at the transient good of one's body when it was a question of the eternal good of our soul.'

At the age of thirty Blaise gave up all his worldly ways and worldly friends, made a retreat, and laid down two principles or maxims that would henceforth govern his life. First, to renounce all pleasures; and second to give up everything superfluous. He did without domestic help as much as possible, made his own bed, went to the kitchen himself and served himself. He even tried to do without his physical senses, or at least not to derive any pleasure from them. Gilberte gives two examples. When the cook prepared something succulent, and he was asked whether he had liked it, Blaise would respond: 'You should have warned me about it in advance, for now I do not remember, and I swear to you that I paid no attention to it.' And when he was asked whether he liked the meat, he replied; 'That it is a sign that one eats to please one's palate, which is always an evil, or at least that one is conforming one's language to the sensual, which is not fitting for a Christian: he should never say anything that does not have an air of holiness.' He refused all sauces, all ragouts, oranges, grapes, and anything that would excite his appetite, even though he naturally liked all such things. At the beginning of what Gilberte calls 'his retreat' he laid down principles for how much food he needed to satisfy the demands of his stomach, and never deviated from these rules. That Pascal was not suffering from anorexia nervosa is clear from the fact that even when he did not feel like eating the amount that his rules prescribed, he forced himself to eat it. When asked why, he responded that it was to satisfy the stomach, not the appetite. With his characteristic abruptness and intransigence, Pascal had discarded the role of the man of the world and donned the robes of the ascetic.

Renouncing all pleasures, Pascal seems to have taken a perverse pleasure in the repugnant medicines that his doctors prescribed for him. Applying his second maxim – to get rid of anything superfluous – he had the tapestries in his rooms taken down. He was also dismantling his collection of friends to the point that 'he did not want to see anyone at all.' 'That is how he passed five years of his life, from thirty to thirty-five, working ceaselessly for God and for his neighbor, or for himself, trying to perfect himself more and more.' Gilberte adds that those were the final years that he *lived*, for the following four years were nothing but 'a continuous languor.' It was not a new illness that overtook him, but the same 'indispositions' of his youth that grew more severe. 'During all that time he could not work an instant on the great work that he had undertaken for religion,' by which Gilberte means the *Apology for the Christian Religion* for which we have but the notes, the *Pensées*. Nonetheless, many of his friends remained faithful to him, and visited him in his retreat – 'friends of condition,' Gilberte assures us. Pascal seems also to have taken on the role of religious mentor, caught between not wanting to take any pride or pleasure in his powers of counselling and still wanting to help others. He found an unusual way out of this difficulty: 'the spirit of mortification, which is the same as that of charity, inspired him to have a steel belt studded with sharp points and to wear it on his bare flesh whenever he was warned that any of his gentlemen friends were coming to see him.' Even this device seemed insufficient to mortify the flesh. Whenever a vain inclination overtook him, or conversation gave him some pleasure, he would elbow himself so that the sharp studs would dig in harder. 'This practice seemed so useful to him that he also used it as a precaution against the lack of application that he began to observe in himself during the final years of his life.' Yet all these strange practices were performed in secret: 'we knew nothing at all about it, and we did not learn about it until after his death, from a person of very great virtue . . . ' Pascal's time was largely spent in prayer and in reading the Bible, which became increasingly one and the same activity. 'He used to say that the Holy Scriptures were not a science of the mind, but of the heart.' He believed that the Scriptures can only be understood through charity, and only to the degree that one hates oneself – '*se hait soi-même*.' According to Gilberte her brother literally knew the Bible by heart.

When commenting on the Bible, Pascal avoided learned words and metaphors, and used a style that anyone could understand easily and pleasantly. 'And his style of writing – naive, accurate, agreeable, strong and natural – was so much his own that when the *Provincial Letters* began to appear, people judged that they were by him, in spite of the effort he had made to conceal the fact.'

As an aside Gilberte mentions that it was at this time (1656) that her daughter Marguerite, who had suffered for three and a half years from a fistula of the eyes 'which the most able doctors of Paris pronounced incurable,' was healed after being touched by one of the thorns from what was believed to be Christ's Crown of Thorns. 'This miracle was attested to by many surgeons and doctors, and vouch-safed by the solemn authority of the Church.' Pascal was evidently most impressed by the miracle; Gilberte contends that the event filliped him into reflection upon the nature of miracles in the Old and New Testaments. Gilberte herself reasoned that if there were mira-cles, there must be something higher than nature; and given that her own daughter was the object of a miracle, it is simply a question of determining the criteria for distinguishing the true from the false. One has the impression that Gilberte believed her brother had resolved the matter, because 'he unravelled all that with an admirable light, and when we heard him speak about it, and when he expatiated upon the times during which the miracles of the Old and New Testaments were reported, they seemed clear to us.'

As Gilberte writes further about her brother, we cannot help observing that she too had been attacked by the '*esprit geométrique*,' outbreaks of which seemed to occur throughout continental Europe in the seventeenth century. The only correct way to construct a philosophy was in the style of Euclid. Even landscapists such as Le Nôtre believed that geometry held the key for correct, and therefore beautiful, landscaping. Showing first symptoms of the geometrical bug, Gilberte often writes of 'first principles' and of how 'all truths are drawn one from the other.' She records how her brother had grown violently opposed to atheists, and how he hoped to refute them utterly. 'But God, who had given him the requisite intelligence for such a grand accomplishment, did not give him sufficient health to bring it to completion.' Contrary to her propensity for seeing behind natural events some transcendent plan, Madame Périer offers no conjecture concerning this apparent oversight on God's part. But Gilberte is not to be faulted for her silence on this point, since it is a silence that anyone of a religious bent must avow. Even the most flinty-nosed scientist must acknowledge the flukes of nature – what Lucretius, following Democritus and the Epicureans, called the '*clinamen*' – an irrational swerve. Pascal calls attention to the same point in the *Pensées*, when he remarks that 'Had Cleopatra's nose been shorter, the whole face of history would have been changed.'

It is clear that Gilberte understood the nature and purpose of her brother's final project. 'He wanted to show that the Christian religion had as many marks of certitude as those things commonly received in the world as the most certain. He did not make use of metaphysical proofs – not that he held them in contempt when they were used in their way – but he found them far removed from the reasoning of the ordinary man; moreover, not everybody was capable of understanding such proofs, and even those who were, an hour after they had used them, did not know what to make of them, and feared being deceived. He also said that those sorts of proof can only lead us to a speculative understanding of God, and to understand God in this way was not to know Him. He was not to use, moreover, ordinary reasoning by which one takes the works of nature' (as proofs for God's existence). 'He respected such proofs, even so, because they are in conformity with Scriptures and with reason; but he believed that they were not proportionate to the mind and the disposition of those whom they were intended to convince.' Metaphysical proofs dissuade better than they convince. Gilberte writes of 'blindness' or '*aveuglement*,' and of course no one can be argued out of his blindness: all that can be done is to restore sight, and this is what she believed her brother hoped to do in his *magnum opus*, the *Apology for the Christian Religion*.

Gilberte gives the impression of having carefully studied some of her brother's writings, for suddenly she breaks out into quasi-Pascalian homiletics. 'The Christian divinity is not only a god who is simply the author of geometrical truths: that is the view of the pagans. Nor is the Christian divinity one who exercises his Providence on the lives and well-being of men, in order to give a happy life: that is the view of the Jews. But the God of Abraham and of Jacob, the God of the Christians, is the God of love and of consolation . . . a God who makes persons feel within themselves their misery and his infinite pity . . . who makes them feel at the same time that they will have no other joy than by loving Him. Self-love and concupiscence . . . are intolerable . . . ' She continues in this homiletic vein, giving the impression of some female French counterpart of Savonarola who had mounted the winding stairs to the pulpit and was thundering down on the awed parishioners below: 'Thus those who search for

God without Jesus Christ find no light able to satisfy them . . . so that they fall into atheism or deism, two things which the Christian religion abhors almost equally . . . For, not only do we know God only through Christ, but we know ourselves only through Christ.' Although Gilberte writes that 'These words are his, word for word,' referring to her brother, she has so incorporated them into her own being that they seem to be her words as well: she too has been converted.

Pointing out that the secret of her brother's style of eloquence was to afflict and to console at the same time – a sort of literary *aigre-doux* – Gilberte writes that her brother wanted not only to be understood by everyone, but to be ardently desired by everyone. Moreover, Pascal held two truths to be certain: 'that God had left perceptible signs, particularly on the Church, to make Himself known to those who sincerely searched for Him, and that nonetheless He has covered these marks in such a way that they can only be apperceived by those who search for them with all their heart.' Thus, when he argued with self-confessed atheists, Pascal never began with philosophical arguments or first principles, but tried to determine whether his interlocutor was sincerely searching for the truth. Pascal's method began with a Socratic 'opening-up,' an avowal of ignorance coupled with an ardent yearning for truth.

Pascal was about thirty-four when he began work on his great project of the defense of Christianity. He spent at least a year in preparing his materials, which consisted in gathering various thoughts, *'pensées,'* that came to him. But in his thirty-fifth year 'he fell back into those infirmities in such an overwhelming way, that he could do nothing for the next four years that he had to live . . . ' The return of Pascal's illness or, in all likelihood, illnesses, was heralded by toothaches so severe that he was robbed of sleep. It was during these bouts of insomnia that Pascal's mind returned briefly to his scientific interests. Many mathematicians in Europe were at that time interested in the problems surrounding the cycloid, or as it was called at that time *'la roulette.'* During several successive nights, thoughts on the subject came to Pascal with extraordinary rapidity. 'Finally a multitude of thoughts succeeded one another; they revealed to him, in spite of himself, the explanation of the cycloid by which he was himself surprised.' For a while Pascal was not interested in writing up an account of his discoveries 'because he had long since renounced such things.' But someone for whom Pascal had great deference 'persuaded my brother to write down everything that had come into his mind on the subject, and to have it published.'

Gilberte does not identify the person; it was, however, the duc de Roannez. Nor does she describe how her brother set about making known his solution to the problem, apparently not finding anything unusual in the proceedings, as indeed there was not at the time. In the scientific world it was a common practice to announce a challenge to anyone who could find the solution to a certain problem; whoever won the competition would receive a prize. Pascal wrote an anonymous letter in June 1658 to European mathematicians, inviting them to enter the competition. Their solutions were to be sent to Pierre de Carcavy, president of the jury. Carcavy, incidentally, was keeper of the king's library. Pascal wrote another anonymous announcement of the competition in July and in October of the same year. Meanwhile he worked feverishly on writing down his own solution to the problem. 'It is incredible with what precipitancy my brother put all that down on paper. He wrote as fast as his hand would go, and he finished it in just a few days . . . They were also publishing other things of his even as he was writing it, and so he was giving the printers two quite different things.' The other work was astoundingly different in kind: 'Cinquième Ecrit pour les Curés de Paris' – 'Fifth Communication for the Priests of Paris.'

Pierre de Carcavy received two replies to the competition, but on 10 November the 'Histoire de la Roulette' appeared, written by Pascal in collaboration with Personier de Roberval. The jury gave Pascal the prize for his solution, which appeared in his letter entitled 'Lettre d'A. Dettonville à Monsieur de Carcavy.' Pascal signed with the psuedonym Amos Dettonville. Even in his severe and final illness, Pascal enjoyed boyish pranks: 'Amos Dettonville' is an anagram of the pseudonym used for the *Provincial Letters*, Louis de Montalte. More importantly, it can be argued that Pascal's work on the cycloid contains elements of the foundations of the infinitesimal calculus.

Pascal's condition worsened, but he bore his sufferings with great patience. He composed a prayer entitled 'To ask God for the Right Use of Sickness.' A few years before, Pascal had written a letter concerning the death of his father in 1651. Gilberte recalls the letter written to herself and her husband (dated 17 October 1651) in order

to interpret her brother's acceptance of his own imminent death. Life
is to be regarded as a sacrifice, and events gain importance only in so
far as they help or hinder the interpreting of life as a sacrifice. Thus,
Pascal regarded his own illness and suffering 'with joy.' But given
Pascal's belief in the reality of original sin, and his faith in Christ,
death was not only a just, but a holy experience. For the same reasons
Pascal believed strongly in penance, and regarded 'these sufferings
like a fire slowly burning away his sins by a daily sacrifice.' But
Pascal's piety was hardly confined to himself. 'He had always had
such a great love of poverty that the idea was always present in him'
and 'he never refused alms to anyone, although he did not have all
that much.' It appears that he had sometimes given so much money to
the poor that he had to borrow money himself – never from friends,
but from his own income and annuities. Gilberte implies that her
brother's desire to help the poor led in large part to what she calls 'the
business of the carriages.'

'*L'affaire des carrosses*' refers to Pascal's plan to found a system of
public transport for the poor of Paris. In January 1662 Pascal received
a patent for 'carriages at five sous' which was the first omnibus
system in Paris, inaugurated on 18 March of the same year. Pascal had
originally hoped to help the poor in and around Blois with the
proceeds, but although the idea of the omnibus was successful, the
poor of Blois had already been helped from some other source.
Gilberte does not say who this benefactor was, but only repeats what
her brother had said so many times: 'that he desired to have wealth
only to help the poor.' Yet just as Pascal was opposed to grandiose
philosophical or theological systems, so he was in general opposed to
grandiose enterprises to help the poor. He believed that the average
citizen does best by helping others in a particular and private way.
Pascal's social views, which we know largely through the details of
his life, reflect the chief characteristics of the *Pensées*: concern with
the individual, interiority, and the avoidance of pomp and system-
building.

Gilberte relates that her brother's strictures became even more
severe. Remarks that seemed innocent to her, such as mentioning that
she had seen a beautiful woman that day, were pernicious to him. She
ought never to mention such things in front of 'lackeys or young
people because one never knew what thought that might give them.'
He even complained to his sister about the caresses that she received

from her own children and 'maintained that it could harm them and that one could show them tenderness in a thousand other ways.' Finding the last admonition unusually difficult to accept, Gilberte nonetheless bows her head in her prose, and says that her brother was ultimately right.

About three months before his death 'God wanted to give him an opportunity to show to the outside world the zeal that He had given him for purity.' Gilberte recounts how her brother was returning from the church of Saint-Sulpice where he had heard Mass, when a girl of about fifteen approached him and asked for alms. Immediately Pascal saw what danger the girl was in – just arrived from the country, her father dead, her mother recently carried to hospital. Pascal took her to the nearby seminary, gave money to the priest, and instructed him to find a safe place for the girl. The next day Pascal sent a woman with more money to find the girl some proper clothes. The priest did not know Pascal's name, but deeming his actions so kindly, he was determined to find it out; but the woman whom Pascal had sent had been instructed not to disclose his name. The priest begged her to get permission to tell him who the benefactor was. Again Pascal refused, and apparently the priest never found out.

Gilberte writes that her brother's greatest love was for their younger sister, Jacqueline, who was now Sister Sainte-Euphémie. 'Assuredly their hearts were only one heart, and they found in each other consolations which can only be understood by those who have tasted something of the same happiness and who know what it is to love and to be loved with confidence . . . ' Sister Sainte-Euphémie died ten months before her brother. When he received the news, all he said was 'Would that God gives us the grace to die in such a Christian way.' He then proceeded to recount the many virtues of his sister's life. When Pascal saw that Gilberte was in tears, he told her that 'it was not right, and that one should not have such feelings about the death of the just.' Gilberte adds: 'Thus he showed how he loved without attachment.'

'He distinguished two sorts of tenderness, one affective, the other intellectual, holding that the former was of little use in dealing with the world.' The distinction becomes more clear in light of the ethical theories of the great German philosopher of the following century, Immanuel Kant, who distinguished sharply between inclination and duty. Inclination is a psychological, emotional, and even physical predilection; duty is dictated by reason, and is therefore impartial and universal. The great difference between Kant and Pascal is that the latter subordinates the dictates of reason to God, 'who must be the unique end of all the tenderness of Christians' – 'qui doit être l'unique fin de toute la tendresse des chrétiens' – as Gilberte puts it. Gilberte quotes her brother as saying: 'A heart is hard when it knows the interests of its neighbor, but resists the obligation to take any part in them. On the contrary, a heart is tender when the interests of one's neighbor readily enter into oneself, so to speak, by all the feelings that reason wishes each to have for the other in similar situations . . . ' In Pascal's mind such tenderness is closely related to the highest virtue, charity. Although Pascal had many friends, and valued friendship, 'he felt no attachment to others, and did not want anyone to feel attachment to himself.' What Gilberte must mean is what used to be called in religious life 'particular friendships,' against which both male and female novices were strongly warned. Gilberte found this a hard teaching, and openly confesses that she was strongly attached to certain persons, and certainly to her brother, whom she esteemed so highly. Gilberte complained to Sister Sainte-Euphémie about their brother's stricture against attachment. Jacqueline tried to comfort her by pointing out that Blaise had always affectionately helped her. But Gilberte did not understand 'this conduct of reserve,' which she terms 'a mystery,' until the day of her brother's death. 'A person of the most considerable intelligence and piety . . . told me that my brother had always made him understand, as a fundamental maxim of his piety, never to let someone love oneself with attachment, and that this was a fault upon which one did not examine oneself sufficiently, and that it had grave results, and that it was all the more to be feared when it seemed to us less dangerous.'

Gilberte does not give the name of the person, but it was probably the duc de Roannez, Pascal's most intimate friend. Gilberte cites a further proof of the same maxim by recalling that when her brother died he was clutching a piece of paper which he had often been seen reading. It read as follows:

It is unjust that anyone should attach himself to me, even though with pleasure and voluntarily. I would disappoint anyone in whom I caused such a desire to be born, for I am the goal of no one, and I do not have what would satisfy them. Am I not ready to die? Thus the object of their attachment will die. Therefore, as I would be guilty of causing a falsehood to be believed, though I do it gently and may derive some pleasure from it; even so, I am guilty if I make myself loved, and if I draw people to me; for they must spend their lives and their cares in attaching themselves to God and to looking for Him.

Gilberte calls this statement 'the first principle, the foundation of Christian morality,' and says that her brother's commitment to the divine order in everything made him an ardent royalist. Pascal believed in the divine right of kings, and opposed the talk of rebellion circulating in Paris. He held that rights are better guarded by a monarchy, supported by God, than in a republic such as Venice. He held that civil war is the greatest evil one can commit against one's neighbor; moreover, the early Christians taught patience, not revolt, when the rulers did not acquit themselves adequately as regards their duties. According to Gilberte, her brother placed revolution and civil war on the same level as theft or murder.

After eulogizing her brother's character, Gilberte remarks that it was not without faults. 'The extreme vivacity of his mind made him so impatient that he could hardly contain it.' But his intellectual impatience was countered by his total lack of 'amour-propre' – 'self-love.' He used to say that 'Christian piety annihilates the human self' – 'le moi humain' – and that 'human civility hides and suppresses it.'

Gilberte writes that her brother had the piety of a child, and that during the last months of his life, when he could no longer work, he went from church to church, day after day. He made himself a sort of almanack that recorded when and where certain religious relics or devotions would be. Yet none of his behaviour struck anyone as hypocritical or affected. He often read in his breviary, and had an especial fondness for Psalm 118 – the longest by far of any in the Psalter. An alphabetic psalm of didactic nature, it is a prayer inculcating the excellence of keeping the divinely revealed law. Its development, sometimes logical, sometimes exclamatory, is closely akin to Pascal's own style in the Pensées.

Her brother's last illness began with 'a strange nausea' – 'un dégoût étrange.' Pascal had lodged a man and his family under his own roof out of charity, and one of the children had come down with smallpox. Gilberte, who was taking care of her brother, did not want to pass the disease on to her own children, and so urged her brother to have the girl sent somewhere else. Blaise refused. 'He was already very ill, but said that there was less danger for himself than for this child to be transported . . . and in effect he had himself transported to our house.'

It should be added to Gilberte's account here that her family were living in the parish of Saint-Etienne-du-Mont. It was on 29 June 1662, that her brother had himself transported to the Périer residence.

Revealing herself once again as her brother's best and most believable biographer, if not hagiographer, Gilberte sees in her brother's act of pity for the young girl 'the marks of predestination in the Gospel, so that when he came to die, in these two acts of charity provided the testimony that God would pardon him his faults, and give him the kingdom prepared for him.' Her brother had forgiven others, and he had helped those in need.

After he had been with the Périer family for three days, Pascal had a violent attack of colic, but insisted on getting his medicines himself. Because he had no fever, the doctors did not diagnose his condition as grave. 'But my brother, not wanting to risk anything, after the fourth day of colic, and even before being confined to his bed, sent for the priest of Saint-Etienne, and made his confession, but did not take Communion.' During this time Pascal drew up his last will and testament. Towards the end he had nothing 'in his heart and mind but the poor.' He asked Gilberte: 'Why is it that I have still done nothing for the poor, even though I have always felt such a great love for them?' Gilberte replied: 'Because you have never had that much wealth.' Pascal replied, as if forgetting that he had already made provision for the poor in his will, that if he recovered from his illness, henceforward he would devote all his time to the poor.

Still wanting to take Communion, Pascal insisted that the doctors allow the priest to come for the Sacrament of Extreme Unction, or as it is now called, Last Rites. The doctors still did not consider his condition sufficiently grave to do as he wished; moreover, they did not want him to fast to receive the Host. After being treated with various remedies of the time (of which one can form a macabre picture by reading medical handbooks of the period) Pascal complained of a crushing headache. Both doctors and friends assured him that his condition was not serious, and that it was better for him to wait to go to church to take Communion, for there was still hope.

'You do not feel my pain, that is where you will be mistaken. The pain in my head is something extraordinary,' Pascal replied. Then he turned to Gilberte and said that since they refused to let him receive Communion, he begged her to have some poor, sick person sent from the parish so that he or she could receive the same medical attention that Pascal himself was receiving. 'That will diminish the pain that I have for lacking nothing, which I can no longer tolerate, unless you give me the consolation of knowing that there is some poor person here being treated as well as I.'

Gilberte immediately sent word to the priest, who replied that he had no one (apparently in the seminary or hospital) sufficiently ill to be transported to the abode of the Périers. The priest also believed that Pascal would be cured, and promised that he would place an old man in Pascal's charge. When Pascal was told that his second request could not be granted, he begged Gilberte to have him transported to the hospital for incurables, 'because he had a great desire to die among the poor.' Gilberte replied that the doctors would find such a move inappropriate, though promising that she would do so if her brother's condition improved.

It did not. The doctors still attributed his symptoms to 'migraine and vapors.' Pascal had never believed in their 'science,' and at this point Gilberte also sensed that the end was near. Without telling the doctors, she sent for a priest to keep vigil over her brother all night, and prepared candles so that he could receive Communion the next morning.

'These preparations were not in vain, but they were required sooner than one had thought; for, around midnight, he had such a violent convulsion that, when it was over, we thought he was dead. And we had the extreme displeasure of seeing him die without receiving Communion, after he had so often, and with such insistence, asked for this grace. But God, who wanted to reward him for such a fervent and just desire, interrupted the convulsion as if by a miracle, and gave him back total awareness and judgment.' Thus, when the priest came in with the Viaticum, and called out 'Here is what you so much wanted to have brought to you!' Pascal awakened. Pushing himself up in his bed as the priest asked whether he believed in the chief mysteries of the Church, Pascal replied: 'Yes, Monsieur, I believe all that, and with all my heart.' Gilberte relates that, while receiving Extreme Unction, her brother was in tears. After thanking everyone, and receiving the final blessing, Pascal said: 'Would that God never abandons me!' – 'Que Dieu ne m'abandonne jamais!'

These were his last words. The convulsions overtook him again. They did not cease until his death, which was twenty-four hours later, 'to wit the 19th day of August 1662, at one o'clock in the morning, at the age of thirty-eight years and two months.'

2
A WITCH'S SPELL

Marguerite Périer, Pascal's niece whose eyes had been healed by the Holy Thorn, left a record of the earliest event known of his life. When Pascal was one year old, 'something very extraordinary happened to him,' Margeurite Périer writes in her 'Mémoire sur la vie de Monsieur Pascal.' Pascal's mother was 'very pious and very charitable' and gave a small sum of money each month to a large number of poor families and to impoverished women. Among the latter 'there was one who had the reputation of being a witch: everyone told her this; but his mother, who was not one of those credulous women but had much intelligence, made light of their opinion and still continued to give her alms.' At this time it happened that the child (Pascal) 'fell into a languor similar to what one calls in Paris an intestinal disorder . . . ' Marguerite uses the phrase 'tomber en chartre,' which is a popular way of describing a mesenteric disorder. But the child's additional symptoms were most unusual: Pascal could not look at water without having violent transports; he could not bear the sight of his father and mother close to each other. He allowed his parents to caress him separately, but if they both approached him, 'he cried and behaved with excessive violence. All that lasted a year, while the evil grew; he fell into such an extreme state that he was believed to be near death.'

Everyone told Pascal's parents that the witch had cast a spell over him, but they refused to believe it. The supposed witch was still allowed free access to the house and still received alms. Finally Pascal's father ordered the woman into his study and charged her with having cast a spell over the boy. The woman denied it in a docile tone, alleging that people had invented the story out of envy for the alms that she received. He then threatened to have her hanged if she did not tell the truth. The woman went down on her knees and begged him to save her life if she told all. She reminded Etienne Pascal that she had asked him to handle some legal matter for her; he had refused because he did not consider her claim legitimate – whereupon she promptly cast a spell over the infant Blaise, seeing how tenderly he loved his son. She said that the spell was deadly – 'le sort était à la mort' – and could be removed only if it fell on another person, or even on an animal. Margeurite continues: 'My grandfather offered her a horse; she told him that he need not go to such expense, that a cat would do. He had one brought to her; she took it away and in going down the stairs she found two Capuchins coming up to console my grandmother for the extreme illess of the child . . . she took the cat and threw it out of the window, from which it fell only six feet, but fell dead. She asked for another cat; my grandfather had it given to her.' He did not realize that the woman was engaged in a mockery 'since it was necessary that, in order to break the spell, a new invocation to the Devil be made . . . '

That evening the witch came again and told Pascal's father that she needed three leaves of three different species of herbs, and that they must be gathered by a child not yet seven years of age. The apothecary offered the services of his daughter; the herbs were given to the witch, who made a poultice out of them, which was to be placed on Blaise's stomach – all to no avail, for at midday he seemed to be dead. The father caught sight of the witch and struck her violently. She explained that she had forgotten to mention that the child would indeed appear to be dead, but he was not; he would come round at midnight. 'However, the child appeared dead; he had no pulse, no voice, no sensation; he grew cold, and had all the signs of death.' Close to one o'clock in the morning he began to yawn; they started warming him and gave him some wine with sugar in it. The wet-nurse gave him suck. As he revived, Blaise was his mother and father close together and began screaming. Although not cured, Blaise was at least alive. 'About six or seven days later he began to be able to tolerate the sight of water . . . and in three weeks the child was entirely cured . . . '

In her 'Mémoire' Marguerite Périer writes that during her uncle's sojourn in Rouen he led a life of great piety which 'inspired the entire family, but that he fell into an extraordinary state, caused by the assiduousness with which he applied himself to the sciences: for the spirits having risen so strongly into the brain, he found himself in a sort of paralysis from the waist down, and he could not walk without support. His legs and feet were cold as marble, and every day slippers soaked in *eau-de-vie* had to be put on his feet to give them some warmth.' She tells of her uncle's scientific studies, and of how he plunged with equal fervor into the delights of society. Pascal had decided to get married and have a family, and went to discuss it with Jacqueline, who was now a nun at Port-Royal. Jacqueline 'moaned to see the one who had shown her the nothingness of the world plunge himself into it with such dedication.' But the time for his ultimate turning had not yet come, and did not come according to Marguerite until the Feast of the Immaculate Conception. On that day, having gone to Port-Royal to see his sister, Pascal talked with her in the parlor while Nones was being said. Jacqueline left him and went to sit with the other nuns behind the rood screen, while Pascal went into the church to hear the homily. According to Marguerite this was about giving up the world, consulting God in everything. Pascal was moved, decided to give up his worldly connections and went 'to the country to get out of his element' – '*pour se dépayser*.' The comte d'Archourt went to Pascal to offer the hand of Mademoiselle de Mesmes in marriage, 'the best in the Kingdom by wealth, birth and person' Marguerite assures the reader in her generally hyperbolic style; Pascal 'did not hesitate to refuse, believing that he owed God this sign of fidelity.' The Count called Pascal 'mad.'

Marguerite describes how her uncle wrote when 'by an order of Providence' he was 'to work against the atheists.' Pascal composed everything in his head, without setting anything down on paper. 'Thus he kept in his memory the ideas of everything he intended to write until he had it at a stage of perfection, and then he wrote. But as he grew sicker, during the last five years of his life, he jotted down ideas as soon as they came to him, and these are the parts so written, bit by bit, found after his death, that we have given and the public has received with so much pleasure.' These 'bits and pieces' are the *Pensées*.

As for Descartes, Marguerite's uncle agreed with him on some points – on the automaton, and disagreed on other – 'subtle matters.' The reference must mean that Pascal shared Descartes's views on mechanics and self-moving bodies, but not on his view of the pineal gland as the seat of communication between – in Pascal's language – 'the order of bodies' and 'the order of minds.'

Marguerite describes Pascal's autopsy with the dispassion and precision worthy of a modern-day medical student. His stomach and liver were 'withered away,' the intestines were 'gangrenous.' 'Still, it could not be determined whether he had suffered from colic because of the state or the other way around. When his skull was opened, the doctors were surprised to find that the cranium had only the lamb-doidal suture,' which apparently caused the headaches from which Pascal suffered all his life. 'He had had the frontal, but for some reason it had remained open so long in his infancy that it had not properly grown together, and a callus had grown over it large enough to be easily touched by the finger.' 'As for the coronal suture, there remained not a vestige of it. The doctors observed that there was a prodigious amount of brain, the substance of which was so solid and condensed that they judged it to be the reason for which, the frontal suture not being able to close, nature provided the callus.' Finally, most remarkable in the autopsy, 'was that inside the cranium, along the ventricles of the brain, were two impressions, like a fingerprint in wax, which were filled with curdled and infected blood which had begun to spread gangrene through the dura mater.'

How could Marguerite have known such details? No woman of her time ever studied medicine, and *dure-mère* – dura mater – the tough, fibrous membrane which envelops the brain and spinal cord – is not a term used by a layman of either gender in any period. One surmises that Marguerite Périer scrupulously interrogated the physicians, took precise notes, and then sat down with scientific piety to write something worthily scientific about her uncle.

3

PIOUS APPRAISALS

In the *Mémoires du Père Beurrier* the author notes at the beginning of Book III that he intends to recount 'the most remarkable things that happened during the twenty-two years that I have been priest of Saint-Etienne' (Saint-Etienne-du-Mont, the parish where Pascal died). Chapter 11 treats 'Of the malady and death of Monsieur Pascal and of what happened on that occasion.' Father Beurrier tells us that he assisted Pascal during his last illness, 'which lasted six whole weeks,' and administered 'the last Christian obligations after his death.' Rumor had it that Pascal had died without Extreme Unction. The archbishop of Paris, Monsieur de Péréfixe, asked Father Beurrier to give an account of the last days of this man who had helped foment so much controversy.

Beurrier had not known Pascal before his final illness, which Beurrier describes as 'bilious and nephriticolic.' Given the gravity of Pascal's condition, Beurrier did not counsel a detailed confession. Pascal mentioned his retreat two years before during which he had made a 'very exact general confession.' He mentioned also that he had amassed a great quantity of materials to refute atheists and heretics 'of which there are a great number in Paris.' 'These materials were diverse thoughts, arguments and reasons that he had couched in few words at various times without any order,' and out of which he had hoped to make a book that would bring all the stray sheep back into the fold of the Church. Pascal said that for the past two years he had withdrawn from all public religious controversy out of prudence 'in view of the great difficulty of the questions of grace and predestination, even according to the view of St Paul.' Pascal cited Romans 11:33. As for the infallibility of the pope, Pascal implied that silence was the best policy since he had never studied scholastic philosophy and his own father had been his only teacher. Nonetheless, Pascal 'wanted to have a perfect submission to the Vicar of Jesus Christ, who is the Supreme Pontiff.' Finally Pascal promised that if his health were restored to him, he would write the book that he had been planning on the defence of the true faith. Father Beurrier heard his confession the next day and gave him the Blessed Sacrament, 'which he received with a singular devotion.'

Beurrier mentions that several of the religious who had been forced to leave Port-Royal by order of Louis XIV had rented a house near his church. Beurrier has learned more about the character and life of Pascal from some of these nuns and novices, and from Gilberte Périer. After mentioning Pascal's precocity in mathematics, his invention of the 'arithmetical machine' at the age of twenty, Father Beurrier writes that at the age of thirty Pascal 'showed so strongly that he wanted to quit society that society finally quit him.'

After his retreat two years before his death, Pascal gave away considerable sums to charity and 'sold his carriage, his horses, his tapestries, his fine furniture, his silver, and even his library, except for the Bible, St Augustine, and a few other books, and gave all the money to the poor.' The 'few other books' were undoubtedly the writings of Arnauld, Saint-Cyran, and some prayerbooks. 'I admired the patience, humility, charity, and the great detachment that I noticed in Monsieur Pascal every time that I went to see him during the last six weeks of his illness and his life.'

Although Pascal had asked to be buried without an epitaph, Father Beurrier writes that he was inhumed in his own church, Saint-Etienne-du-Mont, and that his brother-in-law, Florian Périer, had a funeral plaque in black marble with an epitaph placed over the tomb. Pascal's enemies created such a stir about the epitaph that the archbishop of Paris sent for Father Beurrier, who assured him that Pascal had died piously.

In a letter dated 3 September 1662 addressed to Monsieur de Saint-Calais, Pierre Nicole, a theologian and philosopher, writes that few people will regret Pascal's death because few knew him, but that he will be greatly mourned by those who did know him. Describing Pascal as 'perhaps one of the finest minds that has ever existed,' Nicole contrasts him to many of the voguish thinkers such as Pico della Mirandola, who were 'so many fops compared to him.' After praising him for his courage during his long illness, and for his charity, Nicole writes that 'he will hardly be known by posterity, given that what he left us in his works is not capable of making known the vast extent of his mind . . . ' Nicole's prediction was not to prove true; in his statement that 'nonetheless what remains of this great mind is only two or three little works of which some are distinctly unuseful,' Nicole concludes his letter with lavish praises of Pascal's morality and spirituality, but consigns him to oblivion.

To a Jansenist or to someone sympathetic to Port-Royal, Pascal would have seemed like a persecuted saint; to someone not sympathetic to Jansenism, or hostile to the kind of piety that Jansenism preached – for example, the Jesuits – Pascal would have seemed like a persecuting fanatic. The literary and philosophic texts behind Jansenistic piety are principally the following: *Augustinus* by Cornelius Jansen, *De la fréquente communion* by Antoine Arnauld, and the popularized doctrines by the abbot of Saint-Cyran (Jean Duvergier de Huaranne), *Defense of the 'Chaplet Secret' of the Blessed Sacrament*. Jansenist piety was premised on the conviction that human nature was thoroughly corrupt. Man is caught between the forces of fleshly desire and the ineffable attraction of efficacious grace. Damnation was no figure of speech, as it is in the Miltonic metaphor 'The mind is its own place, and in itself / Can make a heav'n of hell, a hell of heaven' (*Paradise Lost*, book I, 1.253). Damnation is real, eternal, and irreversible. With Pascal damnation is like the state invoked in the *Pensées*: 'The eternal silence of these infinite spaces terrifies me.' The Jansenist view of morality is rigorous to the point of inflexibility. Sacramental absolution did not remit sins, but simply made known that they had been forgiven. Moreover, absolution was valid only if the person confessing already fully loved God.

Although there is no evidence that Mère Agnès de Saint-Paul Arnauld had read *On Divine Names* by Dionysius the Pseudo-Areopagite, the 'Chaplet Secret,' her work popularized by Saint-Cyran, reveals the same form of mysticism and turns of phrase. Dionysius writes of God as ineffable, incomprehensible, incommunicable – in effect so beyond human thinking and language that theology should be strictly impossible. Mère Agnès follows the same mystical bent, leaving the reader with the feeling that God is a metaphysical absolute before which the only proper human gesture is self-annihilation, self-abnegation. There is none of the rosy intimacy, the conversational rapport between the soul and God, to be found in the mystical writings of St Teresa of Avila. Solitude, penitential rigor, and extreme asceticism are the admonitions of Mère Agnès. Again, many mystical writers of the sixteenth century, such as St Teresa and St John of the Cross, looked upon Jesus as a man of great tenderness, sympathy, even an impassioned lover. The Jansenists looked upon Him as a severe and inaccessible redeemer and judge.

Part of the Jansenist zeal for ecclesiastical, sacramental, and educational reform is reflected in Pascal's 'Comparison of Early Christians with Present-day Christians.' Pascal also shared the Jansenist distrust of the Church in its then institutionalized state and hierarchy. It is not unfair to say that many Jansenists were spiritual snobs who believed that they constituted 'the elect' among Catholics and Protestants in general. The richly humanistic tradition represented by Aquinas was also repugnant to the Jansenists, not only because of its emphasis on humanity, but also because of its Aristotelian roots. Dogmatists, the Jansenists were suspicious of theological reasoning; elitists, they thought they were charismatically illumined by God. The resulting attitude was a tendency to prefer private insight to the public teachings of the Church, and contumacy to obedience.

Images of dizziness, of debilitating finiteness, and of self-hatred abound in the *Pensées*: they are the literary rashes, the clinical symptoms of the profoundly pessimistic and malignant view of human nature developed by Jansenism. Pascal succumbed to the dichotomies between the flesh and the spirit, the sensible and the spiritual. It is not surprising that many churchmen of the period viewed Pascal as Calvinistic in attitude, and profoundly antihumanist in doctrine.

4

THE 'MÉMORIAL'

On Monday evening, 24 November 1654, 'from around 10:30 until about 12:30 in the morning,' as he himself scrupulously recorded, Pascal had a mystical experience that changed the course of his life. Language broke down and could not bear the strain of what Pascal experienced. He could find only one word to act as an aegis or symbol of his experience, and he wrote the word in capital letters at the head of the sheet of paper on which he recorded his experience: 'FEU' − 'FIRE.'

To shed light on this most intimate and transfiguring experience in Pascal's life, let us first look at the curious history of how the text was transmitted to posterity, and then examine some of the events that led up to the mystical experience itself. I shall then give a translation of the text, and lastly, some reflections on it.

A few days after Pascal's death, one of the household servants noticed by chance that Pascal's doublet seemed to have something sewn in the lining, one part being thicker than the rest. The servant unstitched the lining and found a small piece of parchment, folded, in Pascal's handwriting, and in the parchment a piece of paper, also in his hand. The one was an exact copy of the other. The domestic immediately gave the papers to Gilberte Périer, Pascal's older sister, who showed them to several of her friends. Everyone agreed that the papers must have served as a sort of '*mémorial*' or memoir of some extraordinary event in the author's life, and that he wanted a constant physical reminder of it. For eight years Pascal had gone to the trouble of sewing it into every new doublet that he bought. Although the original parchment has been lost, a copy in the hand of Pascal's nephew, the Abbé Louis Périer, entirely authentic, has come down to

us; still preserved, however, is the paper on which Pascal noted his
ecstasy and the thoughts which he believed God had inspired in
him.

The 'Mémorial' is usually construed as the record of Pascal's
second conversion, revealing the spontaneity, impatience, and elliptical style that characterize both his life and his writings. The first
conversion had taken place eight years earlier in Rouen, but Pascal
left no record of it. All we know with certainty is that Pascal and his
father had their first encounter at that time with disciples of Saint-
Cyran, and thus with the movement later to be called Jansenism. All
we can say of the first conversion is based upon Gilberte Périer's
biography of her brother. Pascal's father died in 1651; Pascal
promptly wrote a pious letter to his sister. But a few days later he was
leading a worldly life and fraternizing with such persons as Damien
Mitton and the Chevalier de la Méré, who were known to be 'libertins.' Pascal had tried to keep his younger sister, Jacqueline, from
becoming a nun, and especially from entering the austere convent of
Port-Royal. Finally resigning himself to his sister's vocation, Pascal
refused to visit her at the convent for more than a year. Then in
September and October of 1654 Pascal began to visit Port-Royal
frequently, and began to open his soul to Jacqueline, confessing his
sudden distaste for society and the pleasures of the world. Pascal also
related to her how repugnant he found the idea of placing himself
under the spiritual direction of a confessor, a practice strongly
stressed at Port-Royal. He found the nuns' confessor at Port-Royal,
Antoine Singlin – there is a portrait of him by Philippe de Champaigne – particularly crude and uneducated. Nonetheless, Jacqueline
saw 'grace growing visibly' in her brother. It was then that he was
overcome by the mystical experience that he records as follows:

Year of Grace 1654

Monday 23 November, day of Saint Clement, pope and martyr,
and others in the martyrology.
Eve of Saint Chrysogonus, martyr, and others.
From about ten-thirty in the evening until
about half an hour after midnight

FIRE

God of Abraham, God of Isaac, God of Jacob
not of the philosophers or of the learned
Certainty. Certainty. Feeling, Joy, Peace.
God of Jesus Christ.
Deum meum et Deum vostrum.
Your God will be my God.
Oblivion of the world and of everything excepting God.
He is found solely by the ways taught in the Gospel
Grandeur of the human soul.
Just Father, the world does not know You, but I know You.
Joy, Joy, Joy, tears of joy.
I am separated from it.———
Dereliquerunt me fontem aquae vivae.
My God, do you leave me?———
That I be not separated eternally.

This is the life eternal that they know you to be the sole truth
God and the one you have sent J.C.
Jesus Christ———
Jesus Christ———
I separated myself from him. I fled from him, renounced, crucified
him.
That I may never be separated from him!———
He is preserved only by the ways taught in the Gospel.
Total and sweet renunciation.

Total submission to Jesus Christ and to my director.
Eternally in joy for one day of exercise on earth.
Non obliviscar sermones tuos. Amen.

Jacqueline called her brother 'a rejoicing penitent.' Leaving Paris
during the first week of January 1655, Pascal made a retreat near
Port-Royal des Champs, first in the château de Vaumurier, which
belonged to the duc de Luynes, with whom Pascal would later
collaborate on a new translation of the New Testament. He then
continued his retreat at the farm of the Granges de Port-Royal until
21 January of the same year.

To try to explain what the 'Mémorial' *really* means would be an exercise in pretension. The image of fire has an ancient tradition in the rhetoric of mysticism, from the burning bush appearing before Moses to the tongues of fire at Pentecost, from the Pseudo-Dionysius' *On the Divine Names* to the poetry of St John of the Cross and the experiences of St Teresa of Avila. Pascal joins the vast company of mystics using the same image: whether he had an actual visual apparition of fire, whether it was an experience of the imagination, whether it was the sensation of fire, or whether he chose fire as an 'objective corollary' of his meaning, cannot be stated for certain. What is certain, not only from the 'Mémorial' but from everything that Pascal wrote thereafter, is that he had come to the central thesis of all his thought: human reason is a cul-de-sac. Reason cannot give any certain proof of God's existence – 'not the God of the philosophers or the learned.' St Thomas Aquinas had already shown that all *a priori* proofs, or proofs based upon definition, are invalid. Pascal implies that *a posteriori* proofs – proofs by design or effects – are also untenable. Coming out of his ecstasy, Pascal affirms that only the 'grandeur of the human soul' testifies to God's existence. He accuses himself of having neglected God, and then begs not to be separated from him forever. The human soul is unique in that it can both receive and lose grace. The final three lines of the 'Mémorial,' which give the impression of having been added a day or so after the experience, show that Pascal had even resigned himself to having a '*directeur*' – a director of his conscience, or confessor. In his mathematical and scientific studies Pascal always sought to dominate nature and to refute those who disagreed with him; but in his religious experiences he not only wanted but demanded to be dominated. Here again emerges the fundamental dichotomy of Pascal's thought: reason and the heart, 'the order of minds' and 'the order of charity.'

Pascal's retreat at Port-Royal was brief, in part because he wanted to remain 'in the world' to keep abreast of intellectual affairs, in part because out of prudence he did not want to be linked with the '*messieurs*' living in the solitude of Port-Royal. The Port-Royalists had already earned the contempt of the Court, and Louis XIV saw in them a recrudescence of the Fronde. Thus, only after several years of literary fights and illnesses would Pascal fulfill his promise in the 'Mémorial' of 'Oblivion' of the world and of everything excepting God.'

5

PROBING NATURE AND THE HEART

Pascal had intended to write a major treatise concerning the nature of the vacuum; like so many of his works, it was never completed. All that we possess of this project is a remarkable fragment, 'Préface pour le Traité du Vide,' written in 1647. The copy on which the present-day text is based was made by Father Beurrier, who transcribed it from what he called a highly imperfect copy, filled with lacunae. Bossuet was the first to publish the 'Préface,' at the beginning of his edition of the *Pensées*. Bossuet gave the 'Préface' the title 'De l'autorité en matière de philosophie' – 'Concerning Authority in the Matter of Philosophy.'

In the 'Préface' Pascal reveals another facet of his self-image. Squarely entering the battle of the ancients and the moderns, Pascal argues that the ancient philosophers receive such adulation that all their thoughts are turned into oracles and their obscurities into profound mysteries. 'It is not my intention to correct one vice by another, and to accord no esteem to the ancients, because they are given too much. I do not intend to banish their authority in order to establish solely that of reason . . . ' In effect Pascal argues that authority and reason have different but not opposing domains. In such subjects as history, jurisprudence, and 'above all theology,' recourse to authority is essential. But in such subjects as geometry, arithmetic, music, physics, and medicine, reason reigns supreme, and the mind enjoys 'a total liberty to expand itself: its inexhaustible fecundity continuously produces . . . ' Pascal laments both those who try to build the sciences on authorities, ignoring reason and experimentation, and also those who attempt to write theology based solely upon reason, ignoring the Scriptures and the Fathers of the

Church. In Pascal's eyes the great evil of the epoch lay in espousing new ideas in religion that have no roots in authority, and rejecting new ideas in the sciences because they are incompatible with the dicta of the ancients.

Without succumbing to a form of materialism in the style of Spinoza, who habitually wrote '*Deus sive Natura*' – 'God or Nature,' Pascal writes about nature with a quasi-religious awe: 'The secrets of nature are hidden; although she is always active, one does not always discover her effects: time reveals them from age to age; and although she is always consistent, she is not always consistently known.' The leitmotif of the 'grandeur of the human soul' returns: insects like bees can only continuously repeat themselves, building basically the same hive for millennia. 'It is not the same for man, who is produced only for infinity.' But another theme surfaces, which would be strongly denied in Pascal's later thinking: the possibility of unlimited human development through the sciences: 'by a particular prerogative, not only does each person daily advance in the sciences, but mankind is making a continuous progress even as the universe is growing older . . . ' Such a rosy certainty in the advance of humanity through the sciences would soon hold sway in the age of optimism, the Enlightenment. After a deeper look, Pascal would reject it out of hand in the *Pensées*.

Pascal intended to introduce his treatise on the void with philosophic observations because the ancient philosophers generally held that 'nature abhors a vacuum.' Recent experiments had shown that nature does not mind a vacuum at all. Pointing out that when we say that gold is the heaviest of the elements, there is the implicit understanding of 'among the elements known to man,' Pascal points out that he is not actually contradicting the ancient philosophers, for they should be construed as having maintained that nature abhors a vacuum 'according to the experiments we have run.' Pascal was beginning to see himself as a subtle, scientific diplomat, a kind of peace-maker.

Whether Pascal actually wrote 'Discours sur les passions de l'amour' – 'Discourse on the Passions of Love' – may never be known for certain. Victor Cousin discovered the first copy in the archives of Saint-Germain; it bore the note 'attributed to Monsieur Pascal.' Augustin Gazier found the other known copy in the Bibliothèque

Nationale; it did not give any attribution. Many leading Pascal scholars have accepted the 'Discours' as Pascal's, among them Léon Brunschvicg, Victor Giraud, and Gustave Lanson. Other recent scholars, such as V.L. Saulnier and A. Ducas, have denied its authenticity. There is a preciosity and mannerism about the style, and the frequent use of the impersonal *'l'on'* – 'one' – which do not harmonize with Pascal's general style. Yet few authors, except very poor ones, write in the same style throughout their writing careers; moreover, if we assume that the 'Discours' was written during what is known as his 'worldly period,' when he could readily have been reading the *Maximes* of the duc de La Rochefoucauld and other bitterly epigrammatic works on love, we can readily believe that Pascal was the author. Unless one prefers to ascribe it to some totally unknown master of seventeenth-century French prose, it is more reasonable to assume that the 'Discours' is Pascal's, for the work furthers the understanding of Pascal's highly elaborate self-image.

The work begins with a conventional distinction of the period, an image that Pascal would elaborate upon in the *Pensées*: man is both a thinking and an acting being, one given to ideas and to *'passions'* or feelings. The two chief feelings are love and ambition, 'which hardly have any link with each other.' Actually, they tend to be opposed to each other, for a person can have but one *'grand passion,'* however intelligent he or she might be. Both love and ambition demand *'beaucoup de feu'* – 'much fire,' the central image of the 'Mémorial.' He defines a happy life as one that begins with love and concludes with ambition. For Pascal a *'passion'* is not some passive feeling that one undergoes (as the root of the word, from *patior*, would suggest), but something intellectual, involving thoughts, and thoughts *about* something: they are intentional. Thus, Pascal draws the corollary that the greater the mind, the stronger the passions. If any doubts remain about the authorship of the 'Discours,' they must be dismissed by the statement 'There are two sorts of intellects, the one is geometrical, the other one might call the intellect of finesse.' The geometrical mind is slow, hard, and inflexible, while the second turn of mind is flexible and goes to the heart of things. 'When one has both turns of mind together, what pleasure love gives! For one has both force and flexibility of mind, which is essential for dialogue between two persons.'

As the 'Discours' develops, love becomes as central in Pascal's understanding of psychology as it is in St Augustine's and St Thomas's. But again one senses the author's scientific interests: 'However, although man searches for something to fill the great vacuum that he has made in leaving himself, even so he must not be satisfied by any sort of object.' So much attention is given in the 'Discours' to explaining love between man and woman and the importance of female beauty, as to have given rise to the speculation that Pascal had himself fallen in love, perhaps with Charlotte de Roannez. This must remain an idle conjecture; in tone and style the 'Discours' is dispassionate and analytical, giving no hint of personal involvement. Much passion can lie behind elegant Alexandrines, as Racine proves in his tragedies; but behind the nicely turned epigrams of the 'Discours' one senses a passionate intellectual more eager to write like a man of the world than to have an affair. The void, movement, distances in time and space, silence and language: such are Pascal's typical images for describing the phenomena of love. 'In love silence is worth more than language.'

Pascal's passion for antithesis erupts: 'This forgetfulness that causes love, and this attachment to the one we love, gives birth to qualities never seen before. Someone becomes magnificent, without ever having been so. Even a selfish person in love becomes liberal.' Yet his spirit of conciliation tries to cap the volcano by arguing that it is a mistake to oppose love and reason, 'for they are the same thing.' As if anticipating the development of computers and automata, Pascal brilliantly argues that if we took love away from reason 'we would be very disagreeable machines. Let us not exclude reason from love; they are inseparable.' Clearly for Pascal love is not some devouring or obsessive force, as it emerges under Sartre's scalpel some three hundred years later, but a strong feeling based upon strong reason and strong respect. 'When one loves deeply, it is always a new experience to see the beloved; after a moment of absence, one finds an emptiness in one's heart.' A lover in such a state can deserve only compassion; but as his thought progresses, Pascal will sense that only a transcendent Being can satisfy the 'fire' in his heart.

6
COMING TO TERMS WITH GOD

'Sur la Conversion du pécheur' – 'On the Conversion of the Sinner' – was probably written toward the end of 1653 when, according to his sister Jacqueline, Pascal 'had a great contempt for society and an almost unbearable distaste for the people in it.' In this brief work Pascal views himself as a redeemed sinner. 'The first thing that God inspires in a soul that He deigns to touch truly is an understanding and a perspective altogether extraordinary by which the soul considers itself and all things in an entirely new way.'

This 'new light' brings with it fear; what gave pleasure before only stirs up scruples. Confusion and disorder set in as one vanity after another, one solid object after another from the soul's previous state, slips away. What had seemed so solid – 'the sky, the earth, one's mind, one's body, parents, friends, enemies . . . ' – fades into nothingness. Wondering how one could have lived so long in the blindness before conversion, and astounded that so many persons still content themselves with perishable goods, the soul 'enters into a holy confusion and a state of astonishment which bring about a salubrious turmoil.' Humility banishes the soul's pride, making the convert realize that he should love only what cannot be taken away from him. 'This elevation is so eminent and transcendent' that it can only come to a halt at 'God's throne.' Divine grace inspires penitence, prayers, and a resolution never to return to the state of the former self. Pascal compares getting to know God better to a lost traveller asking for directions. What is most striking about Pascal's self-image in this document is that he is totally alone, searching directly for God. No mention is made of the Church, let alone the intercession of the saints, or the other two persons of the Trinity, or the Virgin Mary. If this were the only description that Pascal left us of his conversion one could only assume that he had been converted to Unitarianism before it was founded.

The opusculum entitled 'Comparaison des Chrétiens des premiers temps avec ceux d'aujourd'hui' – 'Comparison of Early Christians with Present-day Christians' – reveals Pascal as a zealous religious reformer. The work also reveals an eagerness to oversimplify and a tendency toward religious romanticism. 'At the birth of the Church one could only find Christians who were entirely consumed by all the points necessary for salvation; whereas today one finds an ignorance so gross that it makes those who have a feeling of fondness for the Church groan.' After a typical series of sharp antitheses, which demonstrate, moreover, a dramatic ignorance of church history, Pascal argues for a sharp and implacable distinction between the Church and the world. He clearly wants to present himself as a religious purist, but only succeeds in appearing as an intransigent dogmatist. He criticizes infant baptism on the grounds that the infant neither knows what the sacrament means nor asks to receive it. This criticism illustrates Pascal's tendency to subjectify religious practices and beliefs. When he further argues that in the early Church baptism was deferred to maturity so that one would understand the sacrament, Pascal has his facts wrong. From St Augustine's *Confessions* and other sources we learn that baptism was delayed as long as possible out of the belief that any sin contracted after being christened would be all the more difficult to absolve. Deathbed baptisms were not uncommon in the early Church. The 'Comparison' breaks off so abruptly that the reader is left with the impression that Pascal had only just begun his litany of complaints against the Church. Whether he intended to criticize the ways in which the other six sacraments were currently administered, as opposed to how he imagined they were once administered by the early Church, we can only surmise.

Revealing an entirely different side of his personality, and one that is vastly engaging and unmarred by censoriousness, is 'Entretien avec Monsieur de Saci' – 'A Conversation with Monsieur de Saci.' Monsieur Le Maître de Saci, grandson of Antoine Arnauld the elder, was the spiritual director introduced to Pascal shortly after his conversion during his two-week sojourn at Port-Royal des Champs. Monsieur de Saci is the '*directeur*' referred to in Pascal's 'Mémorial,' to whom he has 'total submission.' The conversation between the two must have been written down immediately by de Saci's secretary, Fontaine. Sainte-Beuve believed that de Saci's older brother, Antoine Le Maître, was also present at the dialogue. Although the 'Entretien' records the vivacity and 'fire' of Pascal's temperament, it is a reconstruction by de Saci's secretary, perhaps with the aid of notes from Pascal himself, and perhaps with advice from Antoine Le Maître. The 'Conversation' has the air of a Platonic dialogue. The other important figure in the 'Entretien' is Antoine Singlin, the confessor of the nuns of Port-Royal, the priest whom Pascal found 'harsh and uncultivated.' Father Singlin is recorded as having found all that Pascal said on the occasion 'quite right,' but 'it was nothing new.' Everything of importance that Pascal had said had already been said by St Augustine. 'Monsieur Pascal is much to be admired in that, never having read the Fathers of the Church, he has by the penetration of his own mind discovered the same truths that they discovered. He finds them surprising because he has never encountered them before. As for ourselves, we are accustomed to finding them everywhere in our books.' After such a cruel compliment, one can appreciate Pascal's dislike of Father Singlin.

De Saci is described as far more amiable, and certainly more skillful as a conversationalist. Always adapting his conversation to the person with whom he was speaking, de Saci would talk about painting with Philippe de Champaigne – another frequent visitor to Port-Royal – or about medicine with Dr Hamon. Thus, De Saci knew that it would be fitting to talk about philosophy with Pascal, and asked him what authors he read most frequently. Pascal replied, 'Epictetus and Montaigne.' A perfect conversational opening established, de Saci begged him to explain their views 'in depth.'

Pascal explained that Epictetus, a pagan philosopher, was among those who best understood man's duties. God is man's principal object, and man must submit himself to all that happens. 'Always keep the idea of your death in mind, as well as what seem to you the most intolerable evils; thus you will never have any low ideas or desire anything in excess.' The quotations from Epictetus in the 'Entretien' can be readily traced to an old translation by Brother Jean de Saint-François, which appeared in 1609.

After describing the merits of Epictetus' philosophy, Pascal begins to enumerate what he deems to be his errors: that everything is in man's power, that the soul is part of the divine substance, that pain and death are not evils, and that suicide is sometimes laudable. In effect, Pascal salvages from the ideas of the first-century Stoic what is compatible with Christianity and discards what is not.

Turning to Montaigne, Pascal describes him as a philosopher who, although a Catholic, tried to determine what sort of morality reason could discover on its own, without any aid from faith or revelation. Montaigne begins with a sweeping doubt of everything; but even to say that he doubts is too positive, or that he does not know. Taking as his motto, '*Que sais-je?*' – 'What do I know?' – Montaigne is a pyrrhonist or extreme skeptic. 'From this principle all of his writings and *Essays* proceed . . . in this spirit he makes fun of all received opinions.' Rejecting any preconceived rules or principles, Montaigne contented himself with recording his impressions, pointing out how fluid and ephemeral all beliefs are. Applying the same spirit to theological disputes, he tried to expose the bigotry of the heretics of his day, those who claimed to know what a certain passage in the Scriptures really meant. Montaigne applied the same skepticism to the dominant philosophies of his time, Aristotelianism and Thomism, and to what were taken as the first principles of physics. 'And since we do not know what the soul is, or the body, or time, or space, movement, truth, God, not even being, and are not able to explain the idea we form of these things, how can we be certain that it is the same idea in everyone . . . ?' Even geometry is based upon uncertainties, both in its axioms and in its key terms, such as 'point,' 'extension,' and 'movement.' Pascal interprets Montaigne's method as a way of showing how essential faith and revelation must be, for without them mankind would sink into idiocy.

Monsieur de Saci thanks Pascal for such an enlightening presentation, but says: 'I certainly believe that this man was intelligent, but I am not sure that you have not imputed to him more intelligence than he had by this careful linking together of his principles that you have done.' De Saci calls skepticism a silly position, disproved centuries before by St Augustine. Montaigne wasted the fine intelligence that God gave him and made a 'sacrifice of it to the Devil.' After expounding some tenets of St Augustine's philosophy, in particular his refutation of the Academics – the fashionable skepticism in Rome in St Augustine's time – de Saci succeeds in nettling Pascal.

Pascal, 'being still full of his author,' reveals how sympathetic he is to Montaigne's extreme skepticism. Certitude is to be found only in faith. He praises Montaigne's form of Stoic virtue as 'naive, familiar, pleasant, playful, even a bit mad.' Explaining why he was so eager to expound the philosophies of Epictetus and Montaigne, Pascal says that 'they were certainly the two greatest defenders of the two most celebrated sects of the world, and the only ones conforming to reason, since man can follow only one of these two routes, to wit: either there is a God, and he places his highest good there; or he is uncertain, and then the true good is uncertain also, because he is incapable of it.' Pascal explains that the fundamental error of Epictetus was that he did not understand the nature and effects of original sin; his views therefore led to self-satisfied pride. Montaigne, on the other hand, understood the doctrine, but concluded that nature is necessarily unstable and truth impossible to attain. 'For the one establishing certainty, the other doubt; the one the grandeur of man, the other his weakness,' the two philosophers cancel each other out. Pascal proposes a synthesis of these two extremes 'by the truth of the Gospel . . . Unifying all that is true and eliminating all that is false, it brings about a truly celestial wisdom in which contraries are harmonized . . . ' Only in the person of the '*Homme-Dieu*' – 'Man God' – can the opposing dialectical avenues of Epictetus and Montaigne be synthesized. Pascal apologizes for having departed from philosophy and entered the realms of theology, but he argues that it is an inevitable and necessary step. By now the two men are enchanted with each other's dialectical skills, and de Saci praises Pascal for being able to read such authors and extract a higher truth, 'knowing how to draw pearls out of a dung heap' and '*aurum ex stercore Tertulliani*' – 'gold out of Tertullian's dung.' Clearly, only those strong in the true faith should be allowed to read such authors.

Pascal agrees. Although Epictetus is important for showing that the true goods are interior and related to God, he is pernicious because his philosophy can lead to pride and self-sufficiency. (Neither de Saci nor Pascal mentions Pelagius or Pelagianism in this context, but Epictetus is their pagan counterpart.) Montaigne is valuable for destroying the intellectual pretensions of heretics and unbelievers, but his philosophy is equally useful for those with a penchant for impiety or vice.

The 'Entretien' concludes most congenially, like a pastorale: 'And such was the manner in which these two brilliant persons finally agreed on the way to read these philosophers; and they came to the same conclusion, though in different ways: Monsieur de Saci arrived there at once by the clear perspective of Christianity, and Monsieur Pascal got there only after many windings round the principles of his philosophers.'

The 'Entretien' expresses a new self-image of Pascal, one that he was eager to expose to his spiritual director: the exuberant dialectician, the intellectual athlete of God. What is also revealed, however, is a penchant for one of the oldest heresies of the Church: fideism – the belief that reason is categorically incapable of giving any satisfactory argument for some of the major articles of faith, such as the existence of God and the immortality of the soul.

7

THE NASCENT POLEMICIST

Of crucial importance in understanding how Pascal moved from his geometrical studies to his investigations concerning man and God is 'De l'esprit géométrique et de l'art de persuader' – 'On the Geometrical Mind and the Art of Persuasion.' The date of composition, although uncertain, is usually given as around 1658. The tone of the short monograph is magisterial and precise; one senses that Pascal had in mind certain pupils for whom he was writing. We know that at about the same time Pascal had written a Preface for an essay on the elements of geometry for the Petites Ecoles de Port-Royal. Given that Pascal always had a clear idea of the audience he was attempting to reach, we can safely assume that he had the puils of Port-Royal in mind.

'One can have three principal purposes in the study of truth: one, to discover truth when one searches for it; the other, to demonstrate truth when one is in possession of it; and finally, to distinguish the truth from the false when one examines it.' After announcing that he will not speak of the first, Pascal reasons that the third purpose is contained in the second. What he wants to show is how truths already discovered can be given 'invincible proof.' For Pascal geometry follows two principles: the giving of proofs for particular propositions, and the right ordering of the propositions. Consequently he divides his treatise into two parts, the first section entitled 'Concerning the Method of Geometrical Demonstration,' and the second 'Concerning the Art of Persuasion.'

In common with many seventeenth-century thinkers, Pascal believed that only geometry had discovered the true or valid rules of reasoning. It is thus the method of geometry that sets it high above all other human sciences. This method lays down two demands: that all terms must be precisely defined, and that no proposition can be advanced unless it is based on previously known truths. Although definitions should be univocal, there must be 'primitive words which cannot be further defined.' Similarly there must be some principles which are so clear that they admit of no further proof: the axioms. 'From which it appears that man is in a natural and unchangeable powerlessness to pursue any science in an absolutely accomplished order.' Nonetheless geometry provides the paradigm of reasoning even if it cannot define everything and prove everything. Exhibiting his penchant for finding a just mean between two extremes, Pascal argues that geometry sins neither by trying to define everything nor by neglecting definitions and proofs.

Taking an Augustianian tack, Pascal says that the primitive terms such as 'space' and 'equality' are simply *known* – like the term 'man.' Like Molière in his satires of pedants in *Le Malade imaginaire* and *Les Femmes savantes*, Pascal ridicules those who define one word by the same word. 'I know those who have defined "light" like this: "Light is a luminary movement of luminous bodies." ' As a prefiguration of his distinction between the heart and the mind, Pascal writes that nature gives man the ideas of the primitive notion, and that it is both useless and impossible for the mind to define them precisely. Although not everyone has the same understanding of such general, primitive notions – such as 'time' – there is sufficient shared understanding of time for the mere utterance of the word *temps* to bring all minds to bear on the same object. Pascal is a nominalist, but a careful one: 'nothing is more free than definitions.' We naturally understand what time is; but once we redefine it in a certain philosophical or scientific way, we must be ready to bear the consequences. Departing from the ordinary understanding of the terms designating the coordinates of man's existence, such as 'time,' 'space,' or 'existence' itself, one moves from the realm of primitive terms to that of propositions which must be demonstrated.

Despite being attracted by nominalism, Pascal often invokes 'natural light' or *'clarté naturelle'* (sometimes *'lumière naturelle'*) to show that only geometry, making use of the mind's fundamental mirroring of nature, follows the right method. The mind can conceive of a vaster space, a longer time, a faster movement than is postulated; and so too, of a smaller space, or shorter time, or slower movement.

Man's mind oscillates between the two infinites; yet neither end can be proved in fact – whether the universe is infinite in space and eternal, or finite and temporal. Geometry is of no use in solving such conundrums or puzzles; therefore, the lesser human sciences should learn to be silent about such matters.

Pascal introduces the second section of 'De l'esprit géométrique' not with a definition but with a suggestion. 'The art of persuading has a necessary relationship to the way in which people consent to what is proposed to them, and to the state of affairs that one wants to make believable.' Understanding and will are the two avenues of opinion – believing for good reason and believing out of will. Although everyone holds that the latter is an unworthy route, many follow it in the belief that it is the avenue of the understanding. 'I do not speak here of divine truths, which I am wary of subsuming under the art of persuading; for they are infinitely above nature. Only God can place them in the soul, and in the way that pleases Him. I know that He wanted them to enter by the heart into the mind, and not by the mind into the heart in order to humiliate the proud power of reasoning, which pretends to be the judge of what will chooses, and in order to heal this infirm will, which has corrupted itself with unclean attachments.' A major theme in Pascal's thought and self-conception emerges. In regard to human affairs and sciences, one must first understand them before one can love them; as for divine matters, one must first love them before one is able to understand them. The schism between the supernatural and the natural is again reinforced. Much of what reason assents to is rationalizations premised upon the yearnings of the will; and as a final step of hubris, reason makes itself believe that nothing is beyond its ken. There are two ways of persuading: the one involving reason, the other based upon pleasure. Pascal declares himself incapable of giving any rules for the art of persuading by pleasure or '*agrément*' mainly because 'the principles of pleasure are not firm and stable.' They vary from man to man, and depend on social conditions, and age. 'But what I call the art of persuasion, which is nothing but the conduct of perfect and methodical proofs, consists of three essential parts: defining the terms that are needed in clear terms; proposing the principles or axioms needed for proving the case at hand; and always substituting mentally in the demonstration the definitions for what is to be defined.'

What follows is the '*batterie de logique*,' the logical tools, so to speak, that Pascal will use in later works on philosophy and theology. Attempting to give the fewest rules possible concerning definitions, axioms, and demonstrations, Pascal describes 'the entire method of geometrical proofs of the art of persuasion: (1) Do not undertake to define anything known in itself unless you have clearer terms to define it. (2) Admit no obscure or equivocal terms, without definition. (3) Employ nothing in a definition other than terms perfectly understood, or already explained.'

Rules for axioms prescribe that they be clear and self-evident; rules for demonstrations naturally demand that all steps be self-evident. One hears in all these sage and sound admonitions Pascal the schoolmaster, the quick respondent to objections to his proposals – prolepsis, as it is called in classical rhetoric – the combatant girding his loins to make war on those who dare challenge his faith. A new self-image emerges: didacticist, champion of the geometrical method, scorner of rationalism – that the human mind can possibly fathom the fundamentals of existence – and fighter.

The young Pascal criticizes the most revered French philosopher of the time, Descartes, by pointing out that his *'Je pense, donc je suis'* can be traced to St Augustine, who had developed the same arguments in his 'Soliloquies' twelve hundred years before. 'In truth, I am far from saying that Descartes was not the true author, nor even that he may have learned it from reading this great saint; for I know how great a difference lies between writing something by chance, without making any thorough investigation of it, and perceiving in the utterance an admirable linkage of consequences that prove a distinction between the spiritual and the physical . . . ' Small wonder that when the two men did meet in 1647 (Pascal was ill, staying with his sister Jacqueline in Paris), two of the best scientific minds in France, and in Europe, got along so badly. Two brief evenings, or early afternoons, on 23 and 24 September, were recorded by Jacqueline. In the context of the monograph on geometrical reasoning, Descartes must have appeared to the young and ardent author as one of those who pretended to be able to prove everything, from his own existence to God's. What Pascal implies in this brief work is that arguments for God's existence are as ridiculous as those for one's own. God exists, if one has love for Him; and, curiously, one is, if one realizes one's own finiteness and longing for the infinite. The two infinities reappear: self and God, both of them intensely real to

Pascal, yet equally beyond the sweep of geometrical analysis, or experimental demonstration.

8

LETTERS TO FAMILY, FRIENDS, AND SAVANTS

Pascal's younger sister, Jacqueline, states in a letter dated 24 October 1656 that he suffered from an insurmountable laziness when it came to writing letters. Only some dramatic miracle, like that of the Holy Thorn (which his older sister, Gilberte, recounts in her biography of her brother), or some significant secular event, could fillip him into writing a letter. While we possess literally hundreds of letters by Pascal's great contemporary, Leibniz, we possess only fifteen by Pascal. Yet the letters are so revealing that if they were the only extant writings of Pascal's that came down to us we could reconstruct an illuminating biography.

The first letter, dated simply 'from Rouen, the last Saturday of January,' is the earliest autograph of Pascal known to exist. It dates from 1643, when the young Pascal accompanied his father, who was employed in the monarchical tax bureaucracy, to Rouen. Gilberte had married Florian Périer in 1641, but following the custom of the time, Pascal addresses his married sister as 'Mademoiselle.' In a brief, gallant letter, employing the familiar *tu*, Pascal expresses his concern about not receiving letters from his sister and about her state of health.

The next three letters date from the period when Pascal had returned from Rouen to Paris with his father and younger sister. While in Rouen, Pascal's father, Etienne, had slipped on the ice and broken his hip; he was treated by two lay brothers who had connections with Port-Royal. New spiritual doors were suddenly opened for Pascal; it was while he was living in Rouen that he experienced what is called his 'first conversion.' Elements of his new religious concerns and ideas that will find their way into the *Pensées* emerge from the letters. Pascal wrote to his older sister (26 January 1648) explaining that he had not written for four months because of bad health and lack of time. He mentions his visits to Port-Royal and his discussions there with various religious who were obviously trying to convert him to their way of thinking. In the following letter (1 April 1648) Pascal mentions having a copy of 'De la vocation' – 'On the Religious Vocation' – by Saint-Cyran, one of the most important thinkers at Port-Royal. 'Recently printed, without ecclesiastical approval or sanction, it has shocked many people.' Pascal promises to send it to Gilberte as soon as he has read it himself. The letter expresses great tenderness for his sister, which Pascal attributes to their new spiritual interests. Citing Saint-Cyran, Pascal calls their new relationship 'the beginning of life' and says that 'it has pleased God to join us as well in his new world by the mind as He did in the earthly world by the flesh.' He writes that corporeal things are only images of spiritual things and that God represents the invisible in the visible. 'This thought is so general and useful that one should not let a moment pass without giving it serious attention.' God is the only true principle, and the origin of all vice lies in adoring images rather than what lies behind them. Rich with spiritual longing, the letter abounds in signs of Pascal's second conversion recorded in the 'Mémorial.'

Jacqueline had increasingly expressed her desire to take vows at Port-Royal and to lead the life of a sequestered nun. Her vocation had found favor neither with her brother nor with her father. On the afternoon of 5 November 1648 Blaise and Jacqueline wrote to their sister from Paris. They allude to the domestic dispute over Jacqueline's plans. In a strangely ceremonious and circuitous letter, they wonder first of all how Gilberte could have found out about Jacqueline's vocation, since neither of them had told her, nor had their father. Blaise and Jacqueline suggest that only God could have told her. After assuring Gilberte that they were trying to behave as responsibly as possible, and that 'we must be on the watch continuously to purify the interior, which always sullies itself with new stains while holding on to the old ones, since without assiduous renewal one will not be able to receive the new wine, which will never be put into old vessels.' It is a preachy letter, showing much more of Blaise's style than Jacqueline's. It reveals the aggressive side of Blaise, who did not want Jacqueline to take vows at Port-Royal in part because of his ambivalence about the type of austere religiosity being practiced there. The letter also shows the peremptory side of Pascal's character, for in effect he is telling Gilberte to mind her own business and not to influence or encourage Jacqueline's wish to take vows – all this, artfully done, under the guise of a joint letter, a prefiguration of the bent of mind that was to produce the *Provincial Letters*. The letter also reveals a touch of anti-Semitism in Pascal: in none of his writings does he use the adjective *'judaïque'* – 'judaic' – other than pejoratively. In the present letter he writes: 'Thus one should never refuse to read or to hear holy things, no matter how known or common they might be; for our memory, as well as the lessons that it retains, is only an inanimate and judaic body without the spirit which must vivify it.' Lastly, if the violent side of Pascal's psyche were not already revealed in this letter, there is his occasional sanctimoniousness. Gilberte's husband was having some work done on their homes just outside Paris. In the last paragraph Blaise gives a report to Gilberte on how the work is going, but writes that the project is too elaborate and that she and her husband should restrict themselves to the bare essentials – *'le simple nécessaire.'* Blaise goes so far as to add his own prayers, and reminds her that it is much more important to build 'a mystic tower' than a mere house. Sister Jacqueline is allowed to add a postscript: 'I hope to write you in my own name about my affair, about which I shall give you the details; meanwhile, pray God for its outcome. If you know some good soul, have him pray to God for me as well.' Although God may have informed Gilberte about her sister's plans, it seems more likely – given, perhaps, the number of affairs that God must attend to – that Jacqueline had already sent a note about it to Gilberte.

Pascal's father died in Paris on 24 September 1651. Three weeks later (17 October) Pascal wrote a long letter to Gilberte and her husband to give the entire family some consolation. It is a highly 'composed' letter, bringing together the ancient, pagan model of consoling epistles and Christian beliefs. Pascal's main thesis is that one should not try to understand sickness and death in terms of proximate or natural causes but rather as part of God's Providence. Pagans such as Socrates and Seneca conceived of death as a natural event; from the Scriptures, argues Pascal, one sees that death is a punishment for original sin. Death 'without Jesus Christ is horrible, loveable, holy, and the joy of the believer.' Death is not simply an event but a sacrifice, an oblation. The letter has the tone of an elaborate homily; one can imagine Pascal delivering it in one of the vast echo-filled baroque churches of Paris, such as Saint-Sulpice or Saint-Honoré. Pascal confesses that he is the 'most interested party' in holding these views about death: 'If I had lost him six years ago, I would have been lost myself . . . '

On 14 May 1652 the Abbé Bourdelot wrote to Pascal from Stockholm to beg him to send his calculator – the *'machine arithmétique'* that Pascal had invented – to Queen Christina of Sweden. 'You are one of those geniuses that the Queen is searching for; she loves clarity in reasoning and solid proofs better supported than on appearances.' Bourdelot assures Pascal that the queen will relish 'the clearest and most penetrating mind that I have ever seen.' Queen Christina had already summoned Descartes to Stockholm so that he could teach her geometry; unfortunately for Descartes, the queen wanted her lessons at dawn. Descartes soon caught a chill and died in the queen's palace in 1650. Perhaps this event predisposed the queen not to ask Pascal to accompany his mechanical calculator to Stockholm. However that might be, Pascal sent a copy of his calculator to the queen with a letter dated June 1652. The letter not only reveals Pascal's self-esteem as an accomplished inventor but also foreshadows his fundamental distinction between the corporeal and the spiritual orders, both of which he will later subordinate to the order of charity – *'l'ordre de la charité.'*

'Had I as much health as zeal,' Pascal writes to the queen, 'I would go myself to present to Your Majesty this work that has taken several years, that I now dare offer her from so far away; and I would not have allowed other hands than my own to have the honor of placing it at the feet of the greatest princess of the world.' In his most gallant and courtly style, Pascal explains that his machine performs mathematical calculations automatically. Making a deep literary reverence, Pascal writes that the queen possesses the two traits that he admires the most: sovereign authority and solid science. Begging the queen not to take offense, Pascal writes that either of these traits without the other is 'defective.' 'However powerful a monarch may be, something is missing in his glory if he does not possess intellectual preeminence; and however enlightened a subject may be, his condition is lowered by being a dependant.' With Racinian grandeur, Pascal praises the queen for being the first to unite monarchy with the 'lights of science': 'Rule therefore, incomparable Princess, in a manner entirely new, so that your genius will subject all that is not under the submission of your arms. Rule by the right of your birth for years to come in many a triumphant province. But rule always by dint of your merit across the globe.'

The cosmopolitan grandiloquence of the letter to Queen Christina is far removed from the note Pascal sent to his brother-in-law Florian Périer on 6 June 1653, reflecting a domestic squabble. 'I have just received your letter, together with that of my sister, which I have not had time to read, and moreover it would be useless to do so. My sister took her vows yesterday, Thursday, 5 June. It was impossible for me to postpone it: the gentlemen of Port-Royal feared that a slight delay would entail a longer one, and wanted to hasten it because they hoped to put her into their care soon . . . ' Soon after their father's death, Jacqueline vowed to enter the convent of Port-Royal, professing that Blaise himself had inspired the fervor for her vows. Although her brother begged her to wait a year, 'to help himself resolve his unhappiness,' she left Paris for Port-Royal on 4 January 1652. By the laws of the *ancien régime* Jacqueline would give up her part of the inheritance to the oldest male in the family upon taking religious vows. Blaise was not acting out of avarice by trying to block Jacqueline's vocation, but could not bear her taking the habit so soon after their father's death. Upon her entreaty Blaise acquiesced, and was present when Jacqueline took her first vows, as a novice, on 26 May 1652. On the evening before her final vows, Jacqueline decided – perhaps under pressure, although there is no evidence of this – to give her part of the inheritance, her dowry, to Port-Royal, a decision that was against both the custom and the law then in effect. Not only was she breaking with the hierarchical Catholic Church of France, she was challenging the laws of the State concerning the rights of inheritance. In seventeenth-century France both Church and State were largely cut from the same cloth. Both Blaise and Gilberte protested that although their sister had the right to transfer her dowry to Port-Royal, it could not be transferred until their father's affairs had been settled. Pascal went to Port-Royal, talked with Jacqueline, and saw how unhappy she was. He must have spoken with the severe Mother Superior – Mère Angélique – whose visage we know from Philippe de Champaigne's portrait (Plate 7). Pascal gave the required sum, or even more, as Jacqueline attested to the prioress of Port-Royal in June 1653.

From September 1656 to March 1657 Pascal wrote a number of letters to Charlotte de Roannez, the sister of his closest friend, the duc de Roannez. Pascal's original letters were destroyed in 1683 upon the death of Mademoiselle de Roannez, but copies of parts of them were made by Marguerite Périer. Nine fragments have been preserved. During his correspondence with Charlotte de Roannez, Pascal was embroiled with the composition and controversy of the *Provincial Letters*. The Jansenist dispute, which will be discussed at length in Chapter 10, formed the background for the *Provincial Letters*. Pope Innocent X had already censured the 'five propositions' of Jansen – the supposedly heretical propostions that many believed to be contained in his book on St Augustine. Alexander VII censured the five propositions again on 16 October 1656. In March 1657 the doctors of the Sorbonne devised an oath imposing acknowledgment of the papal bull of Innocent X – the *'Formulaire,'* or 'Formulary' – which all religious, including those of Port-Royal, were forced to sign. The condemnation of the five propositions, and the oath, brought about the composition of the *Provincial Letters*. Charlotte de Roannez had a religious experience on 4 August 1656 as she was concluding a novena before the Holy Thorn; she vowed to enter the convent of Port-Royal in Paris. She spoke with the same priest that Pascal had encountered at Port-Royal des Champs, Father Singlin. The nine fragments not only reflect the religious tumult of the period but also depict new aspects of Pascal's character.

In the first fragment Pascal sees the religious and social upheavals of the day prefigured in the Gospel according to St Mark, who speaks of miracles, of the presence of the Holy Spirit in the relics of the dead, and of God's unceasing protection of his chosen. 'But it serves no purpose to tell you what you already know so well; it would be better to tell it to those persons whom you spoke about, but they would not listen . . . ' The second fragment rests upon a typically Pascalian image of two opposing forces with man caught in the middle: the force of God pulling from above, and the force of the body tugging from below. In the third fragment Pascal writes that 'the essence of sin consists in having a will opposed to that which we know is in God.' Pascal alludes to the persecutions being carried on by the theologians of the Sorbonne and by the Jesuits. In the next fragment Pascal indulges in his penchant for paradox, attempting to show why miracles must occur, but only rarely: 'If God showed Himself continuously to men, there would be no merit in believing in Him; and if He never revealed Himself, there would be little faith. But ordinarily He keeps Himself hidden, and reveals Himself rarely to those whom He wants to engage in His service.' The practical corollary is apparently to seek solitude. Pascal describes nature as a veil that covers a hidden God. 'All things cover some mystery; all things are veils that cover God.' What is peculiar to Catholicism, Pascal states, is that 'it is only us whom God illumines to that point,' i.e., of recognizing God hidden behind the appearance of bread in the Eucharist. The sixth fragment is important because it expresses Pascal's strong support of the papacy, and praises Charlotte de Roannez for sharing the same view. Pascal swears that he will never separate himself from the head of the Church, 'who is the pope'. Fragment seven shows that Pascal was acquainted with some of the works of Tertullian (c. 155–220), whose fiery genius, eloquence, and love of paradox have a strong affinity with Pascal's own style. The last two fragments counsel profiting from evil and following Christian precepts because they give more consolation than 'the maxims of the world.'

Two fragments survive of letters to Father Lalouère concerning the nature of the cycloid, dated respectively 11 and 18 September 1658. His death only four years away, Pascal returned to his scientific and mathematical interests. The tenth letter, dated 6 January 1659 and addressed to the astronomer and physician Christian Huyghens at The Hague, also deals with the problem of the cycloid. Pascal says how flattered he is that his name has come to the attention of such a great scientist as Huyghens. The eleventh letter is only a fragment from 1659 of what must have been a vehement objection that Pascal made to his sister Gilberte on her plan to marry off her daughter, who was fifteen years of age, to 'a gentleman of condition.' Pascal was horrified. 'Moreover, as for husbands, although rich and wise according to society, they are in truth bold pagans before God.' He tells his sister that she is about to commit one of the greatest sins: 'It is a kind of homicide and deicide in their persons.'

Pascal wrote to Pierre de Fermat, the mathematician, on 10 August 1660. After expressing his regret that ill health prevented him from visiting Fermat in Toulouse, Pascal writes that 'although you are the one that I hold to be the greatest geometer in Europe, it is not for that quality that I would have been drawn to you, but it is what I can imagine to be the intelligence and honesty of your conversation that would have made me search you out.' Pascal refers to geometry as 'a good trade,' but only a trade or job along with others. Writing from Bien-Assis, near Clermont, Pascal explains that he can no longer walk without a cane or mount a horse, and that it took him twenty-two days to make his journey from Paris. The doctors had prescribed the 'waters of Bourbon' for the month of September. Pascal mentions going by riverboat to Saumur to stay with the duc de Roannez, who was governor of Poitou.

In December of 1660 Pascal wrote to the marquise de Sablé to thank her for bringing to his attention the work of Dr Menjot, who belonged to the reformed church and had just published a book entitled *L'Histoire et la guérison des fièvres malignes* – 'History and Cure of Malignant Fevers.' Pascal simply records how impressed he was with the way in which the author reconciled the immateriality of the soul with the powers of matter to alter its functions and to cause delirium. The book did nothing, however, to alter Pascal's state of health. The last two letters, one addressed to his sister Gilberte, the other in all probability to his legal consultant Domat, both date from 1661. Pascal is clearly concerned about his relationship with Port-Royal and the 'Formulary,' which on 1 February 1661 the Assembly of the Clergy required all ecclesiastics to sign. Pascal's final concerns center on the truth and self-righteous certainty, arguing that one should fight for the truth but not attempt to conquer with truth, and that self-interest may readily disguise itself as impartial service of God. Pascal's last extant letter ends with a lament for 'those who want absolutely that one should believe the truth because they have demonstrated it, which Jesus Christ did not do in His human form: it is a mockery and it seems to me to treat . . . ' There is a lacuna in the text, but it is clear that Pascal still has the papal bull condemning the 'five propositions' in mind. What led to the condemnation by Innocent X and Alexander VII figures into the background of the *Provincial Letters*. Although not a relativist, Pascal scorned those who did not understand the attractions of relativism in matters concerning both faith and morals, and perhaps ultimately in science. The relativist is comforted by his belief in the pervasive relativity of values. Pascal found no comfort in relativism: he demanded the certain, the absolute, which he believed was not to be found in human relationships, nor in science, nor even in mathematics. Although fully aware of the risk, Pascal turned to God.

1 This portrait of Pascal, which is neither dated nor signed, was executed after the portrait by François II Quesnel, which is the sole source—and even that portrait was made after Pascal's death—of depictions of Pascal. Long attributed to Philippe de Champaigne, the portrait is now described as of the French School. Bernard Dorival writes in his definitive work on Champaigne that 'this portrait, moreover quite mediocre, has nothing in common with the painting of Philippe de Champaigne' (*Philippe de Champaigne*, 2 vols, Léone Laget Librairie. Paris: 1976. Vol. 2, p. 326)

2 Cardinal Richelieu, by Philippe de Champaigne

3 Port-Royal des Champs, general lay-out. Gouache by Madeleine de Boullongne

4 Port-Royal des Champs, viewed from a hill. Gouache by Madeleine de Boullongne

5 Louis XIII, by Philippe de Champaigne

7 Mère Angélique Arnauld, by Philippe de Champaigne

6 Ex-voto of 1662, by Philippe de Champaigne. Unlike the Italian and Spanish schools, in which ecstasy is translated into baroque movement, the French school in the seventeenth century attempted to express religious subjects through emphasis on the inner states of mind, harmonious composition, and studied silence

8 The Crucifixion,
by Philippe de
Champaigne.
The Jansenist
Christocentric view is
emphasized through
the portrayal of the
human nature of
Christ

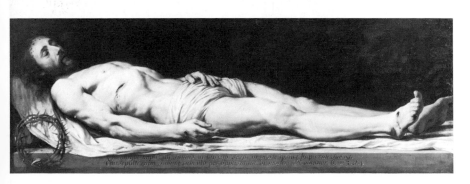

9 The dead Christ on his shroud, by Philippe de Champaigne

10 The Last Supper, by Philippe de Champaigne

11 Jérôme Le Feron, provost of the Guilds of Paris, and the municipal body of the City of Paris, by Philippe de Champaigne. From the middle of the sixteenth century the *Corps de Ville* of Paris had commissioned a group portrait of themselves – first at irregular intervals, then every two years. The portraits included the four *échevins* or aldermen, the prosecutors of the king and of the City of Paris, the registrar, and usually the tax officer. Dominated by a Jansenist-type crucifix, this portrait expresses the individuality and interiority characteristic of the spirit of Port-Royal

LES PROVINCIALES
OU
LES LETTRES ÉCRITES
PAR
LOUIS DE MONTALTE
A
VN PROVINCIAL DE SES AMIS,
&
AUX RR. PP. JESUITES:
Sur le sujet de la Morale, & de la Politique de ces Peres.

A COLOGNE,
Chez PIERRE de la VALLÉE.
M. DC. LVII.

PENSÉES
DE
M. PASCAL
SUR LA
RELIGION,
Et sur quelques autres sujets.
EDITION NOUVELLE.
Augmentée
De beaucoup de Pensées , de la
Vie de l'Autheur, & de quelques
Dissertations.

Sur la copie imprimée ,
A AMSTERDAM,
Chez HENRI WETSTEIN.

Anno M. DCCIX.

12 Title Page of the *Provincial Letters* (Cologne, 1657)

13 Title page of the *Pensées* (Amsterdam, 1709)

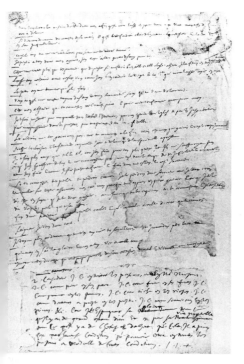

14 Page from the folio of the *Pensées*, folio 89 (553). Reproduced from the edition edited by Léon Brunschvicg, *Original des Pensées de Pascal* (Paris: Librairie Hachette, 1905). Text of folio 89. The upper left line begins: 'Nous implorons la miséricord de Dieu . . .' ('We beseech the mercy of God . . .'). The original is in the Bibliothèque Nationale, Paris

15 Portrait sketch of Pascal as an adolescent
by his friend Jean Domat

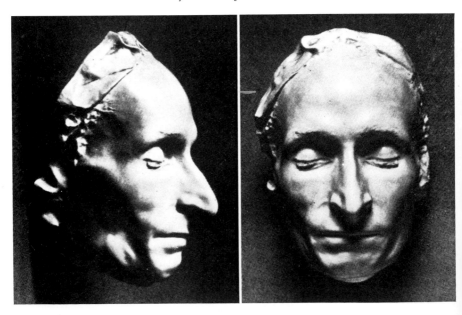

16 Death mask of Pascal

9

GOD'S CHAMPION

Written sometime between May and September 1660, the 'Prière pour demander à Dieu le bon usage des maladies' – 'Prayer to Ask God for the Right Use of Sickness' – is one of the most fervent and spiritual meditations ever written. Towards the end of his life, Pascal suffered again from many ailments which are difficult to diagnose from the impressionistic evidence that remains. But from his sufferings emerged the 'Prière' which is both a prayer, a dialogue between Pascal and God, and an introspective homily to anyone suffering from a terminal disease. The 'Prière' was first published in a collection of devotional works in 1666 entitled *Divers traités de piété*, edited in the formal 'you' – *vous* – instead of the familiar form, *tu*, which has long been the sole correct form for addressing God among French Catholics. French Protestants, such as the Huguenots, have always used the familiar form.

The meditation is divided into fifteen sublime strophes, reminiscent of the solemn oratorios of a contemporary of Pascal's, the great composer Marc Antoine Charpentier. In the first strophe Pascal begs God not to let him react to his illness like a pagan, but to see in his plight a sign of God's goodness. In the second strophe Pascal confesses that when he was healthy he had used his energy for secular interests; his present sickness must therefore be turned to the divine. The third strophe echoes with antiphonal lamentations of '*O Dieu*' – 'O God' – recalling the Last Judgment. Pascal prays to see his sickness as a prefiguration of the hour of death, when he will be separated from all earthly things and set naked before God. The fifth strophe argues that the Church and the Sacraments, even the Crucifixion, are powerless to convert him without God's grace. 'You alone were able to create my soul: you alone can create it again. You alone were able to form your image in it: you alone can re-form it and reimprint your defaced portrait, Jesus Christ my Savior, which is your image and the sign of your substance.' The next few strophes develop, contrapuntally, the themes of beatitude, patience, penitence, and repentance. Pascal asks God 'to re-form my corrupted reason, and to make my feelings conform to yours.' The Incarnation and Passion are invoked to interpret his own physical sufferings. In strophe 11 Pascal prays that he will be able to bear his sufferings as a Christian, and will not be deprived of the Holy Spirit, 'for that is the curse of the pagans and the Jews.' In his typically paradoxical way Pascal prays for both continuing suffering and divine consolation. Strophe 13 develops the theme of total submission to God's will. 'Lord, I know that I know only one thing: that it is good to follow you, and that it is bad to offend you.' The final strophe, a supplication to the second person of the Trinity, concludes like a paean played on an organ with full stops. A new self-image of Pascal is revealed, that of the total penitent. The incarnate oxymoron – the sinner, the saved, the finite, the infinite, the worldling, and the recluse – has found his psychic resolution.

The three little discourses or sermons on the obligations of the high nobility that Pascal gave in the autumn of 1660 first appeared in Pierre Nicole's treatise *De L'Education d'un prince* in 1670. Nicole observes of the 'Trois Discours sur la condition des grands' that although it had been a long time since Pascal had given these discourses, 'nevertheless, all that he said had left such a lively impression on the mind that it was impossible to forget it.' The 'Three Discourses,' apparently given to the older son of the duc de Luynes, are a record of Pascal's thoughts and feelings, if not his actual words. They give three simple lessons. First, that being born into a lofty position is the result of fortuitous events, though rendered legitimate by law. High birth does not authorize the belief that those of a lower condition have any natural obligations to their legitimate superiors. Pascal adhered to the view that might, or position, in this world was the foundation of justice. All temporal power was based solely on custom and power, not on abstract principles. Second, there are two sorts of 'grandeurs' – those that result from nature, and those that result from institutions. 'It is not necessary, because you are a duke, that I esteem you; but it is required that I salute you.' Being a good geometer is a 'natural grandeur,' like being *un honnête homme*.' In the seventeenth century *'un honnête homme'* was a man of great civility, culture, and probity. Pascal implies that it is mathematically easy to determine who is higher placed in the social echelon: one has only to calculate the number of servants, of lackeys, of horses drawing someone's carriage – and the number of his coaches or carriages. Yet all these calculations are 'of this world,' and count for nothing. The divine arithmetic is done by God: once again Pascal's oxymoronic bent of mind returns.

It is idle to speculate whether the Revolution of 1789 would have occurred had *'les grands'* – the higher nobility – taken Pascal's three little 'Discours' to heart. Pascal, like his great mentor St Augustine, was a moralist at heart; both demanded that each individual life, as well as the life of nations and empires, be interpreted as a vast moral and divinely providential tale. St Augustine's voluminous work, *On the City of God* (*De Civitate Dei*), is based upon the simple and stark premise that the Roman Empire was failing because the Romans did not worship the true God. Brief as the three 'Discours' are, they give sufficient evidence that Pascal would have interpreted the French Revolution and the awful events of the Terror as corollaries of moral turpitude. The word 'corollary' is of course at home in the language of geometry; but given Pascal's penchant for seeing what he deemed basic through the eye of the geometer, he would have extended its application to historical events as well. In fact, the next work to be discussed, the 'Abrégé de la vie de Jésus-Christ' – 'Summary of the Life of Jesus Christ' – reads like a treatise on geometry, with definitions, axioms, propositions – and corollaries. As for the 'Discours,' they are a sobering, if not a brazen bit of advice for a geometer from a family of minor nobility, *'de la Robe,'* to give to a future duke of the realm, a member of the higher nobility, *'de l'Epée.'* The roots of the 'Discours' show that Pascal adhered to a positivistic conception of human law; i.e., justice is what the law has long prescribed, proscribed, and protected. But Pascal believed that he could no more tie the hands of God by human law than he could define the primitive notions of geometry. Both the geometer and the high nobility must submit to a higher, although indefinable, authority.

The 'Summary of the Life of Jesus Christ' appears to have been written sometime after November 1654, though the first idea for it probably goes back to 1649. Naturally based upon the Gospel, the 'Abrégé' also draws from two other texts with which Pascal was in all probability acquainted: the *Lettres chrétiennes et spirituelles* by Saint-Cyran, and the 'Series vitae Jesu-Christi juxta ordinem temporum' which had been published in 1655 as an appendix to the *Tetrateuchus* of Jansen. After a brief introduction or 'Préface,' Pascal arranges his summary into 354 numbered entries, most of which consist of only one proposition.

The 'Préface' begins with the ultimate primitive notion or '*nom primitif*' of the entire system: the Word. 'The Word, which was from all eternity, God in God, through Whom all things including the visible were made, making Himself man, in the fullness of time came into the world that He had created to save the world . . . ' After touching upon other fundamental and indefinable first notions, such as the Crucifixion, Adam, and the Holy Spirit, Pascal explains the motive behind his 'Summary'. The four Evangelists may well have written for reasons which are not entirely known; it is clear that they did not always write with a consistent regard for temporal sequence. Pascal proposes to rearrange every verse of the Evangelists in accordance with strict temporal sequence. Echoing consciously or unconsciously St Augustine's final sentence of his *City of God*, Pascal writes: 'If the reader finds something good in what I have written, let him thank God for it, the sole author of all good. And if he finds something bad in it, let him pardon it because of my weakness.'

Throughout the 'Summary' Pascal incorporates verses by the Evangelists in his own translations from the Vulgate into his own text. Proposition 1 begins with a precise date, 24 September, under the empire of Caesar Augustus, in the reign of Herod in Judea, fifteen months before the birth of Christ, the angel Gabriel was sent to the priest Zacharia. After proposition 15 Pascal remarks cryptically: 'Thus Jesus led a hidden life for twelve years until the age of thirty-one.' Events of the life of Christ are recounted with a dizzying, almost obsessive clarity and rapidity – every miracle, every statement, every teaching is set out with Euclidean precision: 'The Jews come to Him in numbers. He instructs them in the indissolubility of marriage (133). 'The disciples, on leaving the temple, admire its structure but predict its ruin' (173). 'He was then troubled in his spirit' (190). 'Each time that He comes to His disciples He finds them sleeping' 214. 'On being interrogated by Pilate whether he was a king, He admits to it' 241. 'But that His kingdom was not of this world' (242). 'The veil of the temple was torn asunder.' (288). 'Jesus Himself appeared amongst them' (334). Sometimes, as in 399a, Pascal provides a commentary; miracles were useful at the beginning of the Church, but became infrequent so as not to bring about apathy. By 348 Pascal's tone reaches a delirium approaching ecstasy. In the final entry (354) Pascal writes: 'And this kingdom will be without end, where God will be all in all, and where it [the kingdom] will remain united to God in the bosom of God and His elect in Him in eternity. Amen.'

A new image of Pascal arises out of this remarkable piece of biblical reconstruction – that of the impassioned exegete. Let other, later writers, such as Renan, write several hundred pages on the life of Christ; Pascal chose to present what he construed as the essentials without historical padding or literary blandishments. The 'Abrégé' unrolls like an ancient Chinese scroll, several meters long, in which the temporal sequence of events is observed, or at least as Pascal himself unrolled it in his own mind.

Pascal's major works, the *Provincial Letters* and the *Pensées*, amplify the various self-images to be found in these ten brief texts. The complexity of the self-image may be grasped by a synoptic view of the materials. The 'Mémorial' presents an ecstatic mystic, while the 'Treatise on the Vacuum' shows the author as a deft and careful philosophical thinker. The 'Discourse on the Passions of Love' shows Pascal as an elegant, almost dandified literary psychologist; 'On the Conversion of a Sinner,' as someone redeemed by contrition. The 'Comparison of Early Christians with Present-day Christians' fulminates with the zeal of a religious reformer, while the 'Conversation with Monsieur de Saci' presents a skillful dialectician, strongly attracted both to skepticism and to fideism. 'On the Geometrical Mind and the Art of Persuasion' shows us a didacticist, a professorial pugilist, equally opposed to obscurantism and to scientism. The 'Prayer' pulls aside the confessional curtain to reveal the total and fervent penitent; 'Three Discourses' shows a homilist, a moralist, and an old-fashioned tutor in the employ of the high aristocracy. Finally, the 'Summary of the Life of Jesus Christ' presents Pascal as an impassioned exegete, the reconstructionist, and ultimately the evangelizer.

What holds so many roles together, what makes them into one man, is Pascal's literary style, both luminous and hard, and the oxymoron. Those who suffer from multiple personality syndrome speak, write, act in different styles, even in markedly different tones of voice. Pascal's tone is remarkably consistent – consistency being the supreme virtue of the geometrician – from the archness of the 'Passions of Love' to the cry of having found certainty in the 'Mémorial.' Pascal left fragments, for the most part indications of what he might have completed. What would have emerged from the fragments of the *Pensées* is described later in this study. What binds this study of Pascal together is again, the oxymoron.

Part Two
Views on the Works of Pascal

I

The *Provincial Letters*

10

THE POLITICS OF ORTHODOXY

Religious controversies are like family feuds: they have tremendous importance for the families in which they occur, sometimes even leading to rupture; but for persons not in the family, they seem either silly, senseless or, at best, unfortunate. Family counsellors are paid to listen to descriptions of such feuds with a clinical ear, and to offer their advice for appeasement, reconciliation or, sometimes, separation. Friends drawn into family feuds are implicitly expected to take sides; but once they do so, they will invariably be wounded by the other side – and usually also by the side they took, at some later date. Prudence dictates impartiality. Religious controversies are more elaborate, and the language used to describe them is highly charged emotionally: they are called heresies, schisms, and reformations, and those engaged in such fights are called heresiarchs, schismatics, and reformers. There are counter-reformations, movements within movements; there are orders, and reform movements within orders, or the movement to abolish all orders. Splinter groups, excommunications, interdictions, anathemas – Christianity has been plagued with such things since its inception, with Donatism, Pelagianism, monothelitism, and Arianism, to name but a few. In family feuds, if blood is spilt, it remains in the family; in religious fights, violence can spread between families, cantons, cities, even nations. Lucretius remarked on the potency of religion in persuading to evil deeds: '*Tantum religio potuit suadere malorum.*'[1] Again, unlike family feuds, there is no impartial counsellor who can be paid for his advice. To have a religion is by definiton 'to be tied' – '*ligare*' – to a particular tradition; to appeal to someone outside of that tradition to settle a dispute is in effect to give up one's religion. Appeal to civil force is a way of eliminating one's opponents, but not of convincing them. When St Augustine appealed to the Roman governor of North Africa to help him squelch the Donatists, Augustine got his way and the dreaded Donatists – people who believed that a priest's personal sins invalidate his ministry – were clubbed, robbed, and chased out of the province. Coming closer to Pascal's own period to appreciate the violence of religious disagreements, we need only remember the night of 24 August 1572, St Bartholomew's Eve, when the bells of the church of Saint-Germain-l'Auxerrois began tolling and a gigantic massacre of Protestants began in the streets of Paris: the Massacre of St Bartholomew.

The major controversy in seventeenth-century France centered upon the movement called Jansenism. It spilled over into the Low Countries, excited accusations of Calvinism, and brought about solemn condemnations from Rome. Jansenism has all the classic symptoms of a religious controversy: it assumed enormous importance for those involved in it, but to outsiders and later generations many elements of the controversy seem silly, senseless, or unfortunate. Jansenism led to ruptures within the Catholic Church that could only be brought to a halt by a form of ecclesiastical amnesty – '*pax ecclesiae*' – a way of saying, 'Please, let's not talk about it any more.' Jansenism brought some of the best minds to fight on its side, Blaise Pascal being the foremost one. And Jansenism was finally rooted out by the State, in this case the monarchy. Louis XIV swore that he would demolish Port-Royal, the geographical center of Jansenism, and this was no idle threat. The king had the twelfth-century chapel of Port-Royal blown up, the religious houses sold block by block, the nuns dispersed, and even the nuns' cemetery destroyed and the bodies transported to a common grave. Clearly, Jansenism was taken seriously: it was condemned by two popes, and was extirpated by the most powerful monarch of seventeenth-century Europe.

To explain Jansenism, which forms the background of Pascal's *Provincial Letters*, it is useful to begin with the event already referred to, the Massacre of St Bartholomew. This took place in the reign of Charles IX, at the instigation of the Queen Mother, Catherine de Medici, and of the duc de Guise, the day after the marriage of the Protestant Henry of Navarre and Marguerite, sister of Charles IX. The Protestant leaders such as Coligny, Ramus and La Place had their throats slit. Only those who abjured their faith were spared: the young Caumont La Force, the Prince de Condé, and Henry of Navarre himself. The direct consequence was a new civil war. In 1598 Henry of Navarre, now King Henry IV of France, issued the Edict of Nantes, which favored the Protestants. The edict included both religious and civil clauses; it gave the Calvinists the right to practice their religion where it had been previously authorized; and it gave them legal, political, and military guarantees. The Edict of Nantes restored religious peace to France. But during the minority of Louis XIV, the provisions of the edict were systematically curtailed, until the king abrogated it in 1685, causing many of the French Protestants, the Huguenots, to emigrate. Although Jansenism was a movement within the Roman Catholic Church, it was seen by members of the Catholic hierarchy as too close to Calvinism for comfort; it was seen by the monarchy as too closely allied with the leaders of the Fronde to be tolerated. Thus condemned by both Rome and Versailles, the Jansenists cast about for someone sympathetic to their movement, yet a devout Catholic, someone who was highly gifted intellectually and respected by the scientific world, and who also had the gift of popular communication. In short, the Jansenists wanted a superior writer and a devout genius on their side, most of their own writers being exceedingly dull and pedantic, like Bishop Cornelius Jansen (1585–1638), who was called Jansenius in Latin. The Jansenists found their champion in Pascal, who managed to produce, out of their often pointless and arid controversies, what great writers as different as Bossuet and Voltaire have called the greatest masterpiece in French prose.

It is the chief mark of great writing that the reader is swept away, transformed, enchanted, by the writing itself, and not by what it is about, or alleged to be about. What Pascal was basically writing about in the *Provincial Letters* was a book that few could or would care to read today, a work in Latin by Bishop Jansen: *Augustinus, seu doctrine S. Augustini de humanae naturae sanitate, aegritudine, medicina adversus Pelagianus et Massilienses.* The title can be briefly translated as *St Augustine, His Doctrine on Human Nature, and Arguments against Heretics.* The most influential work on theology in seventeenth-century France, *Augustinus* was published posthumously in Louvain in 1640.

Family feuds rarely survive a generation; religious feuds, on the other hand, persist for decades, even centuries, with each side attempting to establish its orthodoxy by citing the dicta and dogma of the earliest writers. Jansenism is no exception. The problem confronting Catholic theologians, after the Protestant bombardments in the second half of the sixteenth century, can be simply stated: how to reconcile the dogma of divine grace with that of free will. Before the Reformation, the prevailing views had been based upon Augustinian and Thomist teachings. Although Augustine viewed human nature as more seriously damaged by original sin than did Aquinas, both philosophers agreed that salvation was only possible through divine initiative, and admitted predestination and efficacious grace. It is always a mistake to invoke Catholic monolithism, simply because it has never existed in the history of the Church. Enough agreement has always been possible to expel chaos, but never absolute agreement to kill the spirit. So, too, with the concepts of grace, human freedom, predestination, and divine omnipotence. The Jesuits, in particular, were advocates of a more optimistic reading of human nature, which they introduced into college curricula. Conflicts inevitably occurred between the rigorous Augustinian position, and the newer humanistic tradition advocated by the Jesuits. In 1552 a professor at Louvain, Michel Baius, argued for propositions closely similar to Calvinism. The Jesuit Leonard Lessius was teaching at the same university, and won the day. The pope condemned the teachings of Baius. The Calvinists, and the Catholics who sympathized with John Calvin's teachings, tended to support the role of predestination at the expense of human freedom. The official teaching body of the Church, the *magisterium*, unequivocally supported the doctrine of free will, together with that of divine grace. That the pope himself pronounced in favor of the Jesuits could have been expected to stop the controversy; it did not.

The Spanish Jesuit Luis de Molina published *Concordia liberi arbitrii cum divinae gratiae donis* . . . (Lisbon, 1588) in order to show how free will and divine grace for salvation could be reconciled. Molina's argument can be stated in the simplest of terms: God, through His Son, has provided sufficient grace to save everyone, and therefore everyone is predestined regardless of merit, or what one does or fails to do. Molina's book raised protests, and it was examined by Rome from 1598 to 1607. Pope Paul V, however, refused to promulgate censure of Molina's position, which came to be known as Molinism.

The papal condemnation of the Calvinistic interpretation of St Augustine did not keep it from being taught at universities, particularly at Louvain. Cornelius Otto Jansen, who was of Dutch origin, studied at Louvain in the atmosphere of controversy, and stayed in France for a long sojourn with his friend Jean Duvergier de Hauranne, the future abbot of Saint-Cyran, who became spiritual director of Port-Royal in 1634. After obtaining a teaching post at Louvain, Jansen was struck by what he interpreted as St Augustine's views on grace, and converted Saint-Cyran to them. Believing that the Jesuits were far from the truth as expounded by St Augustine, Jansen, who became bishop of Ypres in 1636, vowed to expound Augustine's orthodoxy and expose the errors of others in a vast work. Dying prematurely in 1638, Jansen left *Augustinus*, a long and laborious work, entirely finished. Friends saw to its publication.

That it interested such a remarkable mind as Pascal's makes a case for the importance of *Augustinus*. Sir Isaac Newton was soon to publish his great work on physics, the *Principia* (1668), based upon the mysterious factors of gravity and light. Newton did not call these 'forces' in any way mysterious, even though his theological interests ran deeper after his remarkable discoveries in physics. Jansen based his book, by its nature without the accoutrements of mathematics, on what he conceived to be the two mysterious factors of human existence: original sin and divine grace. Pascal, of course, died before the publication of Newton's great work, but its ideas and mathematical concepts would have been easily understood by him, and of course by Leibniz, who invented the infinitesimal calculus concurrently – without any collaboration – with Newton. The passion shared by these thinkers is for first principles, but also for certain fundamental but ineffable ideas, or '*noms primitifs*,' as Pascal called them. Pascal's father broke his hip in Rouen: an effect of gravity. Yet it brought the entire family into touch with what would develop into the essential traits of Jansenism. Blaise Pascal would regret his former worldly ways: an effect of physical illness, perhaps; but he would interpret it in light of his own sinfulness, and the larger doctrine of original sin. Physics has its secrets no less than those that theology has, to paraphrase the best-known aphorism from the *Pensées*.

Augustinus begins in a scholarly fashion by presenting St Augustine's refutation of the Pelagians and the Semi-Pelagians. This heresy, named after a French monk from Marseilles, Pelagius, is based on the view that man can earn his salvation by acts of his own merit. St Augustine's basic refutation is that if Pelagianism were true, there would be no need for divine grace or for the Incarnation. After stating what the relationship between philosophy and theology ought to be, Jansen argued that the Church had given St Augustine the final authority on settling questions pertaining to grace. The central idea of *Augustinus* is that it is necessary to distinguish between two states of nature corresponding to man 'before' and 'after' the Fall brought about by original sin. Moreover, two sorts of grace correspond to the two states of nature. Jansen paints a very pessimistic picture of man in his present state – 'after' the Fall – for now concupiscence has absolute power over free will. The third volume of *Augustinus* stresses the importance of Christ the Redeemer, and the Augustinian thesis that grace is required for every good work. Grace works infallibly without eliminating human freedom. Predestination is absolutely gratuitous: those who are predestined are so irrespective of any merit of their own.

A scholarly martinet, Jansen invoked St Augustine like some Juggernaut, systematically citing his most rigid and implacable formulae. For example, man naturally and habitually prefers evil to good in his present state; man can peform no good act without divine grace; free will still remains, but only to do evil. It can safely be said that such views are not those of someone with any tenderness for mankind. Jansen spurned the sane and accurate view of St Thomas Aquinas, that liberty is capable of opposites, and that the will is not naturally inclined to evil. Again following Augustine's lead, Jansen argues that human love naturally centers upon self or physical objects, and that grace is required to set it right. In order to be efficacious grace must be constant and irresistible, not as an exterior force – for then there would be no free will – but as an interior and divine force which determines someone at a given moment to do good. That which leads the will to assent, Jansen calls '*delectatio victrix,*' 'victorious delectation.' He thus incorporates the Aristotelian view concerning the voluntary and the involuntary: one acts voluntarily if the cause or reason is 'inside' oneself. It is like the difference between, say, choosing to recite a poem and being forced to do so at gun-point. What complicates this straightforward explanation of human agency is Jansen's insistence that grace must be irresistible; by placing grace 'within' the person, Jansen believes that he has salvaged human freedom.

Like many theologians of the time, Jansen thought it a problem that some are saved and some not. It was taken as a matter of empirical fact that many would not be saved – criminals, the greedy, the slothful – Calvin even added the poor. Jansen argues that Christ's death was indeed for all, but that His death gave 'gratuitous' grace. Out of His own inscrutable wisdom God gives 'efficacious' grace solely to His elect. Jansen added an appendix to his work entitled the 'Parallelon,' in which he tried to show strong parallels between the repeatedly denounced heresies of the Pelagians and the new views of the Molinists, which he wanted to be denounced.

Augustinus was immediately accused of being Calvinistic, fatalistic, and of denying the reality of free will. The Jesuits managed to have the work condemned first by the Inquisition on 1 August 1641, and then by the bull 'in eminenti' of Pope Urban VIII, promulgated on 19 June 1643. The bull had little effect, at least in France. *Augustinus* found its defenders, among them Saint Cyran, who at least had the good taste to find its style repugnant. After the death of Cardinal Richelieu, who abhorred Jansen and his theological position, *Augustinus* gave rise to a controversy over two related problems. In his book *De la fréquente communion* (1642) Antoine Arnauld had presented a set of Procrustean ideas on penance and the Eucharist; Saint-Cyran had also come to the defense of *De la fréquente communion*; it had enjoyed a great success, and though delated to the Inquisition, the Holy See had refused to condemn it. Secondly, in 1643, Arnauld wrote a vituperative book entitled *Théologie morale des jésuites*, an attack on Jesuit casuistry and indirectly the morality of the order itself. The stage was set for Pascal's *Provincial Letters*.

Cardinal Mazarin inherited Richelieu's power, and also his abhorrence of the Jansenists, not only because he disagreed with their theology, but also because he saw in Port-Royal a challenge to the absolute power of the monarchy. Mazarin directed the syndic Nicolas Cornet to propose to the Faculty of Theology an examination of seven propositions. No mention of Jansen or his book was made, but the doctors of the Sorbonne knew who and what was at stake. After little debate, the faculty, hastily convened, decided to censure five of the seven propositions. They were as follows:

1   Some of God's commandments are impossible for the just to obey, even with a strong endeavour, because they lack the requisite powers; the grace that would make the fulfillment of some of God's commandments is also lacking.

2   In the state of fallen nature, no one can or ever does resist interior grace.

3   In the state of fallen nature, to have merit or demerit it is not necessary that man be free from internal necessity; it suffices that man be free from external constraint.

4   The Semi-Pelagians admitted the necessity of interior prevenient grace for every action, but they were heretical in that they held that man could either obey or resist such grace.

5   To hold that Jesus Christ died or shed His blood for all mankind, excepting no one, is Semi-Pelagianism.

One wishes that Philippe de Champaigne, who was a staunch friend of Port-Royal and one of the greatest portraitists of the age, had been commissioned to paint a group portrait of the learned theologians after they had censured the five propositions. With his deft insight into the workings of the human spirit, Champaigne would have portrayed bewilderment in the faces of some of the theologians. With so much ambiguity in the language of the propositions, many theologians were not sure how to vote. Champaigne would have revealed duplicity in the countenance of the doctors with Augustinian leanings; they sided with what they believed to be the spirit of the propositions, but had agreed to censure them if the Sorbonne so wished. Other theologians believed the propositions to be patently false: Champaigne would have portrayed them as simply censorious. And still other doctors censured the five propositions out of deference to Cardinal Mazarin: Champaigne would have caught the curl of the sycophant's smile.

At the end of 1650, under the leadership of Isaac Habert, bishop of Vabres, more than ninety French bishops agreed that the now infamous 'five propositions' were heretical and attributed them to Jansen's *Augustinus*, and delated the matter to the Holy See. About a dozen bishops protested in favor of Jansen. Both sides sent delegates to Rome, where long and learned controversies ensued.

Rome was pleased to see France, 'the first daughter of the Church,' whose Gallican, or nationalistic, leanings had almost led her the way

THE POLITICS OF ORTHODOXY

of Anglican England, defer to the Holy See for the final judgment. Carinal Mazarin lost no time in denouncing Jansen in a letter written in the name of the young Louis XIV. A committee appointed by Innocent X found the five propositions both 'heretical and execrable.' The bull 'Cum occasione,' promulgated on 31 May 1653, condemned the propositions, simply ascribing them 'to the work of Jansen.'

Mazarin was also pleased. Since the Church need never be shackled by any philosopher or theologian, the papal bull did not even explicitly endorse the doctrine of St Augustine. Mazarin imposed the acceptance of the bull on parliament. The Jansenists seemed discomfited. In 1654 Father Annat, a Jesuit and confessor to Louis XIV, published a pamphlet entitled 'Chicaneries des jansénistes,' in which he cavalierly stated that the five propositions were to be found word for word in Jansen's book. Arnauld replied that only the first proposition could be found in *Augustinus* and only in near similar terms; the other four could only be called inferences of Jansen's thought. Bishop Bossuet, the supreme religious orator of the time, champion of the monarchy and of Catholicism, pronounced that even if the five propositions were not literally to be found in *Augustinus*, they constituted 'the soul of the work.' Arnauld replied that if the pope had condemned the propositions as heretical, they could express neither the meaning of St Augustine nor that of Bishop Jansen. Arnauld's arguments had little effect, for the Assembly of the Clergy, held in 1654 and 1655, confirmed the condemnation.

Pascal remarks in his *Pensées* that 'Had Cleopatra's nose been shorter, the whole face of the world would have been changed' (180). History is riddled with the fortuitous, with the unpredictable: and it is only the flinty-nosed positivist who believes that the right 'covering-law' is to be found. Nothing could have predicted the existence of a priest named Picoté, who changed the course of Jansenism and the history of French literature. On 1 February 1655, Picoté found the duc de Longueil guilty of having his grand-daughter brought up at Port-Royal, and of sheltering in his Parisian house a notorious Jansenist, the Abbé Amable de Bourzeis, who had written a book entitled *Saint Augustine Victorious over Calvin and Molina*. The duke protested to Picoté's superior, Jean-Jacques Olier, who upheld the priest. Arnauld promptly brought the matter to the public in his 'Lettre d'un docteur de Sorbonne à une personne de condition'

(24 February 1655). In his letter Arnauld claimed that he had not found the five propositions in *Augustinus*; moreover, Arnauld cited St Peter's denial of Christ as a case in point of a just man sinning because he lacked grace.

Louis XIV's confessor immediately replied in a letter of his own. The king, naturally, would have many confessors during his long reign – among them Le Tellier and La Chaise (after whom the famous Parisian cemetery is named). Father Annat, a Jesuit, had translated his name – François Canard – into Latin, Annat, from the word for duck, *anas*. Born in Rodez in 1590, Annat became rector of the Jesuit college in Montpellier, then the college of Toulouse, then the Provincial of the order, and finally confessor to Louis XIV. He kept up a constant battle with the Jansenists, being the instigator of the bull of Innocent X, of the 'Formulary,' and the author of many works against Arnauld and Pascal. Apart from his fiery theological views, Annat seems to have been a modest man. Louis XIV remarked about him: 'I never knew whether Father Annat had any parents or relatives.' The king ordered the Sorbonne to investigate Arnauld's position.

The Faculty of Theology decided to deal with the matter by posing two questions, one *de facto*, the other *de juris*. (1) Was Arnauld presumptuous in writing that the five propositions were not to be found in *Augustinus*? (2) Was Arnauld heretical in writing that St Peter was a just man to whom grace was lacking? The Faculty voted on 14 January 1656 to condemn Arnauld on the first question, thereby debarring him from the Sorbonne. Fearing that he would also be condemned on the second question – *de juris* – Arnauld appealed to Pascal for aid. The result was the first of the *Provincial Letters*, published on 23 January 1656.

The *Provincial Letters*, which Pascal's contemporaries called the *Petites Lettres*, or the 'Little Letters,' comprise eighteen letters. The first ten carry the heading 'Lettre écrite à un Provincial par un de ses amis'; the other letters have various titles. Published with neither the author's nor the publisher's name, the *Provincial Letters*, appeared as soon as they were written in little pamphlets of between eight and twelve pages in length. After the publication of the first letter, which had the additional heading 'on the subject of the current disputes at the Sorbonne,' the disputes mounted and the police attempted to discover the publisher. By the time the last letter appeared, on 24

March 1657, one of the greatest publishing successes of the *ancien régime* had been accomplished: more than ten thousand copies of the letters had been printed, selling for a pittance (*'deux sols six deniers'*). Many of the pamphlets were distributed for nothing. After deciding not to publish a 'Dix-neuviène Provinciale,' even though he had made notes for it, Pascal allowed the eighteen letters to be collected and published together, probably under the editorship of Pierre Nicole. In 1657 two editions appeared, both with the same title: *Les Provinciales ou les Lettres écrites par Louis de Montalte, à un Provincial de ses amis et aux RR. PP. Jésuites: sur le sujet de la Morale et de la Politique de ces Pères.* 'Louis de Montalte' was Pascal's pseudonym, Montalte from the Latin *Mons alta*, 'high mountain', the Puy-de-Dôme in Pascal's homeland. Surely in choosing his pseudonym Pascal also had in mind the 'high mountain' upon which Christ was tempted by Satan. The publisher is given as Cologne 'chez Pierre de la Vallée'; actually the publisher was Elsevier in Amsterdam. Whether 'Peter of the Valley,' corresponding to 'Louis of the Mountain,' is an allusion to Descartes's ontological 'proof' of God's existence (just as a valley necessarily implies a mountain, so God's total perfection necessarily implies his existence) and is Pascal's gnomic way of satirizing Descartes's ridiculous 'proof' must remain speculative, even with all the evidence of Pascal's love of acronyms, puzzles, and linguistic acrobatics. What is certain is how quickly the *Provincial Letters* were translated into other languages – first Latin, then English – and how avidly they were read, even by persons not especially interested in religious controversies. The explanation is once again Pascal's style: it compels attention, it stirs feelings, it blinds by its clarity, it makes highly abstract issues seem part of life-and-death reality, and it charms, it entertains, it dazzles with wit. The austere and arid stylists of Port-Royal needed such a defender as Pascal. The Jesuits had only donnish stylists, and mediocre polemicists, to bring to their defense. Nonetheless the Jesuits won, at least in the politics of France and of Rome. Before turning to the reasons for the defeat of the Jansenist cause, let us examine each of the eighteen letters, translating liberally from them, to show the issues involved and give some sense of the literary acrobatics Pascal so much enjoyed.

11
AN INNOCENT ASTONISHED

The fundamental trope, or structural turn, behind the first ten letters is the timeless one of the *'naif,'* the provincial of good heart and adequate intelligence, earnestly trying to find out whether what is being said is actually true. The assumption behind the image of the innocent provincial is that presuppositionless thought is possible, that is, one can just think about some matter without having any special axe to grind, any cause to uphold except to be *'un honnête homme'* – which for the seventeenth century meant 'an upright, forthright, good man.' An 'innocent abroad,' a 'traveller,' someone who 'had lost his way,' a son 'in search of his father' – the variations played upon the theme of the *'naif'* questioning the wise, or those reputed to be so, binds together much of the world's literature. But no other author who had used the device, for example Fénelon or Dante, went so far as Pascal in omitting story or plot: there is none in the *Provincial Letters.* The basic structure is pretended ignorance asking questions of those who should know the answers. Receiving contradictory or unsatisfactory responses, the 'provincial' pretends to be in a quandary, but gives the reader clues for finding the truth. Finally, Pascal, the 'innocent' and the 'provincial,' must defend himself against charges from 'the world' – *'le monde'* – those who do not agree with him and have attacked him in writing. What casts a sinister shadow over all the *Provincial Letters* is that their author is not an innocent, and only a provincial in the sense that he was not born in Paris. The author knows of his great gifts in geometry and mathematics, and has published his results. The author knows of his skills as an inventor, and has secured a copyright on his calculator. The author also believes that he will write the definitive defense of

Christianity; he will die before doing so, leaving the confused but brilliant notes which form the *Pensées*. Pascal begins his attack upon what he deems falsity on a fictional premise: I am not who you might think I am, you may call me whom you please. It is possible to read the *Provincial Letters* as a highly sophisticated attempt to upset one set of fictions by substituting another. Pascal, to be sure, would have rejected this interpretation, believing that he had found the truth beyond all falsifications.

The 'Première Lettre' begins in a straightforward conversational way. 'We were quite misled. I was undeceived only yesterday. Until then I had thought that the subject of the disputes at the Sorbonne was quite important and of extreme consequence for religion. So many meetings of a society as famous as the Faculty of Theology of Paris, and where so many extraordinary and unparalleled things happened, gave one such a vast impression that one could only believe it to be an extraordinary matter.'

Pascal tells his provincial counterpart that the Faculty are simply trying to answer two questions, one of fact, one of right. The question of fact concerns whether Arnauld was audacious for having said in his second letter that the five propositions are not to be found in Jansen's book 'after the bishops have said that they are in it.' Seventy-one doctors took up the defense of Arnauld, arguing that they could not find the dreaded propositions in the book either, and even found assertions opposed to the five. On the other side were eighty secular doctors and some forty mendicant friars who, without even wishing to examine the text, condemned Arnauld's position because of its audacity. Fifteen doctors abstained. Arnauld was condemned. Pascal writes that he fears 'the censure will do more harm than good.' Why refer such a matter to the Sorbonne when anyone can pick up Jansen's book and see for himself whether the propositions are in it or not? 'Whether Monsieur Arnauld is rash or audacious is not a matter for my conscience.' The first question is therefore idle, 'since it is not a question of the faith.'

'As for the question of right, it seems much more considerable in that it has to do with the faith. Thus I took especial care to find out about it. But you will be satisfied to see that it is as unimportant as the first question.' Was Arnauld right in saying that St Peter lacked grace when he denied Christ? Holding the Sorbonne up to ridicule, Pascal tells his friend: 'I became a great theologian in a short time, and you are going to see the signs of it.' The correspondent proceeds to recount how he made many visits to a certain learned doctor who was greatly opposed to the Jansenists. The doctor treated the correspondent disdainfully, informing him that it is only 'a problematic opinion,' according to the Sorbonne, 'that grace is given to everyone.' 'He confirmed this by a passage from St Augustine, which he said was famous: "We know that grace is not given to all men."' Asking whether the other Jansenist opinion is heretical – 'that grace is efficacious and determines the will to do good' – the doctor thunders at the naive correspondent that it is not only not heretical, but is orthodoxy. 'All the Thomists uphold it, and *I* defended it as one of my theses at the Sorbonne.' What then was Arnauld's heresy? 'He does not recognize that the just have the power to obey God's commandments in the sense that we understand it.'

The correspondent recounts his visits to a friend of Port-Royal, who is 'nonetheless a very good man,' then to a disciple of Le Moine, and other theologians. The result came to the following. Along with the doctors of the Sorbonne, Arnauld holds 'that the just always have the power to obey the commandments' but he denies that this power is proximate – '*prochain.*' 'This word was new and unknown to me. Until then I had understood the matter; but this term threw me into obscurity, and I thought that it had been invented simply to muddle things. I asked him for an explication,' but the first doctor made a mystery of it. No one could define the term 'proximate power' – '*le pouvoir prochain.*'

The correspondent tells of visiting other members of the clergy, only to find further disagreement concerning the key term in the controversy. The correspondent is forced to conclude that the dispute is entirely verbal; his opinion of theological disputes has reached its nadir. ' "Then tell me, Fathers, I beg of you for the last time, what must I believe in order to be Catholic?" "You must," they all told me together, "say that all the just have *the proximate power*, abstracting from the sense of St Thomas or any other theologian." – "That is to say, I said in leaving them, that I must pay lip-service to this term for fear of being called a heretic? Is the word in the Scriptures?" "No, they answered." "Is it in the Fathers of the Church, the Councils, or in papal pronouncements?" "No." "Then is it in St Thomas?" "No." "Then what is the necessity of saying it since it is not based on authority and has no sense in itself?" "You are opinionated," they told me: "you *will* say it or you'll be a heretic, and Monsieur Arnauld also; for we are in the majority. And if need be, we shall bring in so many Franciscan friars to win the day." ' Apparently any means are fair so long as they serve to disrupt Port-Royal.

The correspondent concludes with a pun on '*prochain*' which in ordinary usage means 'next' or 'neighbor': 'I leave you nonetheless free to opt for the word "*prochain*" or not; for I love my neighbor too much to persecute him under this pretext. If this account has not displeased you, I shall continue to keep you informed of what is going on.'

The '*prochain*' – the public – were not displeased, they were ecstatic over the 'First Letter.' Someone had dared to hold up to ridicule the most august teaching body in France, the Sorbonne, the right arm of both the State and the Church. In retrospect we see that Pascal had in effect written the prototype of all the future novels based on academia – the machinations, the pretensions, the pedantry, the required lip-service to a slogan, some vague but strongly held notion of orthodoxy protected by the bastion of the faculty.

The 'First Letter' was dated 23 January; a week later the doctors of the Sorbonne voted to censure the second question as well. The same day, Pascal, who had returned from Port-Royal to Paris, was working on the 'Seconde Lettre' in the Auberge of King David, across from the Collège de Clermont, which is today the Lycée Henri IV. The inn provided the anonymity that lay behind the authorship of the 'Letters'. Using documents furnished by Arnauld, Pascal finished the second letter in a few days, showed it to Nicole, who had it printed 'chez Petit.' It was published on 5 February, and produced as lively an effect as the first letter.

In the 'Second Letter' Pascal examines the debate over 'sufficient grace' – '*grâce suffisante*.' 'The Jesuits maintain that there is grace generally given to all men, subject in such a way to the free will that it makes grace efficacious or inefficacious by its choice, without any new help from God, and without lacking anything on its own part for acting effectively. Thus they call it "sufficient" because it suffices for action. The Jansenists, on the contrary, want there to be no grace which is actually sufficient which is not also efficacious, that is to say, all grace that does not determine the will to act effectively is insufficient for action, because they say that one never acts without *efficacious grace*. Such is their difference.' Pascal readily reveals that those who hold to the doctrine of 'sufficient grace' do not agree among themselves as to its meaning, and that the Jesuits do not agree with the Dominicans – the Thomists – for political reasons. But since the Dominicans were a much more revered order, established in 1215, and often championed by the papacy, the Jesuits, relatively new (the order was founded in 1534) were content not to press the Thomists to accept their meaning of 'sufficient grace,' just so long as they both agreed to use the same term. The Society of Jesus 'does not demand that the Dominicans deny the necessity of efficacious grace: that would be to press them too far. One must never tyrannize one's friends.'

The correspondent finds himself in a quandary. If he denies sufficient grace, he is a Jansenist. If he understands it as the Jesuits do, he is a heretic. And if he construes grace in the manner of other doctors, i.e., efficacious grace is necessary, he violates common sense, and according to the Jesuits would be an 'extravagant.' The people turn to the theologians for clarification of what they must believe, and find only discord and confusion.

'Do you want to see a picture of the Church in these conflicting opinions? I see her as a man who, leaving his country to make a trip, meets up with robbers who wound him in many places and leave him half dead. He sends for three doctors from the neighboring villages. The first, having probed the wounds, judges them to be mortal, and declares that only God could give him back his lost strength. The second, arriving next, wants to flatter him, and tells him that there is still enough strength for him to arrive home, and offering an affront to the first doctor, who was not of his opinion, forms a plan to ruin him. The sick man, in this doubtful state, perceives the third in the distance, holds out his hands to him, as if he were the one to decide his case. After examining the wounds, and after listening to the opinions of the first two, he embraces the second doctor's diagnosis, joins with him. The second and third doctor form a league against the first, and chase him away shamefully; for they were stronger in number.' The sick man decides to go along with the verdict of the second doctor, who says that he has 'enough strength' to make his trip. But the sick man – who is assured that legs *naturally* have 'enough strength' for walking – begins to feel them caving in under him. He complains that he thought he had sufficient power to continue. 'Certainly not,' replied the doctor; and you will never walk effectively if God does not send you some extraordinary help to sustain and guide you.' The sick man is furious and sends them both away, chiding them for their treatment of the first doctor. 'After making a trial of his own strength, he recognizes by experience his own weakness ... and remembering the first doctor, puts himself in his hands ... and asks God for the strength that he confesses he does not have. He receives mercy, and by its help, arrives home happily.'

Pascal now emerges as a parabolist, as the conveyer of moral lessons in simple stories, in the tradition of Aesop and La Fontaine, and of course, Jesus. The correspondent assures his provincial friend that 'sufficient grace' is as trivial a notion as 'proximate power.' He also mentions that Arnauld has just been censured on the second question.

The 'Second Letter' was followed by a 'Response of the Provincial' to his friend's first two letters, dated 2 February 1656. The provincial assures his correspondent that the letters were not just for him, but that 'everyone sees them, everyone understands them, everyone believes them. They are not only esteemed by theologians, but are also found agreeable by the ordinary man. They are intelligible even to women.' The provincial reports that a member of the Académie Française entirely agrees with the correspondent's position, and regrets that his 'limited power' cannot banish 'proximate power' from the language. The provincial begs his correspondent to write more.

In spite of the *Provincial Letters*, the Sorbonne condemned Arnauld on 31 January 1656. The king had the publisher Savreux, his wife, and two of his employees, imprisoned on 2 February, believing them, mistakenly, to be the publishers of the 'Letters.' The publishers Petit and Desprez, two other publishers friendly to Port-Royal, were placed under investigation. In his 'Third Letter' Pascal directly attacks the censure of Arnauld, calling it unjust, absurd, and nugatory. The correspondent is insensed that the Sorbonne could waste its time on such trivial issues, while the great religious controversies have been concerned with such fundamentals as denying the mystery of transubstantiation or of renouncing Jesus Christ or the Gospels. Everything Arnauld wrote can be found in the Gospels and supported by the Church Fathers. Drawing chiefly from St Augustine, Pascal attempts to show Arnauld's orthodoxy. The terms of the censure were extraordinarily harsh, so much so that the effect is comic. 'How is it possible, most people are asking, that one can bring so many imprecations into this censure – the assemblage of terms of "pestilence," "horror," "rashness," "impiety," "blasphemy," "abomination," "execration," "anathema," "heresy" – which are the most horrible expressions that one would use against Arius or even against the Antichrist, to combat an imperceptible heresy without even making clear what it is?' The correspondent concludes that it is not Arnauld's beliefs which are heretical, but his person: he is not a heretic for what he said or wrote, but for being Monsieur Arnauld. 'These are disputes of theologians, not of theology.'

On 15 February Arnauld was formally struck off the list of doctors of the Sorbonne. Furious over their treatment by the first three 'Letters,' the Jesuits began intriguing against Port-Royal even more vehemently, both at the Court of Louis XIV and in Rome. Dated 25 February, the 'Fourth Letter' abandons the defensive posture of the preceding letters, and mounts an offensive attack on the Society of Jesus. With brilliance and thoroughness Pascal exposes then denounces the Jesuits' conception of sin. Sin is not only central to Christianity, but to Pascal's own understanding of it. Beginning with 'There is nothing like the Jesuits' the 'Fourth Letter' is the most skillfully constructed and important of the *Provincial Letters*. Pascal sets out to destroy the Molinist doctrine, which he states as follows: 'An action cannot be imputed to sin if God has not given, before committing it, the knowledge of the evil involved, and an inspiration that excites us to avoid it.' The correspondent tells his provincial friend that he had gone with a Jansenist friend to the Jesuits. The Jesuit father, to prove his position on sin, pulls out a book entitled *Somme des Péchés* 'All about Sin' (to translate freely) – by Father Bauny. ' "It's the fifth edition, which shows you it is a good book." "It's too bad," my Jansenist whispers to me, "that the book was condemned by Rome, and by the bishops of France." "Look," said the Father, "page 906 . . . " ' Other authorities are brought out by the Jacobin, the argument beginning to teem with quotations, citations, and glosses. Other authors, including the king's confessor, Annat. Pascal and his Jansenist friend feign astonishment at so much learning, so much authority. But then Pascal cries out: 'Oh, what a good way to be happy in this world and in the next! I had always thought that one sinned more, the less one thought about God; but from what I see now, once one has managed not to think about Him at all, everything becomes pure for the future. No more of these half-sinners, hardened sinners, sinners with any mixture, full and accomplished, hell does not hold them; they have deceived the devil by dint of abandoning themselves to him'.

The Jesuit, whom the correspondent has described as 'extremely clever,' tries to avoid such consequences, and tries to escape adroitly, 'without getting angry, either out of kindness or prudence, he simply answered: "so that you might understand how we save ourselves from such dilemmas, you must understand . . . " ' The Jesuit explains a further doctrine that only those who do not want to be saved are damned, for God clearly gives to all the wish and sufficient knowledge to avoid sin. The arguments pile one upon the other, until the reader is left both exhilarated and dumbfounded. Saints and sinners are thrown into the *mêlée*, even a pagan – Aristotle, whom Pascal cites only once in the *Provincial Letters*, and nowhere else in his other writings. He does it only to trip up the Jesuit. Taking as authority Father Bauny once again, the Jesuit says: 'Look at the reason on which he established his thought. . . . Read what he cites from Aristotle, and you will see that after such an explicit authority, you must either burn the books of this prince of philosophers, or be of Bauny's opinion.'

Hostile to scholasticism, it is hardly surprising that Pascal did not like Aristotle. But to meet his scholastically trained Jesuits on their own ground, Pascal cites a few passages from the *Nicomachean Ethics* (III, I, 17, and III, I, 14–15) to show his Jesuit interlocutor that he has incorrectly interpreted the text of 'the Philosopher' – the 'master of them who know,' as Dante had called Aristotle. Pascal also wanted to show that the Molinists made more of the pagan Aristotle's philosophy than they did of St Augustine's. Pascal, with his fictional aid the Jansenist, shows that Aristotle meant, contrary to the Molinist interpretation, a simple fact of moral experience. Aristotle held that actions are voluntary if one knows while doing them that one could do otherwise; or if one could have known, but was in such a state – say anger or drunkenness – which falls within one's moral sphere. It is only ignorance of fact, the ignorance of which cannot be attributed to carelessness or being in any emotional state, that Aristotle calls 'involuntary.' In all probability quoting from the French translation of the *Ethics* published in Frankfurt in 1628, Pascal shows that Aristotle never held that one could be exculpated for not knowing the difference between right and wrong, such precepts being 'natural to man' and, as the naturalist philosopher further argues, 'need only be developed by proper habit.' Not satisfied with vanquishing the Jesuit with the correct interpretation of Aristotle – and Pascal was right, for the Molinists had carelessly interpreted the 'prince of philosophers' to suit their own interests – Pascal quotes from St Augustine, whom he calls the 'prince of theologians.' Pascal establishes an entire concordance between the two philosophers on the issue, citing Augustine's *Retractiones*, or *Retractions*, a review and correction of all his works that Augustine wrote in his last years.[2]

> The Father appeared surprised to me, as much by the passage from Aristotle as by the one from St Augustine. But, as he was thinking of what he should say, someone came to inform him that Madame la Maréchale de . . . and Madame la Marquise de . . . had come to see him. Parting in haste; I shall speak about it to our fathers. They will readily find some response. We have many a subtle father here.'

Surely no better way could have been found to stop, as opposed to settling, a theological dispute than to have ladies of quality announced. The scene is high comedy, worthy of Molière. 'When I was alone with my friend, I confessed how astonished I was by the upheaval that this doctrine brought about in morality, to which he responded that he was astonished by my astonishment.' Both the 'provincial' and readers of his time eagerly awaited the next 'Letter.'

12

THE WILES OF THE CASUISTS

Persecution of Port-Royal and the Jansenists began to mount in February 1656. Dr Sainte-Beuve, an Augustinian scholar, was expelled from the Sorbonne on 26 February. On 15 March Arnauld d'Andilly received an order from the Court to leave Port-Royal along with the other 'Solitaires.' Evacuation of the Granges de Port-Royal began on 20 March. A week later Pascal's 'Fifth Letter' appeared, dated 20 March; it is an attack on casuistry in general, and the Spanish theologian Escobar in particular. During the twenty-four days between the 'Fourth Letter' and the fifth Pascal had read with incredulity and indignation a book by Antonio Escobar y Mendoza, SJ, entitled *Liber theologiae moralis vigenti quatuor societatis Jesu doctoribus reseratus* ... ('A Compendium on Moral Philosophy drawn from Twenty-four Theologians of the Jesuit Order'). The book is no more than a compilation of twenty-four casuists, all Jesuits. Pascal concentrates on books 7 to 11 to expose Jesuitical casuistry, quoting extensively from the text.

'Casuistry,' from the Latin *casus* or 'case,' is the science, or art, or method of reasoning that attempts to resolve cases of conscience, by applying general principles of morality and religion to particular instances. Although 'casuistry' is often used contemptuously, almost as a synonym for 'sophistry,' the intention of the casuist is hardly contemptible: he tries to answer the ancient question 'What ought I to do?' especially when one finds oneself in a moral dilemma or conflict, or a highly unusual moral situation. No less an ethicist than the twentieth-century English philosopher G.E. Moore wrote in his *Principia Ethica* that casuistry is the goal of ethics.

The casuists whom Pascal attacks in the 'Fifth Letter' might be described as proponents of a new and more relaxed morality. Feigning to be quite surprised by the attitude of the Jesuits, Pascal tells his provincial friend that he went to see his 'faithful Jansenist' to have the Jesuit doctrine of 'probable opinions' explained to him. The Jansenist explains that 'probabilism' is the doctrine that, in a doubtful moral case, it suffices to have on one's side the authority of a single doctor for your opinion to be 'probable,' that is to say, worthy of approbation. It is on the basis of this doctrine that the Jesuits find a means to excuse almost every sin and to reassure even the most tepid Christians of their salvation. Given the complexity of moral experience, and the dramatic changes of the time – the Reformation, the discovery of new continents – the typical seventeenth-century Jesuit argued that it was both futile and sinister to adopt any form of moral rigor. And that the Jesuits had a high opinion of their missions is made unforgettably clear by the beginning of the 'Fifth Letter' where Pascal quotes from a book by and about the Jesuits, *Imago primi saeculi*: 'It is a society of men, or rather of angels, which was foretold by Isaiah in these words: "Go, quick and light angels." They have minds of eagles; it is a troup of phoenixes . . . They have changed the face of Christianity.'

In his wily way the correspondent writes that he went to see a Jesuit acquaintance and told him that he was unable to tolerate fasting. The good father immediately gets down his books on casuistry and promptly finds all sorts of excuses that will apply to the case in hand. One ends up with such absurd propositions as 'He who is tired of something, such as pursuing a girl, is he obliged to fast? Not at all.' Pascal writes to his provincial friends: 'It is by the obliging and accommodating conduct . . . that they give their arm to everyone . . . in that way they keep their friends and defend themselves against their enemies; for, if one reproaches them for their extreme relaxation, they immediately produce before the public one of their austere directors, with some books they have made about the rigor of Christian law. Simple persons, and those who do not delve deeper, are content with these proofs.'

Astonished by the new teachings of the Jesuits, hardly in accord with what he takes to be orthodoxy, Pascal asks the father to provide some explanation for the apparent conflict. The Jesuit explains that though the Church Fathers were excellent in their own times, their ideas are not always in the spirit of the current epoch. Their principles are always used in speculation, but one must turn to the casuists to find out what to do in practice. Pascal protests that casuistry substitutes settling matters in the world for coming to terms with one's conscience. The Jesuit replies by citing other casuists – Sanchez, Vasquez, Layman, Cellot, Reginaldus, and many others: so many, in fact, that Pascal achieves one of the most humorous effects in the *Provincial Letters*. After dismissing Saints Augustine, John Chrysostom, Ambrose 'and the others' as outdated and irrelevant, the Jesuit father begins a litany of the new authors – 'all clever and quite celebrated' – 'they are Villalobos, Coninck, Llamas, Achokier, Dealkozer, Dellacruz . . . ' and some forty other names, only one of which, 'Suarez,' remains in the history of philosophical and religious thought.

The Jesuits were indeed condemned, albeit in vague terms, by Alexander VII in 1665, and by Innocent X in 1679, for what might be called their 'modernist' tendencies in morality, but never for their modes of proselytizing. Pascal unfairly lashes out at the way in which Jesuit missionaries were gaining converts in India, Japan, and China. 'Thus, they have something for everybody, and give what people want. When they find themselves in a country where God crucified seems like a folly, they suppress the scandal of the Cross, and only preach about Jesus Christ the glorious one, not the suffering one.' Exporting a religion is more difficult than exporting a commodity; for the latter one either points out a need for the thing, or gives a false impression that it is needed; with the former, its truth must be forcibly argued without giving offense to those one wants to convert. The Jesuit missionaries had arrived in Japan with crucifixes and Bibles, but their rags and hirsuteness frightened off the court. The Japanese and Chinese could not conceive of scruffy-looking beggars as bearers of the truth, and no one was converted. Changing their attire, bearing gifts, and preaching Christ in kingly glory – which has a much more ancient iconography than the atrociously agonizing images of Christ that Pascal and Port-Royal preferred – the Jesuits made converts. No one can deny the Jesuit's skills in gaining converts, even if some of their means might be deemed dubious; it can be questioned, however, whether Pascal's great *Apology for the Christian Religion*, the notes for which are known as the *Pensées*, would have ever converted anyone. Certainly his 'le Défi' – 'the Wager' – which will be discussed in Chapter 18 as an argument for belief in a

Christian God rivals anything to be found in Escobar for grotesque-
ness and sophistry. Pascal's peculiar form of dogmatism is interesting
when he trips up an opponent or plays the innocent comic; he
becomes as deadly as many of his casuistical opponents when defending a thesis of his own.

The 'Sixth Letter,' dated from Paris, 10 April 1656, reveals his
continued instruction on various points of Jesuit morality. On 23
March the *'Solitaires'* and their pupils had left Port-Royal. Father Le
Conte, SJ, visiting his cousin who was prioress of Port-Royal des
Champs, threatened her and called her a heretic. Madame Racine,
grandmother of the playwright Jean Racine and a nun at Port-Royal,
was present during the scene and fainted. On 30 March a civil deputy
named Dreux-Daubray came to make sure that the buildings of the
bastion of Jansenism were empty, and to try to locate a clandestine
printing-press, which did not exist there. In Paris police began
raiding various printers, trying to discover who was printing the
Provincial Letters. Replies to the letters had begun to appear, but
nothing to match the vigor and wit of Pascal's style. Under his
questioning in the 'Sixth Letter' the Jesuits are portrayed as capable
of finding exceptions to every moral precept, even to simony, by dint
of their specious reasoning. Even more shocking to the correspondent is the discovery in the 'Seventh Letter' of what the Jesuits call
'direction of intention,' thanks to which one may 'correct the vice by
the purity of the purpose.' The practice of duelling is thereby
permitted, 'for what evil is there in going to a field, taking a walk
there while waiting for a man, and defending oneself when someone
comes to attack you?' 'One may, without sin, even kill a man because
he slapped you, or for even less – because of words, signs, or
gestures.' Killing someone for having stolen something is counte-
nanced 'provided that the thing stolen has great value according to
the judgment of a prudent man.'

'In truth, Father,' the correspondent exclaims in the 'Sixth Letter,'
'your doctors give much to profit from: of two persons who do the
same thing, the one who does not know these doctrines sins, while
the one who does them does not sin?' The priest drops more names of
casuists and theologians, and as if to entice his opponent, promises to
give the casuistical maxims applying to *'les gentilshommes'* – 'the
gentlemen' – at their next meeting.

The next four 'Letters,' which complete the first series of the

Provincial Letters, deal almost exclusively with the duplicities of casuistical morality. Dated 25 April 1656, the 'Seventh Letter' appeared against the news of the miracle of the Holy Thorn, which occurred at Port-Royal of Paris on Friday 24 March. The recipient of the miracle was Marguerite Périer, Pascal's niece. The best doctor in Paris had given up in despair after treating the girl for a suppurating inflammation of the eye. The Holy Thorn was brought in its reliquary to the convent of Port-Royal in Paris; the girl knelt before it and prayed; she was healed completely a few days later. Incidentally, the Holy Thorn in question was apparently the one from the Sainte-Chapelle, which King Louis IX, St Louis, had constructed in the thirteenth century as an architectural reliquary for the Holy Thorn and other prized relics. News of the miracle spread throughout Paris; many persons interpreted it as a sign from God in favor of Port-Royal. Even Louis XIV was impressed, and therefore the Court showed signs of being impressed as well. On 23 April Arnauld d'Andilly was permitted to return to live in his little house next to Port-Royal des Champs. The 'Seventh Letter,' which concerns the casuistry of homicide, was greatly admired: even the king had it read to him, as did Cardinal Mazarin. Boileau judged the 'Seventh Letter' to be the finest of the *Provincial Letters* because of the great elegance of its reasoning.

The 'Seventh Letter' examines the casuistical principle of 'direction of intention,' which can be simply stated as follows. In any given action one should aim one's intention away from the evil consequences of the act to the good that will redound from it. When the correspondent objects that such a principle will countenance any action, Pascal's hypothetical Jesuit replies swiftly: 'To prove to you that we do not allow everything, you must know, for example, that we never allow the formal intention of sinning for the sake of sinning. Anyone who is so obstinate as to have no other purpose in evil than evil itself is diabolical, and we would break with him – and that regardless of age, sex, or quality. But when one is not in this unfortunate disposition, then we try to put into practice our method of "direction of intention," which consists in giving oneself as an end of one's actions something which is permitted.' In effect 'direction of intention' is a legerdemain with one's conscience: by not 'intending' to do anything evil for its own sake, but 'intending' to bring about some greater good, one can do something formally 'forbidden' by 'purifying the intention.' Applying the principle to homicide, the Jesuit displays the great diversity of killings that can be justified, and proceeds to illustrate the importance of the principle for politics and the interests of the State. Faced with the objection that such an ethics of expediency cannot be found in the Gospels, the Fathers of the Church, or in the Councils, the Jesuit retreats to citations from the casuists, especially Molina. 'Very well, Father, I am a little surprised by all this, and the positions of Father L'Amy and of Caramuel do not please me at all.' The Jesuit then asks pointedly: 'Are you a Jansenist?' Neither affirming nor denying that he is a Jansenist, the correspondent simply replies that he has been writing from time to time to a friend in the provinces, trying to explain to him what the theological commotion in Paris is all about.

On 12 May the syndic of the priests of Paris, Rousse, demanded that the Assembly of the Clergy should either condemn the *Provincial Letters* if they were mendacious, or should act with rigor against the casuists if what the *Provincial Letters* claimed was true. The 'Eighth Letter,' dated 28 May 1656, continues Pascal's attack on casuistry, as does the 'Ninth Letter,' dated 3 July 1656. More than a month elasped between the publication of the eighth and ninth letters, perhaps because it was becoming more and more difficult to get them published. The Jesuits had tried to persuade the syndic of publishers and printers of Paris to convince his colleagues not to publish more of the letters 'written to a provincial by one of his friends.' We know from Baudry de Saint-Gilles, writing on 18 August, that for two months 'everyone, even the magistrates, is getting such pleasure in seeing in these pieces Jesuit morality innocently exposed, that there is more freedom in having these texts printed.' Pascal considered bringing the *Provincial Letters* to a halt with the 'Eighth Letter,' but their tremendous success encouraged him to continue his campaign. Other events also fired his zeal. The clergy of Rouen, which was at this time the second largest and most important city in France, came out openly against the Society of Jesus. From Rome it was made known that Cardinal Barberini was in no way displeased with the discomfiture of the Jesuits. And so Pascal proceeded to unmask the casuists, showing how they attempted to justify usury, venality, even false oaths of perjury 'provided one had taken care to make a "mental reservation." '

The 'Eighth Letter' begins on a note of amusement concerning the authorship of the 'Letters.' Some believe that the author is a doctor of the Sorbonne, others believe that there are four or five authors, who are 'neither priests nor ecclesiastics.' 'All these false suspicions make me realize that I have done badly in my design to have myself known only to you, and to the good father who always tolerates my visits, and whose discourses I also tolerate, though with much pain.' The correspondent points out that the casuists have even come to the aid of the businessmen by countenancing 'breeding money from money' if some 'greater good' is thereby obtained. The 'Ninth Letter' reaches the heights of Pascal's feigned naive and ironic style. Describing how the 'good Jesuit father' welcomed him at his last visit, the correspondent writes that the priest greeted him clutching a recently published book entitled *Paradise Opened to Philagie by One Hundred Devotions to the Mother of God, Easy to Practice*. In effect the book was a Jesuitical self-help guide to Heaven by means of prayers to the Virgin Mary. The correspondent protests: 'In truth, Father, I know that devotions to the Virgin are a powerful means of salvation, and that the least of them have great merit when they proceed from motives of faith and charity, as with the saints that have practiced them. But to make persons who use them without changing their wicked lives believe that they will be converted at death, or that God will resurrect them, I find more conducive to keeping these sinners in their disorders by the false peace that this rash confidence brings them, than to bringing them to a genuine conversion which only grace can produce.' The Jesuit replies that it makes no difference how you get into Paradise, so long as you get in.

While the clergy of Rouen continued their attack on the Company of Jesus, a Jesuit named Brisacier begged the archbishop of Rouen, François de Harlay, in July, 'to declare the said letters pernicious for faith and for morals.' Pascal's 'Tenth Letter' appeared soon afterwards, dated 2 August 1656. In it he abandons irony, dialogue, and wit; his tone modulates into the new key of virulent moral outrage. The politics of the Jesuits are to make 'confession as easy as it used to be difficult.' Attrition is described as 'sufficient,' full contrition being 'unnecessary.' All manner of 'pious and holy "finesses" ' are introduced, along with 'holy artifices of devotion.' Even the love of God is dispensed with: 'This is the crowning part of the doctrine,' the 'good father' explains. 'You will see therefore that this dispensation of the annoying obligation' – *'obligation fâcheuse'* – 'to love God is the privilege of the evangelical law as against the Hebraic law.'

'It is thus that our fathers have released man from the *painful* obligation of actually loving God. And this doctrine is so advantageous that our Fathers Annat, Pintereau, Le Moine and A. Sirmond even have defended it vigorously when people have tried to combat it.' Quoting from these authors, the 'good father' gives the reasoning behind the doctrine of dispensing with *actually* loving God: 'It was reasonable that under the law of grace of the New Testament God would lift the law of performing an act of perfect contrition in order to be justified; and that He would institute sacraments to fill the gap, with the help of an easier arrangement. Otherwise certainly, the Christians – who are the children – would not now have more facility in placing themselves in the good graces of their Father than the Jews – who were the slaves – had for obtaining mercy from their Lord.' Pascal cries out in his own voice, no longer playing the role of the innocent enquirer: 'It is the height of blasphemy. The price of the blood of Jesus Christ will be to obtain for us the dispensation to love Him! . . . The strange theology of our times! . . . Thus you make those worthy to enjoy God in eternity who never loved God in their entire life! Behold the mystery of fully accomplished iniquity.' With these words Pascal leaves the Jesuit, knowing more than enough to prevent his ever visiting him again.

13

AN INNOCENT ON THE
DEFENSIVE

The new series of letters, which begins with the 'Onzième Lettre,'
reveals two changes in Pascal's attitude. First, he is no longer writing
to a fictional 'provincial,' but henceforth to the Jesuits themselves.
The subtitle of the 'Eleventh Letter,' is 'Written by the Author of the
Letters to a Provincial to the Reverend Jesuit Fathers.' Second, Pascal
changes from the offensive position that he had adopted since the
'Fourth Letter' to a defensive position in order to reply to his critics.
Dated 18 August 1656, it begins with the Jesuits' chief charge that the
author did not write with sufficient seriousness about their maxims,
and that he 'held up holy things to ridicule.' Pascal replies: 'In truth,
Fathers, there is a great difference between laughing at religion and
laughing at those who profane it by their extravagant opinions. It
would be an impiety to lack respect for the truths that the mind of
God has revealed; but it would be another sort of impiety to lack
disdain for the falsities that the mind of man sets up against them.'
Readily marshalling the teachings of the Church Fathers against the
casuistry of the Jesuits, Pascal enunciates three rules for judging
when criticism proceeds from piety and love, as opposed to impiety
and hatred. Although Pascal attributes these 'three rules' to the
'Fathers of the Church,' it is, as always with Pascal, St Augustine on
whom he relies almost entirely; there is, however, a reference to St
Hilary. 'The first of these rules is that the spirit of piety always
inclines to speak with truth and sincerity, while envy and hatred
make use of lying and calumny . . . ' 'The second rule is to speak with
discretion.' Pascal points out that he chose the most widely held of
the Jesuits' teachings, avoiding those that even they held to be
suspicious. Further, pointing out that he never resorted to personal

attacks, Pascal argues that he never violated the second rule. 'The third rule is that when one is obliged to use ridicule, the spirit of piety dictates that one use it only against errors, and not against holy things; whereas the spirit of buffoonery, impiety, and heresy is to laugh at whatever is most sacred.' To conclude his defense, Pascal cannot forebear criticizing an unfortunate poet of the Jesuit Order who wrote a poem entitled 'A Praise of Modesty, in which it is shown that all beautiful things are red, or subject to blushing.'

In spite of the popular success of the *Provincial Letters*, the Jansenist cause took a turn for the worse. The published writings of Arnauld that had been censored by the Sorbonne were condemned in Rome on 3 August and placed on the index of forbidden books. When news of this reached Paris, the General Assembly of the Clergy issued the 'Formulary' on 1 September which all bishops were required to have their priests and religious sign. The Formulary required submission to 'our Holy Father Pope Innocent X,' in his condemnation of the 'five propositions' in the bull of 31 May 1653. Pascal's 'Twelfth Letter,' dated 9 September 1656, is again addressed to the Jesuits. 'I was ready to write to you about the injuries you have caused me for such a long time in your writings, where you call me *impious, buffoon, ignoramous, joker, impostor, calumniator, knave, heretic, Calvinist in disguise, disciple of Du Moulin, possessed by a legion of devils*, and anything else that pleases you.' Arranging his defense by the 'impostures' of the Jesuits, Pascal defends his attacks on their position concerning alms-giving and simony. Obviously aided by theologians of Port-Royal, he cites St Thomas Aquinas to strengthen his defense. Usually offense is rhetorically more engaging and brilliant than defense, and in the 'Twelfth Letter' Pascal reveals himself both shrill and humorless.

By 30 September when the 'Treizième Lettre' appeared, the clergy of Paris was in agreement with the clergy of Rouen that the power of the Jesuit Order must be curtailed, and issued conjointly a notice to all the clergy of France: 'A Notice . . . concerning the wicked maxims of some new Casuists.' The 'Thirteenth Letter' is the most violent invective of the *Provincial Letters*. The reasons behind it are two-fold: the Jesuits accused Pascal of misquoting, or misreading, one of their texts; he accused them of duplicity in the facile distinction between theory and practice. The text concerns a practice long fallen into oblivion – duelling, civilized by comparison with some 'modern' ways of settling disagreements. Still, the frictions between *'theoria'* and *'praxis'* that Pascal deals with in the 'Thirteenth Letter' are familiar to anyone living in the twentieth century. The Jesuits had accused the author of the *Provincial Letters* of having falsely attributed to the theologian Lessius a maxim concerning murder and of having distorted his philosophic position. Lessius had written: 'He who has received an affront may immediately pursue his enemy, even with blows of his sword, not to avenge himself but to restore his honor.' The Jesuits reproached Pascal for omitting the phrase 'I condemn the practice.' But Pascal replies in the 'Thirteenth Letter' that the caveat applies to the following proposition: 'Whether one may kill because of slander.' He vindicates himself on two accounts: he has not falsified Lessius's text, and he can cite other passages in which killing is allowed for even more extravagant causes, e.g., 'that a religious is permitted to defend the honor that he has acquired by his own virtue, even by killing him who attacks his reputation.' Pascal's fury seems disproportionate to the importance of the text, but not to the principle at stake. He was always a meticulous exegete.

The remainder of the 'Thirteenth Letter' concerns Pascal's attack on the Jesuitical distinction between 'speculation' and 'practice.' Hoping to gain a foothold in the lives of the worldly, the Jesuits tended to be tolerant, if not lax, with sin omitted in cases 'in which only religion was concerned.' Difficulties arose when a case involved both religion and the State, such as usury or homicide. 'Brazen before God,' the Jesuits are 'timid before man.' 'Speculatively' they authorize a certain action because they see it only falls within the domain of divine law; 'practically' they forbid the action because they fear the consequences of civil law. When conjoined with the doctrine of 'probable opinion' the slippery distinction between 'speculation' and 'practice' can be manipulated to permit or rationalize almost any action. In the final paragraph Pascal invokes the wrath of God on the casuists for their duplicity and for offering 'two paths to man, thereby destroying the simplicity of the spirit of God, who curses whose who are double-hearted and who make for themselves two paths.'

The 'Fourteenth Letter,' dated 23 October 1656, was written during the turmoil caused by the Formulary. Although Pope Alexander VII had again condemned Jansen on 16 October, his bull was kept in secret and not remanded to the king until March 1656. The bull 'Ad sanctam beati Petri sedem' affirmed that the 'five propositions' were contained in *Augustinus* and that they were condemned in accord with the author's meaning. Arnauld agreed with the papal condemnation in regard to '*droit*': the five propositions were indeed heretical; however, Arnauld believed that the pope was simply mistaken about the matter of '*fait*': the five propositions were not actually to be found in Jansen's book. Arnauld was determined to show his respect for the head of the Church, and was in favor of signing the Formulary if it could be reworded to cover only the question of '*droit*.' His position came into conflict with two groups among the Jansenists themselves: one group, which included a number of recalcitrant and influential women, refused to sign the Formulary on any condition; and the other group, more pacific, thought that the matter should be entrusted to God and that the Formulary should be signed out of simple obedience. The 'Fourteenth Letter' is the most violent of the *Provincial Letters*. Pascal repeatedly pits orthodoxy and the Church Fathers against the specious reasonings of the casuists. He concludes by expressing his contempt for the Jesuits' replies: 'I just saw the response of your apologist to my thirteenth "letter." But if he does not reply better to this one, which meets most of his difficulties, he will not merit a response.'

The Jesuits were disturbed to see the clergy of Paris and Rouen militating against them. The Grand Vicar of Paris had also made known his misgivings about the Society of Jesus. The Assembly of the Clergy had asked Chancelier de Séguier to forbid the publication of Escobar in French. To stem the tide the Jesuits began a series of libels and calumnies against Port-Royal. The 'Fifteenth Letter,' dated 25 November 1656, and the following one, dated 4 December, are both attacks on the use of calumny. The casuists even try to justify or at least attenuate the seriousness of libel by writing that 'it is only a venial sin to calumniate and to attribute false crimes to ruin the credence of those who speak evil of us.' Pascal cites particular lies that the Jesuits had spread; for example, the 'Letter from a Minister to Monsieur Arnauld,' in which it is implied that Arnauld's treatise on 'Frequent Communion' 'had been written with a secret understanding with the ministers of Charenton,' that is, with the Protestants. The Jesuits obviously thought that it was more pardonable to lie than to be a Protestant.

Longer and less trenchant than the other 'Letters,' the 'Sixteenth

Letter' contains the important statement that the author is not himself a man of Port-Royal, but that it is the absurdity of the Jesuits' vilifications of Port-Royal that spurs him into defense. Pascal cites one of the recent libels, the title of which gives the entire content: 'Port-Royal and Geneva in Conspiracy against the Most Blessed Sacrament of the Altar.' Pascal becomes particularly vehement when defending the sisters of Port-Royal who took the name 'Filles du Saint-Sacrament' – 'Daughters of the Blessed Sacrament.' (It will be remembered that Pascal's beloved sister Jacqueline was herself a sister at Port-Royal des Champs.) The 'Sixteenth Letter,' which is not entirely by Pascal, chiefly concerns defending the orthodoxy of Jansen, Saint-Cyran, and Arnauld.

The 'Seventeenth Letter,' dated 23 January 1656, appeared six weeks later, when the Jansenist cause seemed to be doomed. On 12 December the High Council of the king forbade writing against the Jesuits, and on 23 December it was ruled illegal to publish without permission or '*privilège du Roi*' and without the author's name. The casuists stepped up their attacks on the *Provincial Letters*, which made the Jansenists decide upon the publication of the 'Dix-septième Lettre.' Police were keeping publishers and printers under surveillance; it was difficult to find a publisher for the penultimate letter. Nonetheless, Pascal's tone is conciliatory, intended to establish the orthodoxy of the Jansenists rather than attack the morality or politics of the Jesuits. The 'Letter' is addressed to the Provincial of the Order, Father Annat, who was the author of most of the replies to the *Provincial Letters*. Annat had accused the author of being a heretic, employing a syllogism that any schoolboy could understand: he who is writing the 'Letters' is of Port-Royal; Port-Royal has been declared heretical; therefore the author of the 'Letters' is heretical. But Pascal had already declared that he was 'not one of those gentlemen of Port-Royal.' Moreover, it would require extraordinary subtlety to declare Pascal a heretic when he declares: 'The only attachment that I have on earth is with the Catholic, Apostolic and Roman Church, in which I want to live and die, and in communion with the pope, her sovereign head, outside of which I am well persuaded there is no salvation.'

By the time of the last 'Letter,' dated 24 March 1656, the cause of Port-Royal had worsened further. Alexander VII's bull condemning it had been remanded to Louis XIV on 11 March. The Assembly of the Clergy had received the bull on 17 March and had formulated a stricter version of the Formulary. The archbishop of Rouen put an end to the quarrel between his clergy and the Jesuits. Jesuits throughout Paris delivered homilies against Port-Royal, among them Father de Lingendes at the Church of Saint-Merry. But the miracle, as it was widely held to be, of the Holy Thorn continued to bolster the Jansenist cause, and other events also deemed 'miracles' were quick to follow. Causes are often known by the people they attract, and the Jansenist cause became a mecca for some of the greatest lords and ladies of France – Henrietta of France, the Prince de Condé, the Prince Palatine, the duc de Nemours. Power seemed so evenly divided on both sides of the controversy that there was talk of armistice. The 'Eighteenth Letter,' also addressed to Annat, is calm, pious, and conciliatory.

Arguing that Port-Royal's doctrine concerning grace perfectly coincides with the traditions of the Church, Pascal dimisses the charges of Calvinism brought by the Jesuits. He marshalls quotations from Augustine and Aquinas to prove his point. When he turns to the pope's condemnation of Jansen, Pascal reminds the Jesuits that they had also obtained a decree against Galileo regarding his opinion on the movement of the earth: 'Does that prove that the earth does not move?' There are but three avenues to truth, Pascal argues, and none of them involves casuistry. 'From where do we learn the truth of the facts? From the eyes, Father, which are the legitimate judges, just as reason is of natural and intelligible things, and faith of supernatural and revealed things . . . according to the two greatest doctors of the Church, St Augustine and St Thomas, these three principles of our understanding – sense, reason, and faith – each have their separate objects, and their certainty within this scope.' The last lines of the 'Eighteenth Letter' are both pacific and threatening: 'Leave the Church in peace, and I shall willingly leave you. But while you labor to stir up trouble in the Church, do not doubt that there will be children of peace who will believe themselves obliged to use all their powers to maintain tranquillity.'

Around April 1657 Pascal began a 'Nineteenth Letter,' also addressed to Annat, but he wrote only a few paragraphs and left some fragmentary notes. Clearly he was disturbed over the consequences of the Formulary: 'They are attacking the greatest of Christian truths, which is the love of truth . . . ' Holding with Arnauld that the 'five propositions' were not in *Augustinus*, Pascal wrote: 'One is not guilty for not believing.' Why did Pascal not finish the 'Letter'? For one reason many prominent figures of Port-Royal, including Mère Angélique, de Saci and the nuns' confessor Father Singlin, deplored the polemic and the irreligious attention that the controversy was attracting and believed that silence accorded better with Chrisian charity than publishing replies – however brilliant – to attacks on Jansenism. Another reason is that Pascal finally realized that the Jansenist battle was lost, and that public opinion swayed by the *Provincial Letters* had no influence. After the bull of Alexander VII, and its acceptance by Louis XIV and the Assembly of the Clergy, Pascal could only wait to observe the repercussions of his 'Letters.' It is not certain whether Pascal wrote the 'Letter from a Lawyer of Parliament to one of his Friends concerning the Inquisition that they are trying to establish in France on the occasion of the new Bull of Pope Alexander VII.' Doubtless Pascal was gratified to see that the Assembly of the Clergy did publish 'Instructions for Confessors' by St Charles Borromeo, which condemned many of the same casuistical principles exposed in the *Provincial Letters*.

Believing that the Assembly of the Clergy were too divided in their opinion on the Jesuits to condemn them, the Society published a book by Father Picot with a typically lengthy title of the period: 'Apology for the Casuists against the Calumnies of the Jansenists: in which the Reader will find the Truth of Christian Morality so nicely explicated and proved with so much solidity that he will readily see that the Maxims of the Jansenists have only the Appearance of Truth; and that they lead to all sorts of sin, and to great laxities that they blame with so much Severity. By a theologian and professor of canon law.' (With such a title there is no need to read the book.) But the Jesuits outsmarted themselves, for the work was immediately condemned by the clergy of Paris and Rouen, and finally in Rome. Ironically, the clergy of Paris turned to the gentlemen of Port-Royal, and first to Pascal himself, to aid them in their battle against the Jesuits. Pascal was already working on his *Apology for the Christian Religion*. Interrupting this work, he wrote a brief work for the Parisian clergy: 'Address to the Parish Priests of Paris, against a book entitled "Apology for the Casuists . . ." and against those who composed, printed and spread it.' Repeating in succinct form the basic theses of the *Provincial Letters*, Pascal makes his logistics clear in the opening sentence: 'Our cause is the cause of Christian morality. Our adversaries are the casuists who are corrupting it.'

The Jesuits replied with a 'Refutation of the Calumnies published against the Jesuits.' The parish priests responded on 2 April 1658 with a reply written by Pascal in one day. Volley followed volley for several months. Among these 'Pamphlets of the parish Priests of Paris' the 'Fifth Pamphlet' is certainly by Pascal, based on both internal evidence and the testimony of his sister Gilberte in her biography. The subtitle of the 'Fifth Pamphlet' is 'On the advantage that the Heretics Take against the Church from the Morality of the Casuists and the Jesuits.' Pascal develops his argument as follows. The Calvinists depend upon the propositions of the casuists to condemn the morality of the Church; yet the Calvinists are deceiving themselves because these propositions are condemned by the bishops and the parish priests. Nonetheless the Jesuits are guilty of a grave injustice against the Church: because they respect the unity of the Church, the Jesuits are less guilty than the Calvinists, but are heretics in their own way even so.

Among Pascal's papers in his own hand was found a 'Projet de Mandement contre "l'Apologie pour les casuistes" ' – 'Project for a Bishop's Letter against the "Apology for the Casuists." ' It was intended to be submitted to a bishop for his signature. The tone is indeed pastoral: 'The love that we have for our people obliging us to a continuous vigil to prevent all that might injure them, we felt ourselves obligated to double our vigil when the pernicious book entitled "Apology for the Casuists" began to circulate in this dio- cese . . . ' The 'Apology' was condemned on 16 July 1658. Predict- ably the Jesuits replied with 'The Sentiments of the Jesuits on the "Apology . . . " ' Equally predictably, the parish priests could not let their opponents have the last word, and they published a 'Sixth Pamphlet' on 24 July. It has been attributed, though not conclusive- ly, to Pascal. But by this time even Pascal had wearied of the polemics, much as he enjoyed literary pugilism when he thought he was on the right side. He now devoted his time to his great project, the *Apology for the Christian Religion*, and enjoyed the intellectual serenity of his scientific work. In 1658 appeared his 'First Circulating Letter Relative to the Cycloid.'

Thus ended a struggle that had consumed more than two years of Pascal's life. The Port-Royalists decided to have the 'Letters' published together in one volume, which appeared in 1657. The *Provincial Letters* would be published under Pascal's pseudonym until the end of the *ancien régime*. Immediately an English translation appeared (London, 1657) perhaps under the instigation of John Milton, who may have hoped that the *Provincial Letters* would bring about a Gallican schism similar to the Anglican schism. The English title is *Les Provinciales, or, the mysterie of Jesuitisme discovered in certain Letters, Written upon occasion of the present differences at Sorbonne, between the Jansenists and the Molinists, from January 1657 to March 1657* . . . Pierre Nicole translated the work into Latin (Cologne, 1658) with extensive theological notes. A polyglot edition in Latin, Spanish, and Italian appeared in 1684, while the French editions kept appearing: there were at least thirty-five up until 1769. The *Provincial Letters* became the greatest publishing success in the *ancien régime*. As further proof of this, it may be pointed out that the Parliament of Provence placed it on the index of forbidden books. Finally, in 1660, upon the report of an ecclesiastical commission, the Council of State ordered the Latin translation by Nicole (who used the pseudonym Wendrocke) to be burned. It appears, however, that the book was burned more because of the translator than the author: Nicole included among his notes to the text a comment that was interpreted as a defamation of the memory of Louis XIII.

As for his anonymity, few authors have taken such a delight in their pseudonym as Pascal. Few knew that he was the author of the *Provincial Letters*; in fact he took a puckish delight in signing the third 'Letter' 'Votre très humble et très obéissant serviteur E.A.A.B. P.A.F.D.E.P.' No one knew how to decipher the rebus 'et ancien ami Blaise Pascal auvergnat, fils d'Etienne Pascal' – 'and your old friend Blaise Pascal, from Auvergne, son of . . . ' Those who thought they knew who the author was mentioned the names of Le Maître de Saci, Antoine Arnauld, Antoine Le Maître, Abbé Le Roy de Haute Fontaine – which was actually the pseudonym of the mannerist novelist Gomberville. But the Jesuits, clever and persistent if nothing else, quickly suspected that the author was Pascal, and sent a member of their Society, Father de Frétat, to threaten Florian Périer, Pascal's brother-in-law. It was not until 1659, with the publication by Father Vavassor – who used the name Fabi – of his *Notae in notas Willeilmi Wendrockii ad Ludovici Montalti litteras*, that Blaise Pascal was named as the author of the *Provincial Letters*. None but the intimates of Port-Royal knew from the beginning that Montalte was Pascal; he maintained his anonymity by working clandestinely, sometimes in the Auberge of King David, other times at the Collège d'Harcourt or at the townhouse of the duc de Roannez.

Although Pascal was the sole author of the *Provincial Letters*, he readily admitted that many of the materials were furnished to him by Arnauld or Nicole, not being a theologican himself. Pascal admitted that he had not read all the books that he cited, but he had read the whole of Escobar twice. As for the other casuists, 'I had them read by my friends, but I never used a single passage without having read it myself in the book cited, and I always read what preceded and followed the passage, so as not to risk citing an objection for a response, which would have been reprehensible and unfair.'

Bossuet was once asked what work he would have preferred to write if he had not written his own; he replied, 'Les *Lettres Provinciales.*' Bossuet had prepared a censure of the Jesuits' morality which the Assembly of the Clergy did not have time to vote on in 1682, but which was passed, with Bossuet present, in 1700. Seventy-three years later in the pope's bull of suppression of the order one of the major grounds given was the pernicious morality of the casuists.

In his excitement Pascal often confuses casuists with Jesuits; actually, casuistry was practiced in all religious orders: it was simply that the Jesuits practiced it with the greatest vigor. Without being able to foresee how his *Provincial Letters* would be read in the Age of Enlightenment, Pascal unintentionally supplied the techniques and attitudes that would lead some of the best minds in the following century – Voltaire, Condillac, Hume, and Gibbon – to scoff at all revealed religion. By discussing theological issues in a profane and often witty way, and by emphasizing the importance of 'the light of reason,' Pascal opened the gates for a similar examination of the contradictions and extravagant positions to be found in the Church Fathers and even in the Bible.

It must be admitted that many of the issues so heatedly discussed in the *Provincial Letters* are superannuated and dusty, and yet the work survives. One may not believe a single statement in the New Testament, or in the *Aeneid*, and still use them with great success in teaching or learning Koiné Greek or classical Latin. The same holds true of the *Provincial Letters*: they form the most pure masterpiece in the French language. In *The Age of Louis XIV* Voltaire writes of the

Provincial Letters: 'They are the first work of genius that one has seen in prose.' He adds, 'The first letters are worth the best comedies of Molière' and 'Bossuet has nothing more sublime that the last "Letters." ' Every literary genre appears in the *Provincial Letters*. There is not a word in excess. The language perfectly fits the thought. The author never intrudes upon his subject. The result is a perfect expression of classicism. All passion is spent through excess of restraint, and the *Provincial Letters* conclude in beatific calm.

II
The *Pensées*

14

THE SUPREME
APOLOGIST

In the 'Preface' that he wrote for the 1670 Port-Royal edition of the *Pensées*, Etienne Périer, Florian's brother, testifies that Pascal was about thirty years of age when he gave up the study of physics and mathematics and turned all his attention to the study of the Scriptures, the Church Fathers, and Christian morality. The project of writing a grand defense of the Christian religion can therefore be traced to 1653. The archdeacon of Beauvais, Bridieu, familiar with the project from the beginning, writes that 'Monsieur Pascal composed these fragments for eight strong minds of Poitou who did not believe in God; he wanted to convince them by moral and natural reasons.' The first notes that Pascal made for the *Apology for the Christian Religion* concerned miracles, and cannot be dated before 1656, ten months after the miracle of the Holy Thorn and undoubtedly prompted by that event. Gilberte Périer writes that it was not until 1657, when her brother was thirty-four, that he applied himself entirely to the work.

Towards the end of 1658, at the invitation of the '*messieurs* de Port-Royal,' Pascal travelled down from Paris to Port-Royal des Champs to give a lecture on his vast project. Etienne Périer writes: 'The *messieurs* did not want him to write down what he had in mind, but to deliver it *viva voce*. In very few words he developed the plan of the entire work; he presented to them what he had to do with the subject and the material; he gave them an abridgment of the reasons and the principles, and he explained to them the order and the plan of the things which he wanted to treat. And these persons, who were as capable as one can possibly be to judge of these sorts of things, avowed that they had never heard anything so beautiful, so powerful, so moving, or so convincing.' The scholars of Port-Royal were well known and admired for their acuity and discipline; by the time of their meeting with Pascal he must have had the entire structure of the *Apology* worked out in his mind, and certain important parts already written. This mode of composition – working out a subject entirely in the mind and then setting it down on paper at break-neck speed – can be traced throughout all of Pascal's works – scientific, mathematical, and philosophical. Luckily, another Jansenist, Filleau de la Chaise, was also present at the meeting, and left an eye-witness account. He included this account, written under the pseudonym Debois de la Cour, in 1672 under the title 'Discourse on the *Pensées* of Monsieur Pascal in which one tries to show what was his plan . . . '

Filleau de la Chaise included in his 'Discourse' two short treatises by Pascal: 'Discourse on the Proofs of the Books of Moses' and 'That there are demonstrations of another type, but as certain as those of geometry.' These two methods – treating the Scriptures like any other historical document, and ordering philosophical and theological ideas in order to achieve certain demonstrations – are the guiding principles of the *Pensées*. Moreover, there are a few notes in Pascal's own hand entitled 'A.P.R. Pour demain' – 'To Port-Royal, for tomorrow.'

The first edition of the *Pensées* (Paris, Guillaume Desprée, 1669) is so rare that only two copies are known to exist. The title in full is '*Pensées* of Monsieur Pascal, on Religion, and on some other subjects, which were found after his death among his papers.' In his 'Preface' to the 1669 edition, and the much more widely distributed 1670 edition – the first public edition – Etienne Périer gives invaluable information concerning the composition and first editing of the *Pensées*:

> It was thus that he made most of the fragments that one will find in this collection: hence one should not be surprised that some of them seem rather imperfect, too short, or inadequately explained, and that in them one can even find terms and expressions less proper and less elegant. Nevertheless it sometimes happened that having pen in hand he could not keep himself, in following his inclination, from extending his ideas, and of extending them a bit further, although this was never with the same power or application of mind as if he had been in perfect health. And this is why one will find some of the ideas more developed and better written than others.

That is how the *Pensées* were written.

As one knew the plan that Pascal had of working on religion, we took great care, after his death, to gather all the writings that he had made in this manner. We found them all tied together in various bundles, but without any order, without any connection, because, as I have already remarked, it was only the first expressions of these ideas that he wrote down on little pieces of paper in so far as they came into his mind. And the whole thing was so imperfect and badly written that we had all the trouble in the world to decipher it.

Etienne Périer continues by saying that 'the first thing we did was to copy the fragments just as they were and in the same confusion that we had found them.' As for the holographs – all the fragments written on scraps of paper – they were cut into pieces and pasted in an enormous album bound in 253 folios. This album, now in the Bibliothèque Nationale (MS. 92092, *Pensées*, 1711) was used to establish the first edition of 1670.

Actually, Etienne Périer was mistaken: Pascal's notes were not chaotic, but followed a plan that Périer failed to perceive. By a careful examination of the holograph and of the holes for the original strings, one can see that Pascal was jotting down his ideas on large pieces of paper at the top of which he usually drew a little cross. He drew lines between the various entries, and sometimes lines within an individual *'pensée'* to show that it needed to be filled out. When Pascal was asked by the *'messieurs'* of Port-Royal to present his project on 'The Truth of the Christian Religion,' he began cutting up the original large pieces and classifying them under general topics, following the indications of the crosses and lines. He then proceeded to arrange the *'pensées'* into twenty-seven files, which comprise 382 entries. But because his illness became more severe in 1659, Pascal left the other fragments – some 590 unclassified.

From the little notes *'pour demain'* and the current, and most acceptable, rearrangement of the fragments themselves, one can restructure how Pascal described his grand project to the scholars of Port-Royal in the autumn of 1658. The *Apology*, or 'reasoned defense,' was to be constructed along simple, classical lines, in order to produce a compelling and grandiose effect. One is reminded of architectual masterpieces of the same period, such as the colonnade of the Louvre by Perrault, or Versailles. The purpose of the *Apology* was also simple: to convert the unbeliever. Taking the unbeliever as his prime audience, Pascal would first show him the two states of man: his misery and his grandeur. Next, Pascal would prove to him that only the Old Testament is capable of explaining the misery of man by means of the doctrines of Creation and Original Sin; and only the New Testament explains the grandeur of man through the doctrine of the Redemption. Thus, given that the Scriptures afford the best explanation of man's condition and of his destiny, one is rationally obliged to concede, even if one still has doubts, that there is some probability that God exists and that the Bible is worthy of being the foundation, along with the Church, of one's faith.

At this point Pascal would argue with the unbeliever that he must choose, and that refusing to choose – the position of the agnostic or skeptic – is still a choice. The argument based on 'the wager' – 'le pari' – is then developed. It is, incidentally, more exact to refer to this argument by the title that Pascal gave it in the fragments – 'Infini – rien' – 'Infinity – nothingness.' The next step is to show that the Christian religion is not only plausible and desirable, but is the sole true religion. The proofs are not supported by scholastic philosophy, but solely by the unique proof of the person of Christ. He was foreshadowed and hoped for in the Old Testament; He is brought into being and raised up as the model of all mankind in the New Testament. The truth of his perfect humanity and perfect divinity is a truth to which one must submit. Finally, the human and divine drama of Christ has never ceased, and will continue through the centuries so long as there remains one soul to be saved. Such are the broad outlines of the work that Pascal presented to the gentlemen of Port-Royal; they, at least, were overwhelmed by its simplicity and power.

Only the first part – 'Misery of Man without God' – was almost entirely completed by Pascal; the second part – 'Proofs of the Christian Religion' – remains in a state of largely unorganized fragments, many of which are so laconic or illegiible that one can only speculate as to their meaning. Even so, both parts of the *Apology* can be conceptually connected to the fundamentally important fragment (no. 84) entitled 'Disproportion de l'homme,' which is commonly called 'les deux infinis' – 'the two infinities.' Pascal's argument is that the two infinities of man, his smallness and his grandeur, can only be resolved in God. It is as if Pascal, the geometer, realizing that any given point can be diminished or extended infinitely, connected the two infinities in man into a circle, or God, thereby situating man in the universe and revealing his true state and destiny. The theme of 'the two infinities' runs through the *Apology* like a leitmotif in Fauré or Franck; its periodic resurfacing binds together what would otherwise seem like unrelated or extraneous materials. The 'wager' proposed to the unbeliever is but one of the many transmogrifications of the same leitmotif.

Because Pascal was able to bring only the first part of the *Apology* close to completion, or rather the Introduction to the *Apology* itself, a natural misunderstanding of his thought has arisen, which stresses the negative, skeptical, and desperate aspect of his thought. The proofs for the Christian religion, the sublime surge of optimism, and the tranquil mysticism are all related in fragments. It is as if Dante had completed only the *Inferno* and had left only fragments for the *Purgatorio* and a few sketches for the *Paradiso*; as the *Divine Comedy* stands, we have a totally complete and balanced view of Dante's conception of man in the cosmos. With Pascal we must interpolate and meditate upon the fragments that comprise the second part to obtain a synoptic view of the author's plan.

It is also a mistake to read the *Pensées* as if they were a diary or intimate journal. No one can doubt that Pascal experienced the spiritual agonies, the fears of being a small point in infinite space and time, as recounted in the work. Yet all personal references have dropped out of the text: there is no romantic imposition of the self, or even of the first person singular. The author – a believer – sets up a vast dialogue with the interlocutor – an unbeliever. The apologist tries to convince the interlocutor to give up his 'old self' – skeptical, miserable, self-centered – for the 'new self' – believing, tranquil, theocentric. Biographical parallels between Pascal's own conversion and his testimony in the 'Mémorial' are obvious: it is the ascetic of Port-Royal addressing his former self as the 'worldly' skeptic. To begin the dialogue the author demands of his interlocutor, as he did of his former self, that he look deeply into the brute fact of his existence in the world. Just as Pascal conceived of geometry as resting upon nebulous but certain axioms, so he grounded his defense of Christianity upon an equally indefinable but certain datum: one's own existence.

Nonetheless, the *Pensées* can also be read as Pascal's autobiography, although transposed, so to speak, into another key. The author is converted from his early self as a brilliant mathematician to his religious self, as expressed in the 'Mystère de Jésus,' which was not intended to be part of the *Apology* but is now included in the *Pensées*. Read as autobiography, the *Pensées* hark back to St Augustine's *Confessions*. Pascal continued his mathematical and scientific research to the end of his life, proving that the believer is in no way called upon to give up intellectual studies: they, too, are simply transposed to another key. After the publication of his *Principia*, Isaac Newton also turned his attention to theological matters, while keeping abreast of the physics of his day. Like Newton, Pascal demanded that religion entirely satisfy his intelligence. In the Age of Reason, reason must be convinced, or at least strongly persuaded, of the claims of faith.

Pascal's *Apologie pour la religion Chrétienne* should be placed within the context of apologetics in general, one of the most ancient literary genres. 'Apologetics' is ultimately derived from the Greek verb which means 'to answer,' 'to account for,' 'to defend,' 'to give a case for,' or 'to justify.' Specifically 'apologetics' means giving a reasoned defense for the Judeo-Christian tradition. The Old Testament may be viewed as the first work of apologetics, for it is an attempt not only to recount historical events but also to defend God's providential relationship to his chosen people. Yahweh is described as striking a covenant with the Israelites: ' . . . I will be your god and ye shall be my people' (Jeremiah 7:23). Although God's ways are held to be mysterious, once having intervened in human history He directs and shapes events, while still allowing man his freedom and therefore his responsibility. Obedience to the Decalogue is a requirement of loyalty to Yahweh. The prophets and the authors of the Old Testament continually strain to make God's intervention in history both intelligible and righteous. The Deuteronomist does not so much pretend to understand God's ways as to plead for man to accept them because they are God's ways. When the Deuteronomist bewails the people of Israel in exile (4 Kings 17) he does not approach the event as a brute fact but gives an account of it – an apologetics – in terms of God's ultimate justice.

The authors of the New Testament engaged in apologetics when they construed the miracles and words of Jesus as justifications for their belief that He was indeed the Christ, the Son of God. The Holy

Gospels give an account, and justification, of God's activity in Christ. Mark engages in straightforward apologetics when he attempts to answer questions that would occur to early Christians. For example, why did the Jews refuse to believe in Jesus if He performed so many remarkable miracles? Mark answers that most people did accept Jesus as the Messiah; this was why the high priest arranged to have Jesus arrested by stealth and had Him crucified. His great credibility among the people made the Pharisees fear for their own future. Again, if Jesus was the Son of God, why did He undergo the Crucifixion? Mark answers (chs 8, 9, 10) by giving the three prophecies of the Passion, Death, and Resurrection. It was a death that Jesus willingly accepted because it was part of His redemptive task. Old Testament quotations are used apologetically throughout the New Testament. Events are not described as mere happenings, as they would be in a chronicle, but as figures and symbols of a higher and divine intent. The Holy Gospel is the cornerstone of all Christian apologetics.

The strategies of the Greek apologist of the second century were deployed to defend nascent Christianity against both Jewish and pagan attacks. The first sort of argument was based on the miracles of Christ. They were attested to by credible witnesses and must therefore indicate that Jesus was the Son of God. But the early apologists were wary of citing miracles, because the pagans had rather remarkable wonder-workers of their own, and also in part because miracles could be ascribed to demonic assistance. Much more credible in defending Christianity was the extraordinary moral effect of Jesus's teachings, especially concerning love. Writing in about 150, Justin Martyr points out how Christianity had altered man's reliance on magic and a plurality of gods to a fervent belief in one true and good God. Again, Christianity emphasized a sharing of material goods and care for the poor, as opposed to the avarice of the pagans. Christianity elevates humility to a virtue and denigrates self-gratification to a vice. The apologists also used arguments based on the predictions of the Hebrew prophets and of Christ. Lastly, the apologists were careful to point out that Christianity was the fulfillment of the Old Testament, not a new upstart cult, but one whose roots could be traced back to Moses, and therefore more ancient than the sages and poets of Greece. In his *Contra Celsum* Origen (c. 185–c. 254) argued that the highest defense of Christianity was the miracle of the

Resurrection. Tertullian went so far as to defend Christianity by arguing for its continuity with pagan philosophy while superseding and perfecting pagan morality.

Scholastic apologetics is based upon an ingenious assumption: the defense of Christianity is organized on the same principles and forms of argument already espoused by many opponents of Christianity – the philosophy of Aristotle. St Thomas Aquinas, in the *Summa contra gentiles*, sets out to show the continuity of Christianity with the philosophy of Aristotle. In a subtly oxymoronic argument Aquinas proposed that the mere existence of Christianity is proof that it is the true religion. Other religions offer temporal rewards and carnal delights; Christianity promises only spiritual rewards and suffering. That so many people espoused a religion based upon self-abnegation and self-sacrifice shows that miracles did in fact take place. Aquinas wanted to meet the non-believer on his own ground; the Aristotelian method of explication, and its first principles, seemed theologically neutral, and therefore acceptable to atheists and agnostics, as well as to theists such as the Jews and the Muslims. Aquinas was the most natural of all apologists because he believed that faith was connatural to man and a communal possession. He was also the most humble of apologists, recorded as saying towards the end of his life that all his philosophy was 'as straw' compared to what he had finally glimpsed of the truth. Apologetics would not enter its virulent phase until the birth of modern science, which is, in effect, the age of Pascal.

Apologetics in the sixteenth century, the period of the Reformation, was largely involved in defending the authority, necessity, and continuity of the Church in face of Protestant charges and criticism. Although primarily an autobiography, St Teresa of Avila's *Vida*, or autobiography, contains many apologetical passages. Cardinal Bellarmine, Saints Ignatius of Loyola and Francis Xavier, and others, attempted to demonstrate that the marks of the Church of Rome showed that it was the true church, and therefore the supreme arbiter in matters of faith and morals. Sixteenth-century apologetics usually produced more clamor and calumny than it did theological reconciliation. The Scriptures, themselves an infinitely delphic work, were quoted, glossed, and interpreted by both sides to support logically incompatible positions. It must be borne in mind that many of the casuists with whom Pascal spars in the *Provincial Letters* had minutely studied the most subtle casuist of the sixteenth century, the Spanish Jesuit Francisco Suarez, whose *Defensio Fidei* appeared in 1613.[1] An elaborate defense of the papacy, *The Defense of the Faith* argues for supreme papal authority not only in spiritual matters but also in temporal ones.

Apologetics in Pascal's era took an emphatically Cartesian turn, even though Descartes himself never took up the apologetic pen. Descartes's first principle was not to accept anything as true which was not clearly and distinctly perceived to be so by the knowing subject. Secondly, nature would reveal herself only if the enquirer followed the scientific method and the proper use of reason. Vague and riddled with conundrums as Descartes's 'method' is, as described his *Directions for the Use of the Mind*[2] and other writings, apologists, including Leibniz, approached the enterprise in a Cartesian spirit. Miguel de Elizalde's apology, *Forma verae*, was published in Naples in 1662. Even earlier an enchiridion type of apologetics had been published by Hugo Grotius in 1627: *De veritatae religionis christianae*. Cartesian apologetics are dominated by the conviction that only science, guided by the geometrical method, has access to truth, whether in physics or theology. It was precisely against this enlightened bigotry that Pascal's own apologetics was conceived.

15
HOW TO SWAY THE DOUBTFUL

As reconstructed, Pascal's *Apology* begins with a sweeping statement: 'People have contempt for religion; they bear hatred towards it, and also fear that it is true' (1). Pascal announces that he intends to 'heal' that contempt, first by showing that religion is not contrary to reason, then by demonstrating that religion is 'venerable' because it understands the true state of man. Pascal will go on to show that religion is 'loveable' because it promises 'the true good,' and finally that the Christian religion is 'true.' These four theses are to be guided by one supreme principle: 'Two excesses: exclude reason, allow nothing but reason' (3). Thus Pascal clearly states his opposition both to fundamentalism or what one might call 'bibliolatry' or 'Bible-worship,' and to 'scientism' or what later came to be known as positivism. 'If one submits everything to reason, our religion will have nothing mysterious or supernatural about it. If one shocks the principles of reason, our religion will be absurd and ridiculous' (4). Opposed to any form of irrationalism, Pascal also has the audacity to treat the Bible as a historic document without presupposing divine inspiration. But his position would also find disfavor during the following century, the Age of Enlightenment, when such thinkers as Diderot, Helvetius, and Condorcet naturally assumed that man's mind is the measure of all things and confidently predicted that everything would be known by the end of the century.

Without mentioning any particular metaphysical proof for God's existence, such as the 'five ways' in the *Summa Theologiae* of St Thomas, or the ontological proof of St Anselm, Pascal boldly rejects the entire enterprise of using such proofs because 'they are so distant from man's reasoning and so convoluted that they make little impression' (5). Pascal is surely right: few subjects have earned such an energetic use of specious reasoning as has the existence of God. Pascal does not mention Descartes's proofs for God's existence in the *Discours* or the *Méditations*, but he found them both sophistical and wrong-headed: 'In any dialogue or discourse it is essential to be able to ask those who take offense: What are you complaining about?' (9). Thus, in his dialogue with the unbeliever or the atheist, Pascal counsels beginning with piety, but then determining why they have adopted such a position.

Recalling his distinction between '*l'esprit de géométrie*' and '*l'esprit de finesse*' from his earlier essay so entitled, Pascal applies the two ways of persuasion to the method of the *Apology*. The principles of the geometrical intellect can be grasped, as 'palpables,' but are far removed from ordinary concerns; but once the principles are seen fully one would have to possess a completely perverse intellect – '*avoir tout à fait l'esprit faux*' – to reason incorrectly on the basis of them. 'But in the mind of finesse, the principles are in ordinary usage and before the eyes of everyone. One has only to turn one's head, and there is no need to do oneself violence; it is not a question of having good insight; it is *essential* to have good insight. For the principles are so unconnected and so vast in number that it is almost impossible for some not to elude us' (21). The '*esprits fins*' – or 'intuitive minds' – understand things in one fell swoop, often using their feelings and imagination, without making use of first principles or demonstrations. The '*esprits fins*' are nonetheless astonished when presented with geometrical reasoning, 'such sterile principles that they are not accustomed to see in such detail – that they are rebuffed and disgusted by them.' On the other hand, the geometrical mode often allows the diversity and nuances of things to escape scrutiny. 'And thus it is rare that geometers are subtle or artful ['*fins*'] and that the subtle are geometers, because the geometers want to treat geometrically subtle things and make themselves ridiculous by wanting to begin with definitions and then with principles, which is not the way in which to proceed in this sort of reasoning.' Pascal's method for the *Apology* requires a delicate balance between both kinds of mind or spirit; the two are usually not to be found in one and the same person because those who are only artful or subtle lack 'the patience to descend to the first principles of speculative things and things of the imagination . . .' Anyone willing to pick up the challenge posed by the

Apology must possess both habits of mind.

'Those who are accustomed to judging by sentiment understand nothing about things of reason, for they want to penetrate with insight first, and are not accustomed to principles. The others, on the contrary, understand nothing about things of sentiment, trying to find its principles, and not gaining any insight' (23). Pascal assigns 'finesse' to judgment, and geometry to the intellect. But both intellect and sentiment are formed by conversation, as well as spoiled by conversation. 'Thus that makes a circle, from which those who come out are fortunate.' Implying that the style of the *Apology* runs parallel to the content, Pascal states: 'True eloquence makes fun of eloquence . . . To make fun of philosophy is truly to philosophize' (24). Like any serious writer, Pascal faces up to the difficulty of judging his own writing. 'I have never judged the same thing in exactly the same way. I cannot judge my work while doing it; I must do as the painters do and distance myself from it, but not too much. But then, how much? Guess' (28).

'Theology is a science . . . ' (29) simply because there is no reason to adopt a sole model for all sciences, in the same way that 'countryside' covers 'trees,' 'leaves,' 'plants,' 'ants,' 'ant legs,' and so on 'to infinity.' 'Nature imitates herself: a seed, sown on good earth, produces; a principle, sown in a good mind, produces; numbers imitate space, though of such a different nature' (31). Subjects like geometry, medicine, poetry, and theology each have their proper nature; to force one subject to conform to the nature of another inevitably leads to deformation.

'Let no one say that I have done nothing new,' Pascal writes, 'for the disposition of the materials is new; when one plays tennis it is the same ball that both play with, but one places it better' (65). The disposition, the order of the topics in the *Apology*, must follow its natural course. Some order is introduced by showing the vanity of commonly received values, or the vanity of certain philosophies, such as Pyrrhonism or Stoicism. But no human science can construct an order for the *Apology*. 'Mathematics keeps order, but it is useless in its profundity' (70). Pascal states that he will write his thoughts without order, but not perhaps 'in a confusion without design: it is the true order, and it will always designate my purpose by disorder itself. I would give my subject too much honor if I treated it with order, since I want to show that it is incapable of order'(71).

Anticipating the best-known line from the *Pensées* – 'The heart has its
reasons which reason does not know' (477) – Pascal concerns himself
with the objection that the Holy Scriptures have no order: 'The heart
has its order; intellect has its own order, which is by principle and
demonstration; the heart has another. One does not prove that one
must be loved by setting up an ordered exposition of the causes of
love: that would be ridiculous' (72). Christ and St Paul both had what
Pascal calls 'the order of charity,' not the order of intellect. Their aim
was to stir the soul, not to instruct the intellect. Pascal implies that
many philosophies, such as St Augustine's, are elaborate invitations
and exhortations to look at some broad realm of experience in an
entirely new way, drawing on both the order of the intellect and the
order of the heart. The *Apology* will follow the same spirit. 'This
order consists principally in digression on each point that has a
rapport with the end, in order always to show it' (72). Pascal states
the plan of the work with elegant simplicity:

> *First part*: Misery of man without God. *Second part*: Felicity of man
> with God. Or: *First part*: That nature is corrupted. By nature itself.
> *Second part*: That there is a restorer. According to Scriptures. There is
> nothing on earth which does not show either the misery of man or the
> mercy of God, or the powerlessness of man without God or the power
> of man with God. The knowledge of God without that of man's misery
> leads to pride. Knowledge of his misery without knowledge of God
> leads to despair. Knowledge of Jesus Christ forms the middle ground,
> because there we find both God and our misery. (73–5)

Clearly such an enterprise is foreign to the geometric mind as such
because there are no first principles or definitions to which one can
appeal. The apology rests its ultimate case upon what it construes as
empirical facts: the misery and grandeur of man, and the historical
life of Christ. The *Apology* must follow the '*esprit de finesse*,' which
can also be translated as the 'discriminating mind.' The geometrical
mind studies the finite, the expressible, and proceeds discursively;
the 'discriminating mind' attempts to throw some light on the
infinite, the inexpressible, and proceeds intuitively.

Even though Pascal begins his work with criticisms of Montaigne
and the Pyrrhonists, he retains their suspicion of 'first principles'
because he does not believe that they exist. Even the 'first principles'
of geometry must remain indefinable, undemonstrated, and in a way

arbitrary. Nor can one appeal to nature for 'first principles,' because any such principles, even if they date from one's childhood, might be traced to false impressions or to faulty education. Descartes had attempted to distinguish nature from custom by his method of radical doubt. But Pascal asks: 'What are our natural principles but principles based upon custom? . . . A different custom would result in different principles. Custom is a second nature that destroys the first. But what is nature? Why is custom not natural? I greatly fear that this nature is itself a first custom' (119). Descartes sought certainty in his '*Je pense, donc je suis.*' Pascal replies that this motto, this slogan, is no more certain than any other exclamation, for the two key notions – 'thinking' and 'being' – are amorphous and indefinable. Descartes's inference that he is essentially a simple thinking entity is equally sophistical and illusory. It is true that man seeks certainty; it is equally true that man will deceive himself into believing that he has certainty – 'I think, therefore I am' – when he does not possess it. It is fair to conclude that Pascal was highly suspicious of philosophy as such, and of philosophies in particular, for all begin with illusory certainties. Even the skeptics begin with what they claim as a certainty – that there can be no certainties.

Pascal avoids succumbing to skepticism, and to any form of rationalist philosophy, by his belief in what he calls 'the heart,' or, occasionally, 'intelligence.' The heart provides acquaintance rather than knowledge of the realm of principles; it senses intelligently, rather than knows in a demonstrable or geometrical way. That man is not endowed with a pure and unfailing natural light, an immediate angelic intelligence, is just one of the many signs of his fallen or incomplete nature, of the 'misery of man.'

16
MAN WITHOUT GOD

The dialectic of the *Apology* begins with rejection – rejection of a philosophy that epitomizes everything opposed to the entire project of the *Apology* itself: the philosophy of Montaigne. It is a form of extreme skepticism – Pyrrhonism – secular, impressionistic, anti-theological, basically pagan, hedonistic, self-satisfied, and smug. Pascal first chides Montaigne for following no method, and for 'jumping from subject to subject . . . The stupid project that he had of painting himself!' (76). Pascal does not condemn the attempt to know oneself; on the contrary, self-knowledge is the starting point of 'Man without God.' It is Montaigne's self-satisfied silliness, his pretentious foppery, that Pascal cannot countenance. 'For to say silly things by chance or by weakness is an ordinary evil; but to say them by design is intolerable' (76). 'The defects of Montaigne are great. Lascivious words . . . gullible . . . ignorant . . . his feelings about voluntary homicide, about death. He inspires a nonchalance about salvation . . . ' (77). Montaigne's softness, his relativism, his godlessness repel Pascal. 'It is not in Montaigne, but in myself, that I find all that I see there' (79).

Pascal states that his study of the abstract sciences revealed almost nothing to him about the nature of man. When he turned to the human sciences, he found little to enlighten him. 'It is necessary to know oneself: when that does not enable one to find the truth, it at least enables one to regulate one's life, and there is nothing more appropriate' (81). For Pascal ethics and theology must be rooted in the facts of human nature; it is impossible to deduce such sciences from the mathematical or physical sciences, or from abstract reasoning. The first chapter of the *Apology* – 'The Place of Man in Nature:

the Two Infinities' – is an attempt to situate man in the infinite vastness of the cosmos. The most striking characteristic of man is his disproportion with the universe – specks on a small planet, illuminated by a relatively small sun, orbiting in and through incomprehensible vastness. 'It is an infinite sphere whose centre is everywhere, the circumference nowhere. Finally, it is the greatest perceptible characteristic of the omnipotence of God: our imagination loses itself in the thought of it' (84). 'What is man in infinity?' (84). 'But to present to him another prodigy equally astonishing, let him do research on what he knows of the most delicate things . . . let him lose himself in these marvels as astonishing in their smallness as the others are in their extent.' Realizing that one is 'between these two abysses of the infinite and nothingness' one is terrified of oneself and 'will tremble at the spectacle of these marvels' (84).

'After all, what is man in nature? A nothingness in regard to the infinite, everything in regard to nothingness, a mean between nothing and all. Infinitely distanced from knowing the extremes, the purpose and principle of things are invincibly hidden from him in an impenetrable secret, he is equally incapable of seeing the nothingness from which he is drawn and the infinity in which he is swallowed up' (84). Those who have failed to contemplate the two infinities – endless extent and endless division – readily adopt the presumption that man is the measure of all things, and that human science can explain everything. As a man of science Pascal is never anti-scientific; yet he is opposed to the attitude that can be expressed as 'Whatever is, is that science says.' Moreover, because everything in nature bears both its own nature and the image of its author, almost all things have a 'double infinity.' 'Thus we see the infinity of the sciences and the extent of their research: for who doubts whether geometry, for example, has an infinity of propositions to expose?' (84).

Part of Pascal's conception of God is that He is that which reunites the extremities of the 'two infinities.' 'These extremities touch and reunite with each other by dint of being separated, and find themselves in God, and only in God.' The practical corollary of the 'two infinities' is that man ought to know his place: 'We are something, but we are not all; what we have of being steals from us the knowledge of first principles, which are born from nothingness; and the little that we have of being hides from us the view of infinity.' In effect man's intelligence is as limited in the intelligible world as his body is limited in the physical world. 'Our senses perceive nothing extreme: too much noise deafens us, too much light blinds us, being too far or too close hinders vision, a discourse's being too long or too brief makes it obscure, too much truth astonishes us . . . ' Pascal continues with excess of harmony in music, extremes of cold or heat. 'Such is our true state, which makes us incapable of knowing with certainty and of being absolutely ignorant. We sail along on a vast mean, always uncertain and floating, pushed from one to the other . . . Nothing stops for us. This is the state that is natural to us, yet the most contrary to our inclination; we burn with desire to find a firm bearing, and a constant and final base upon which to build a tower that will rise to infinity; but our foundation cracks, and the earth opens up in chasms' (84).

Pascal realizes that it is impossible to know parts of a system without knowing the entire system, and *vice versa*. Yet man's knowledge is made up of bits and pieces, some bits certain – as in geometry and parts of physics – but many pieces simply conjectural – as in medicine. It is not that nature is chaotic; on the contrary, it proceeds according to a vast procession of mediate and immediate causes. It is rather our 'brief duration' on a little planet, our constant change in face of what Pascal takes for granted – 'the fixed and constant immobility of nature' (84) – that prevents us from gaining a stronger foothold ('*assiette*') on nature. What makes our grasp of the universe all the more tentative is our double nature: 'And what caps our weakness for knowing things is that they are simple and that we are composed of two natures, quite opposed and of different kinds: body and soul. For it is impossible that the part of us that reasons should be other than spiritual; and when they maintain that we are only corporeal, that would preclude us from having knowledge of things. Nothing is more inconceivable than to say that matter is aware of itself . . . ' (84). Pascal scrupulously avoids giving any explanation of how the mind and body interact, thereby avoiding the controversies of his day – from Descartes's dualism to Malebranche's occasionalism. It is unlikely that Pascal was acquainted with the views of Leibniz and Spinoza on the relationship between the mind and the body. His self-consciousness is linked with consciousness of the other; the physical remains 'the thing we understand least. Man is to himself the most prodigious object of nature, for he cannot conceive what is body, still less what is mind, and less than anything how a body can be united with a spirit' (84).

To conclude the proof of the weakness of man – as if further proof were needed – Pascal points to the relativity of judgment (85). 'Too young, too old, and one judges badly, just as if one is too far from or too close to a painting. The same with motion: a background is needed to judge. But the same is true of language, which is constantly changing. But where do we find a port of call in morality?' (87). Pascal concludes the first chapter in a tone of controlled hysteria: Why is his life so limited in time? Why was he born at one point in time rather than another? Why is his knowledge so limited? Something arbitrary, unfathomable, seems to intervene. And finally: 'How many kingdoms of which we are ignorant!' (90). 'The eternal silence of these infinite spaces terrifies me' (91).

Editors have arranged the various fragments that comprise chapter 2, the 'Misère de l'homme,' under the chief sources of man's 'delusive powers.' On Pascal's reading of human nature, man's misery can be attributed to nine chief factors: (1) sense and the memory, (2) imagination, (3) custom, (4) self-love, (5) pride and the spirit of vanity, (6) contrariety, (7) the folly of human science and philosophy, (8) diversions or entertainments, and (9) man in society: the injustice of human justice. Just as Descartes had tried to reach certainty by his method of histrionic doubt, so Pascal sought to strip off the comforting layers of artifice and show man totally naked. Descartes's rationalistic method was essentially autobiographical and dangerously solipsistic; oddly, Descartes thought that he had to prove even the existence of 'other minds.' Pascal's method is empirical; and unless one is mad, the heart senses – knows – that there are other 'minds.' Moreover, unless one is totally devoured by vanity or narcissism, one knows that humanity, and its miseries, are of a piece. Man cannot know anything with absolute certainty, either by his senses or by his reason, of the infinite world surrounding him. Even man's self-love is based upon a radical misunderstanding.

(1) *'Les sens et la mémoire.'* 'Man is so happily fabricated that he has no exact principle for the true and several excellent principles for the false. Let us see how many. But the strongest cause of his errors is the war between the senses and reason' (92). Both sense and reason are highly fallible and gullible in themselves, and both powers try to deceive the others. Emotions, or the *'passions de l'âme,'* interfere

with both. 'The mind of this sovereign judge of the world is not so independent that it is free from being troubled by the first hubbub that occurs around it. You do not need the sound of a cannon to hinder its thoughts: the sound of a weathervane or a pulley will do. Do not be surprised that he is not thinking well at the moment: a fly is buzzing in his ear. It is enough to make him incapable of good advice. If you want him to find the truth, chase off this insect that is holding his reason in check and is troubling this mighty intelligence that governs cities and kingdoms. What a marvellous god is man! O most ridiculous hero! (*O ridicolosissimo eroe!*)' (95).

Perhaps recalling St Augustine's comparison of God the Father to the memory, the ultimate sustainer, Pascal points out that memory is fundamental to all the operations of reason, and then, in an ironical afterthought, he writes: 'A thought escaped me, I wanted to jot it down; I write, instead, that it has escaped me' (97). 'Why is it that a lame man does not irritate us, but a lame brain does? Because the lame man recognizes that we walk straight, whereas a lame-brain thinks that we are the limping ones . . . ' (101). Memory is notoriously given to distorting, falsifying, embellishing, and of course failing.

(2) '*L'Imagination.*' The imagination is the dominant part of man, 'mistress of error and falsity' (104). 'Reason cries out in vain, but cannot give the true estimate of things' (104). 'Imagination,' in both French and English usage of the seventeenth century, was almost always pejorative in connotation, ringing of 'fabrication' or 'falsification.' Conforming to this usage, Pascal denigrates 'imagination' as a source of fantasy, conceit, and lack of proportion. When he lashes out at 'imagination,' it is not that he means to befriend dullness or blandness: his own style is so articulated and muscular that it has few peers. What he laments about 'imagination' is the substitution of display and panoply, in religion, law, or art, for purity of line. But imagination is also the subtle cohesive that makes events seem more important than they are, or diminishes things worthy of note. 'Imagination' is used by Pascal to include prejudices of any sort, terrible recollections from childhood, and even the images one inevitably constructs of someone else in society.

In a few phrases Pascal sketches in the lines of love in all its vicissitudes, and all its literary genres. Although he does not apply one of his favorite geometrical metaphors to illustrate the folly of trusting solely in the love of another human being, the implication is clear that no man, or woman, can complete the circle of one's existence. No human link will bring one's being into harmony with itself. 'Two similar faces, neither of which is amusing by itself, together by their resemblances make people laugh' (115). Again, Pascal juxtaposes the extremes, dull in themselves, and equally incomprehensible, to produce laughter – '*font rire ensemble par leur ressemblance.*'

Tertullian had often written of the 'folly of the Cross.' As the last entry under the Circe-like effect of the imagination, Pascal naturally makes an observation concerning the art of painting, which was the best 'showing' that imagination had to offer in the seventeenth century: 'What a vanity it is when painting attracts admiration by its resemblance to things for which one has no great admiration for the originals!' (116). Pascal refused to have his portrait painted – a practice as prevalent in his social class as having one's photograph taken for some event or another in our own time – because he deemed it a mark of pride or vanity.

(3) '*La Coutume.*' 'The most important thing in life is the choice of one's vocation, trade or job; nonetheless, chance takes care of it. Custom makes masons, soldiers, roofers. "He's an excellent roofer," someone says. And, speaking of soldiers: "They're crazy," someone else says. Others say on the contrary: "There's nothing greater than war; all other men are fools." By virtue of hearing these trades praised in childhood, and all the others despised, one chooses. For one naturally loves virtue, and naturally hates folly; the words themselves will decide: one errs only in the application of them. So great is the force of custom that, of those whom nature has only made men, one makes all the conditions of man. For some countries are all masons, others soldiers, etc. It is beyond doubt that nature is not so uniform. Custom has affected all that, for custom constrains nature. Sometimes nature surmounts custom and restrains man in his in-stincts, in spite of all custom, good or bad' (127).

(4) '*L'amour-propre.*' Self-love or self-conceit is for Pascal the most dangerous of man's enemies. He had charted its progress and inroads in himself, in his mathematical and scientific work, and in the way he had vaunted his accomplishments and taken pride in refuting other thinkers. 'The nature of "*amour-propre*" and of this human "me" is to love and consider only oneself. But what will it do? It will not know how to keep this object that it loves from being full of

defects and miseries: it wants to be great, and sees that it is small; it wants to be happy, and sees that it is miserable; it wants to be perfect, and sees itself full of imperfections; it wants to be the object of love and the esteem of men, and sees that its defects only merit their aversion and contempt. This embarrassment in which the self finds itself produces within it the most unjust and criminal passion possible to imagine; for it conceives a mortal hatred against this truth that reproves it and convinces it of its defects. It would like to annihilate it, and, not being able to destroy the truth in itself, the self destroys it as much as it can in its own awareness and in the awareness of others; that is to say, the self takes great care to hide its defects both to itself and to others, and cannot bear to have someone show them to itself or that they be seen' (130).

The picture that Pascal proceeds to paint of the selfishness, the duplicity, the cruelty, and the depravity of the human self is as somber as anything to be found in the *Maximes* of the duc de La Rochefoucauld or the *Leviathan* of Thomas Hobbes. Artifice and dissimulation are the fabric of the self. 'Here is a proof of it that horrifies me. The Catholic religion does not oblige one to reveal one's sins indiscriminately to everyone: it allows one to remain hidden from all other persons; but Catholicism makes one exception – the one to whom one is commanded to reveal the bottom of one's heart and to show oneself as one is. There is only this one man in all the world that the Catholic religion orders us to confess, and it commits him to an inviolable secret, so that it is as if this knowledge in him were not really there. Could one imagine anything more charitable or kindly? Nevertheless the corruption of man is such that he still finds even this law too hard; and it is one of the chief reasons that has made a large part of Europe revolt against the Church' (130).

'Thus human life is only a perpetual illusion; people simply deceive and flatter each other. No one speaks of us in our presence as they speak of us in our absence. Relationships between persons are founded only on mutual deception; and few friendships would endure if each knew what his friend said of him when he was not there, though he might be speaking sincerely and without passion' (130). Where Pascal differs from other moralists who had given a similarly dark rendering of the self is that he unequivocally condemns the self: there is no subtle self-congratulation on being so ingeniously self-centered such as one finds in La Rochefoucauld, who could state quite casually that even a serious misfortune to our best friend gives us a secret pleasure. Pascal finally explodes: 'The "me" is odious' – '*Le "moi" est haïssable*' (136). Even if the Machiavellians and the disciples of Montaigne had pretended to found all sorts of rules of polity and justice on the concupiscence of man, the villainy of the self remains: it is not changed. To change the self, to convert the 'me' to the love of God, is the ultimate objective of Pascal's *Apology*. 'In a word the self ['*le "moi"*'] has two qualities: it is unjust in itself, in that it makes itself the center of everything; and it is troublesome with others in that it wants to subdue them: for each "me" is the enemy and wants to be the tyrant over all the others' (136). As Pascal concludes his description of the self, it begins to sound like an astronomical 'black hole': 'Each is all to himself, for, when dead, all is dead for the self. And from that comes the notion that each believes himself to be everything for everybody. One must not judge nature according to ourselves, but according to nature' (139).

(5) '*L'Orgeuil et l'esprit de vanité.*' 'We do not content ourselves with our own life and being, but want to live in the ideas of other persons an imaginary life, for which we force ourselves to *appear*. We work ceaselessly to embellish and preserve our fictive being, and neglect the true one. And if we have some tranquillity, generosity, or fidelity, we make haste to make it known so that those high traits are attached to our very being . . . ' (145). Pascal begins listing vanities – games, visits, comedies, false genealogies – vanities from cooks to philosophers – and settles on a contradiction in the nature of man: 'Contempt for our being, dying for nothing, hatred of our being' (156).

(6) '*Contrariétés.*' 'Man is naturally credulous, incredulous, timid, foolhardy' (159). 'Description of man: dependence, desire to be independent, need' (160). Man is a victim of the vicissitudes of time, and thereby loses himself in the multiplicity of personages, and his heart is inconstant. People always speak about the weather, as if it had some parallel with their emotional states: 'Weather and my humor have little in common; I have my fogs and my good weather within myself . . . ' (163). Man never lives for the moment that he occupies, but obsessively mulls over the past, or longs delusively for the future. 'Thus we never live, but always hope to live; and making do without being happy it is inevitable that we shall never be so' (168). 'Solomon and Job knew and wrote best about the mystery of man: the one was

the happiest of men, and the other the unhappiest; Solomon knew the vanity of pleasures by experience, and Job the reality of evil' (169). Pascal is fascinated by the absurdity of existence, from the man whose wife and only son have died and who now concentrates his life on playing tennis, to the length of Cleopatra's nose. The judgment of Christ by his own people presents a similar absurdity, though leading to the completion of the 'mystery of Jesus' (181). 'Discourses on humility are good for pride among the vainglorious, and for humility among the humble . . . few speak humbly about humility, or chastely about chastity, or about skepticism with any doubt. We are nothing but lies, duplicity, and contrariousness, hiding and disguising ourselves from ourselves' (187).

(7) *'Folie de la Science Humaine et de la Philosophie.'* Quickly reviewing the history of philosophy from its ancient origins to his own day, Pascal shows that there is no proposition so outlandish that some philosopher has not championed it. He particularly chides Descartes, who 'would have preferred to do without God in his philosophy' (194). 'Descartes is useless and uncertain' (195). 'The science of external things will never console me in my ignorance of morality in times of affliction; but the science of customs will always console me for the ignorance of physical sciences' (196).

(8) *'Les Divertissements.'* 'Our nature is in movement; utter repose is death' (198). 'Man's condition: inconstancy, boredom, anxiety' (199). As for boredom or *ennui*, nothing is more unbearable than being 'in absolute repose, without passions, without a task or diversion or something to occupy the mind. Then man feels his nothingness, his abandonment, his insufficiency, his dependence, his powerlessness, his emptiness. Immediately from the bottom of his soul will rise *ennui*, baseness, sadness, grief, spite, despair' (201). Man prefers the chase to the catch, disputes to truth, the struggle to the conquest. 'We never search for things, but for the quest for things' (203).

The bulk of man's trouble derives from the fact that he is unable 'to keep still in a room' (205). One remembers T.S. Eliot's line 'Teach us to sit still,' from his 1930 poem 'Ash Wednesday.' 'But when I thought about it more closely, and after having found the cause of all our woes, I wanted to discover the reasons, and I found one which is quite effective: it consists in the natural affliction of our weak and mortal state, which is so miserable that nothing can console us when we think about it closely . . . ' (205). Just as the king had a troop of persons round him to keep him entertained, so the ordinary man surrounds himself with intrigues, games, and follies so as not to think about himself. 'The only thing that consoles us in our miseries is diversion, which is, however, the greatest of our miseries. For it is entertainment that chiefly keeps us from meditating on ourselves, and which insensibly makes us get lost. But without it, we would be in *ennui*, and this *ennui* would make us search for a more solid way of escaping from it. But diversion amuses us, and makes us insensibly arrive at death' (217).

The splendid thing about being entertained is that one need not think about one's finiteness, brevity, and transience in the vastness of things: that is worth paying for, fighting for. But even 'serious' things are forms of diversion: 'From infancy men are charged with concern for their honor, their well-being, their friends, and also for the well-being and honor of their friends. Men have to be concerned about business affairs, learn languages, . . . what a strange way to make them happy!' (206). But without all these distractions, diversions, man is thrown back upon himself, and then must wonder – as the painter Gauguin did – 'What are they, where do they come from, where are they going . . . ' (217).

Wedding the 'two infinities' with practical interests – his new idea of public transport for Paris – Pascal emerges with a startling image: 'The grand people and the common people have the same accidents and annoyances, and the same passions; but the great are high on the wheel, whilst the others are near the hub, and thus less agitated by the same movements' (223). The following fragment reinforces the notion of who is at the center and who is at the circumference: 'Whoever had the friendship of the king of England, the king of Poland and the queen of Sweden, would have believed it possible to need a place of retreat or exile anywhere in the world?' The image of Queen Christina of Sweden leaving her native land – familiar from Greta Garbo's film – is not to be compared with the nocturnal vanishment of some distant aunt. But the plight of both is equally absurd, equally part of the continuously revolving wheel of the drama: 'The last act is bloody, however beautiful the comedy might be in all the rest of it: finally they throw some earth on the head, and there it is forever' (227).

(9) '*L'homme en société*.' Pascal apparently had plans to conclude

his analysis of the pitfalls and shortcomings of humanity by examining what humanity calls justice. Never succumbing to the myth of
man 'before society' – unlike Hobbes – Pascal wrote of man in the
natural way as part of a larger structure, even if that structure were
sinister, catching each individual like a fly in a spider's web. And,
needless to say, Pascal never romanticized man as some good and
wholesome being, corrupted 'by society' – as did so many of his
successors, for example Rousseau or Bernardin de Saint-Pierre.
Wanting to have no pride in the individual, Pascal took pains to show
that the individual had no especial dignity before society nor taint
after being part of society. Nor could man's dignity be derived from
some fiery explosion of individualism, from the myth, developed in
nineteenth-century America, of the 'self-made man.' Yet the attractions of what A.O. Lovejoy referred to as 'primitivism,' encourage
the tendency to believe that each member of society can come to
terms with himself without comprehending, or at least envisaging, a
vaster context.

Everything being a mixture of truth and falsity, justice and injustice, law attempts to set limits and constraints, but does so only
arbitrarily. If one adopts a positivist notion of law – 'that each should
follow the customs of his own country' (230) – then the just and
unjust would be determined geographically. 'Truth on this side of the
Pyrenees, error beyond' (230). From incest to the exposure of
unwanted children – every kind of human behavior has found its
sanctions at one time or place or another. 'Doubtless there are natural
laws, but this splendid corrupted reason has corrupted everything'
(230). 'From this confusion it arises that some hold the essence of
justice to be the authority of the legislator, and others the conveni-
ence of the sovereign, and still others the current custom: but what is
most sure is that nothing, based solely on reason, is just in itself;
everything gives way with time. Custom alone makes equity, for the
simple reason that it is received; such is the mystical foundation of its
authority (230). The origins of what is called 'justice' are quite
infantile: '*Mine, thine* – This dog is mine, say these poor children;
there is *my* place in the sun. – Such is the beginning and the image of
the usurpation of all earth' (231).

Pascal's view of human justice is emphatically nominalistic: 'justice' is parallel to 'those in power,' just as 'correct usage' is parallel to
'those who write well.' But Pascal's oxymoronic turn of mind

prohibits him from postulating only human justice, which is based on the customary and the vain; the other, the antithetical justice, is based on God's justice.

If justice were a rational system, then the dictum that one should follow the customs of one's own time and country would be ideal, like saying when in Babylon do geometry the way the Babylonians do. Yet the dictum is widely taken as the foundation of ethics; Descartes made it one of the few maxims in his provisional morality in the *Discours*. 'Empire founded on opinion and the imagination holds sway for a while, and this empire is pleasant and voluntary; the empire of force holds sway always. Thus opinion is like the queen of the world, but force is its tyrant' (243). Pascal doubts whether justice is based on reason or 'first principles.' What passes for justice is generally received custom enforced by authority, surrounded with various sanctions. True justice, however, is what is revealed to the heart by way of the Gospels (246, 252). Once again, in examining man's nature, Pascal believes that he finds indubitable evidence that man is not alone in the vastness of the universe.

After completing his *exposé* of human misery, Pascal begins the first part of chapter III with the title 'Marques de la grandeur de l'homme' – 'Signs of Man's Grandeur.' This grandeur is a natural consequence of man's misery, of his instinct for truth and goodness even in his wanderings. 'The grandeur of man consists in knowing his misery' (255). 'Thought makes the grandeur of man' (257). Turning to his own invention, the '*machine d'arithmétique*,' Pascal writes that the calculator has operations that resemble human thinking more closely than anything to be found among the other animals, but has nothing comparable to will or desire, which are to be found among animals. 'All the dignity of man consists in his thought. But what is this thinking? How stupid it is! Thinking is thus an admirable and comparable thing by its nature. It would have to possess strange faults to be contemptible; but thinking has such faults that nothing is more ridiculous. How great it is in its nature, how low in its defects!' (263).

Given that man's dignity rests solely on his ability to think, Pascal concludes that the guiding principle of morality must be the striving to think well. All the miseries outlined in the preceding chapter are so many proofs of man's grandeur. 'They are miseries of a great lord, miseries of a deposed king' (269). Man's natural struggle to prove things shows that he is not a slave to dogmatism; his instinctual idea of truth makes him immune to radical skepticism. 'Man does not know at what rank to place himself. He is visibly lost, fallen from his true place without being able to refind it. He looks everywhere with anxiety and in impenetrable shadows without success' (275). Even man's overweening desire for 'glory' – *gloire* – his desire to be admired and esteemed, is proof of his grandeur. 'We have such a high idea of man's soul that we cannot bear being despised by it . . . all of man's felicity consists in this esteem' (278).

The varieties of evil, like mistaken solutions to a problem, are virtually infinite, while the good is unique. Most of what goes under the rubric of evil is actually the result of carelessness, insouciance, or banality. But Pascal points out that 'a certain kind of evil is as difficult to find as what one calls good . . . An extraordinary grandeur of soul is required to obtain it, as well as for the good' (279). Thus, even heroic and muscular evil, as typified by Iago or Milton's Satan, affords proof of man's grandeur.

As the next step in his dialectic, Pascal argues that a radical reversal of 'for' and 'against' is required to show the grandeur of man. Man's grandeur does not reside in the acquisition of goods, glory, or 'certitudes' of reason, but in his weakness and his awareness of it. The true grandeur of man lies between the two abysses, the 'two infinities,' in the middle point which is a battleground between passion and reason. 'This doubleness of man is so visible that some persons have thought that man has two souls. A single subject seemed to them incapable of such abrupt changes, from a limitless presumption to a horrible dejection of the heart' (315). It would be so much simpler to exist as a being with pure reason and no passions, or as a being with passions, or feelings, without reason. But man finds himself in an 'interior war of reason against passion' (317). 'Man is neither angel nor beast, and the misfortune is that he who would act the angel acts the beast' (329). 'If he brags about himself, I shall belittle him; and if he belittles himself, I shall vaunt him; and I shall keep contradicting him until he understands that he is an incomprehensible monster' (330). Pascal now believes that he has man poised at the precise point at which he should be able to get his bearings. 'Let man now estimate his worth. Let him love himself, for there is within him a nature capable of good; but let him not *live* himself because of the baseness which is there. Let him despise himself, because this capacity is empty; but let him not despise because of that this natural capacity. Let him hate himself, let him love himself: he has within himself a capacity to know the truth and to be happy; but he emphatically does not have truth, either constant or satisfying' (331). Pascal pits himself against both the optimists and the pessimists of human nature, both the cynics and the Panglosses – to jump a century to Voltaire. 'I can only approve of those who seek moaning' – *'en gémissant'* (333). Perhaps Pascal had in mind the line from the *Salve Regina*: *'gementes et flentes in hac lacrimarum valle'* – 'moaning and weeping in this vale of tears.'

Suddenly Pascal the apologist reappears, hoping now to advance his plan for searching for God. 'Before entering into the proofs for the Christian religion, I find it necessary to show the injustice of those who live in indifference about looking for the truth of something so close to and important for them . . . ' (334). Pascal argues that the immortality or the mortality of the soul is a question of capital importance, the position one takes being a hallmark of one's life. One cannot remain in apathy: 'The immortality of the soul is something that touches us so strongly and profoundly, that you would have to lose all sense to be indifferent . . . ' (335). Pascal gives no arguments for the immortality of the soul, for any such position would be based on 'first principles' – and there are none. 'It is nonetheless an indispensable duty to search, when one is in this doubt . . . I do not know who has put me in the world, nor what the world is, nor what I am; I am in a terrible ignorance of everything; I do not know what my body is, or my senses, or my soul and that part of myself that thinks, that reflects on everything and on itself, and knows itself no more than the rest. I see the frightening spaces of the universe that hold me . . . ' (335)

'As I do not know where I am coming from, so I do not know where I am going. I know only that in leaving this world I shall fall forever either into nothingness or into the hands of a God full of ire, without knowing into which of these conditions I shall be eternally ranged. That is my state, full of weakness and uncertainty' (335). Pascal compares man's state to that of a man in a dungeon awaiting his sentence: how shall he spend his final hour? ' . . . it is against nature that he should not use his last hour to find out whether sentence has been passed, but plays cards. Thus, it is supernatural that man, etc. It is a heaviness from the hand of God' (342). This last *pensée* in the Conclusion of Part 1 uses the figure of asyndeton – the rhetorical device of grammatical disjointedness: '*Dungeon*. I find it good that one should not make Copernicus's opinion more profound: but this . . .! It matters to all life to know whether the soul is mortal or immortal' (346). Pascal thinks that simply the zeal of those who search for God proves His existence, just as the fact that some philosophers have conquered their passions shows that the soul must be immaterial. 'What feels pleasure in us? The hand? The arm? The flesh? The blood? One will see that it must be something immaterial.' Pascal simply assumes that immateriality proves immortality; the obvious reply is that though thinking might be called 'immaterial' in that it is non-spatial, nonetheless it is a mortal function of an elaborate system, just like the 'thinking' of a computer. And Pascal himself implies that the intellect should be conceived of as an automaton – a much more sophisticated version of the '*machine d'arithmétique.*' But Pascal never attempts to set up arguments, simply because he does not employ deductive argument as such. Consistent with the spirit of the 'discriminating mind,' he prefers to suggest, shed light, make people reflect on their state and what *may* be their destiny.

Turning to the atheists, Pascal asks: 'What reason do they have for saying that one cannot be resurrected? Which is more difficult, to be born or to be resurrected; that he who never was, should be, or that he who is, should still be? Is it more difficult to come into being than to come back into being? Habit or custom makes the one easy to us, lack of custom makes the other impossible: a popular way of judging!' (357). Pascal concludes Part 1 with the observation that there are three sorts of persons: 'those who serve God, having found Him; those who endeavor to search for God, not having found Him; and the others who live without looking for Him and have not found Him. The first are reasonable and happy; the last are unhappy and mad; those in the middle are unhappy and reasonable' (364).

17
MAN WITH GOD

The second part of the *Apology*, entitled 'L'Homme avec Dieu,' is much briefer and more fragmentary than the first, being a compilation of notes to himself and allusions often difficult to interpret. Pascal believes that he has now convinced his opponent that God is the sole true object of man's needs, and that man's existence will have meaning and purpose only in the search for God. Having shown the impossibility of certainties in mathematics, science, and particularly in philosophy or theology, Pascal does not intend to give his opponent new certitudes, still less the promise of a mystical vision of God, for God is a 'hidden God' – *'un Dieu caché.'* Indeed, Pascal believes that he has convinced his interlocutor – atheist, skeptic, or 'free-thinker' – to such an extent that he should no longer be called an 'opponent' but a 'fellow searcher.' Pascal believes that one must refind God through the marks and signs that He cared to give of His existence, but not through some facile and sweeping argument based on the 'marvels of nature.' One could readily marvel at the subtlety of nature, as Lucretius does in *De Rerum Natura*, and be a materialist or a decorous polytheist. The reason why apologists for Christianity have failed in the past is that they have presupposed faith instead of bringing it into birth.

'I admire the boldness with which these persons undertake to talk about God. While addressing their discourses to the irreligious, they set up their first chapter to prove the Divinity by the works of nature. I would not be astonished by their enterprise if they were addressing their discourses to believers, for it is certain that those who have a living faith within their hearts immediately see that everything that exists is none other than the work of the God whom they adore. But for those for whom this light is extinguished, and in whom one has the plan of making it come back to life, these persons destitute of faith and grace, and who, searching with all their light everything they see in nature which might lead them to this understanding – *they* find only obscurity and shadows: to say to them that they have only to see the least things that surround them and that they will find God disclosed, and to give them, as the only proof of such a great and important subject, the course of the moon and the planets, and to pretend to have finished one's proof with such a discourse, is to give them cause for believing that the proofs of our religion are quite feeble. And I see by reason and by experience that nothing is more calculated to make them conceive a hearty disdain for it' (566). God is not to be found in nature; and because of the corruption of human nature He cannot be 'read off' as if He were an 'innate idea': such was the faulty route of St Anselm, Descartes, and later the Cambridge Platonists.

Pascal argues that one must depart from absolute doubt, from Pyrrhonism, which paradoxically will end up serving religion. Pyrrhonism helps show that man does not know what he is all about, whether he is of importance or nugatory. It is thus antithetical to the pretensions of dogmatic philosophy and the concentrated self-esteem of Stoicism. Returning to his favorite rhetorical structure, the oxymoron, Pascal writes that 'the Stoics say: "Enter within yourselves; it is there that you will find rest." And that is not true. The others write: "Go outside: search for happines in diverting yourself." And that is not true. Sicknesses come. Happiness is neither outside us nor within us; it is in God, both outside and within us' (465). Philosophies have given moral prescriptions for both extremes, but only the *Apology* will bring about the synthesis. Now that Pascal believes that he has shown the necessity for God, it is imperative to show what He is and that He is the God of the Christian Church. Pascal embarks on one of the first attempts at comparative religion.

'In seeing the blindness and misery of man, in looking at the mute universe and man without light, abandoned to himself as if lost in this corner of the universe, without knowing who put him there, what he has come to do, what he will become by dying, incapable of all knowledge, I become terrified, like a man asleep who has been carried to a deserted and frightening island, and who wakes up without knowing where he is and without any way of leaving. And because of that I admire how one does not fall into despair over such a miserable state' (393). Pascal writes that he looks round and sees many miserable people, and many rival religions, each proclaiming itself to be the true one and denigrating the others. The skeptic or relativist would let the matter go at that: religions are all equally true and equally false simply because 'truth' and 'falsity' cannot be applied to religion. This is of course not Pascal's position; nor does he adopt the posture of the comfortable dogmatist. Rather, he asks whether there are any signs of a true religion, and postulates sincerity, miracles, and prophecies. Before turning to the religion of Israel, Pascal gives short shrift to the pagans, the Muhammadans, and what he vaguely refers to as 'the history of China' (397, 398). Doubtless there are or were sincere pagans, but paganism has no authority and no prophets. All religions contain obscurities, but should not be faulted for that; it is rather on the clear points that they should be compared and judged. The religion of China, as Pascal understood it, contained clear but manifestly false propositions, e.g., statements about astronomy. Pascal implies that the teachings of Muhammad are a farrago, especially the description of Paradise. '*Differences between Jesus Christ and Muhammad.* – Muhammad, not foretold; Jesus Christ, foretold. Muhammad, in killing; Jesus Christ, in having himself killed for his own. Muhammad, in forbidding to read; the apostles, in ordering to read' (402). Finally, 'Anybody can do what Muhammad did; for he performed no miracles; he was not foretold. No one can do what Jesus Christ did' (403). These passages (395–404) are among the most fragmented and elliptical of all the '*pensées*'; clearly Pascal would have had to flesh them out to make them understood. His examination of the religion of the Hebrews reveals much closer acquaintance and greater depth.

Pascal first cites the homogeneity of Judaism as a mark of its validity, though incomplete; he also cites its antiquity: 'In effect, all the other sects cease, while this one still endures, and for four thousand years' (406). 'From time immemorial the Jews held that men had fallen from communication with God, but that He had promised to restore them.' Ancient prophets had foretold the coming of the Messiah and 'the time and the manner in which he would come' (406). Subsequently the Jews were dispersed and were 'everywhere cursed' – '*partout en malédiction*' – and nonetheless survived. Pascal does not want to rest his argument on the miracles of Moses or of Christ, 'because they do not immediately seem convincing' (407). 'I see the Christian religion founded on a previous religion . . . ' which is Judaism (407). Pascal cites the singularity and separateness of the Jewish people as an empirical fact that presages Christianity. 'I see makers of religion in several places of the world and in all times, but they do not have a morality that pleases me or proofs that can convince me, and so I would have equally rejected the religion of Muhammed, or of China, or those of the ancient Romans or Egyptians, for the simple reason that one did not have any more signs of truth than the other, and nothing that would necessarily convince me . . . ' (355). But the strict monotheism of the Jews, their adherence to what they believed to be a divine and universal law, and their doctrine of original sin, reveal the religion of the ancient Hebrews to be unique. 'The law by which this people is governed is altogether the most ancient law of the world, the most perfect, and the only one which has always been maintained without interruption in a state' (408). Both Greeks and Romans founded their laws on it (408). As for the Bible, Pascal deems it unique in that it was written by a people witnessing events and recording them as they happened, unlike Homer, who 'made a novel, that he presented as such and was so received' (412). Once again Pascal reveals not only his ignorance of the Homeric tradition and its close links with history but also his cavalier attitude towards biblical scholarship. But the aim of his dialectic is clear: 'Our religion is so divine that another divine religion was the foundation' (413).

Nonetheless, the religion of the Hebrews knew only the misery of fallen man; Christianity reveals the grandeur of man as well. 'If man is not made for God, why is he happy only in God? If man is made for God, why is he so contrary to God?' (415). The question of man is also a question of God, and *vice versa*, for Pascal. In one aphorism he gives his solution to the problem of evil: 'Nature has its perfections, in order to show that it is the image of God; and its faults, to show that it is only His image' (416). Although Pascal does not develop this thesis, he implies that any reasoning based on bad things happening to good persons misses the point. God being a '*Dieu caché*,' there are no grounds for supposing a perfect parallelism between divinity and nature, and it is a sign of bad faith to suppose that there is. The reality of evil – metaphysical, natural, and moral – has always posed the strongest objection to Christian theism, along with the gratuitousness of God's existence for the mathematical and physical sciences. Pascal nowhere diminishes the reality of man's misery, or the imperfections of nature, expressed not only in events untoward to man – earthquakes, tidal waves – but also the sheer redundancy, the superabundance of nature. 'For myself, I readily admit that once the Christian religion discovers this principle, that the nature of man is corrupt and fallen from God, the eyes are opened to see everywhere the character of this truth; for nature is such that it signals everywhere a lost God, and in man and outside of man, a corrupted nature' (441). Pascal invokes the rhetorical myth of man's former innocence to explain that man has strayed from dominating other creatures to enslaving them, from using his reason to following 'extravagant customs' (423). Pascal's chief criterion for what he calls 'the true religion' is that it is firmly founded on man's condition: 'It must know the grandeur and the smallness, and the reason for the one and for the other. What religion has known it better than the Christian one?' (426). Pascal appears to contradict himself when he lays down as a certitude that any religion is false that is not monotheistic and does not teach a theocentric ethics (430), for this sounds like a 'first principle.' Yet in the '*pensées*' (433–7) this principle is based on the hypothetical scenario of God's existence: the principle is certain *if* there is a God. 'All these contrarieties, which seemed to estrange me the most from any religion, are what have led me the fastest to the true one' (437).

When Pascal directs his attention to what he calls the most difficult of all doctrines to understand – original sin, and the relentless transmission of the effects of the first sin from one generation to another – his reply is starkly simple. Given the unassailable fact of man's misery throughout history, the mystery of original sin explains man's condition better than any other hypothesis. To use the voguish jargon of our own day, the doctrine of original sin is 'the best working construct' or 'model' to explain the facts of man's condition 'It is an astonishing thing, however, that the most remote mystery of our understanding – the transmission of sin – is something without which we could not have any understanding of ourselves. For without a doubt there is nothing that shocks our reason more than to say that the sin of the first man has made guilty all those who seem capable of being part of it, given their distance from the source. This emanation not only seems impossible to us, it also seems very unjust;

for what is more contrary to the rules of our miserable justice than to damn eternally an infant incapable of will for a sin in which he appears to have had so little part, that was committed six thousand years before he came into being?' (438). Pascal overstates his case by adopting St Augustine's view that an unbaptized infant will be eternally consigned to Hell; the Church had never really adopted this view, and had long since consigned such infants to Limbo. As for the date of the 'first sin' – some six thousand years before – it is one of the quaint views that can be found in commentaries on Genesis written in Pascal's day, or, for that matter, fundamentalist vagaries of our own day. Nevertheless, Pascal's paradoxical argument in favor of the doctrine of original sin is not shaken by these two objections. 'Certainly nothing more rudely shocks us than this doctrine; and nonetheless, without this mystery, the most incomprehensible of all, we are incomprehensible to ourselves. The hitch of our condition takes its coils and turns in this abyss, so that man is more inconceivable without this mystery than this mystery is inconceivable to man' (438). Pascal concludes that there are two foundations of Christianity, and that they are supported both by experience and by the Scriptures. The first is that man as created or in a state of grace is above nature and enjoys a kinship with God. The second is that tainted man has fallen from the state and has lost that divine kinship. 'For is it not clearer than day that we feel in ourselves ineffaceable signs of excellence? And is it not equally true that we experience every hour the effects of our deplorable condition? What is this chaos and monstrous confusion crying out to us if not the truth of these two states, with a voice so powerful that it is impossible to resist?' (439).

18

THE WAGER

Pascal knew that the art of persuasion requires more than intellectual arguments to arrive at the truth; the heart, or feelings, and the will, must also be swayed. Up to this point Pascal's dialectic has striven to show the agreement between his empirical reading of human nature and the teachings of the Scriptures. As mentioned earlier, Pascal does not prejudge his case by assuming that the Bible is entirely or even in part revealed; he leaves that question open. Since the dogmas extracted from the Scriptures are in accordance with the facts of human nature, the Scriptures are literally true. Divine inspiration would simply be a bonus and a preternatural consolation. Now his dialectic takes on a new strategy in order to lead his interlocutor from the realm of the intellect to an act of submission

Pascal introduces 'the wager' by a section entitled 'Le Noeud' – which can be translated variously as 'the knot,' 'the hitch,' 'the knotty point,' or perhaps best, because of its Shakespearian overtones, 'the rub.' Pascal first sets out 'to get rid of the obstacles.' The first obstacle is naturally the occurrence of miracles. Pascal treats the obstacle more as a formal or definitional question than a material question. ' "A miracle," they say, "would strengthen my credence." They say that when they do not see it. Reasons seen from a distance seem to limit our view, but when one has arrived there, one begins to see still beyond. Nothing stops the volubility of our mind. They say there is no rule without some exception, and no truth so general that it does not fail in some aspect. It is enough that the general truth is not absolutely universal to give us grounds for applying the exception to the case at hand, and to say: "That is not always true; therefore there are cases in which that does not hold" ' (440). Pascal makes another note to himself: 'After the note "that one must search for God" put the note "get rid of the obstacles" which is the discourse on the "machine," to get the machine ready, to search by reason' (441). Pascal's view of the mind as such re-emerges: it is a dispassionate machine or calculator – necessary but not sufficient for getting at the truth.

Pascal quickly states that his own existence is a mere contingent fact, that he is neither eternal nor infinite: facts, indeed, that any sane person must recognize. God's existence is obviously more difficult to grasp: 'Infinite movement, the point that fills all, the moment of rest; infinite without quantity, indivisible and infinite' (445). 'The eternal Being is forever, if it is one time' (446). Suddenly Pascal breaks down into a series of antinomies – equally comprehensible and arguable points of view: 'that God does exist, that He does not exist; that a soul is united with the body, and that there is no soul; that the world was created, that it was not, etc. that there was an original sin that there was not' (447). A sense of hysteria pervades these fragments. Pascal knows that able minds have argued from both sides. He also knows the indifference of many people concerning the truth of either side. He clearly realizes the effects of custom, or what has come to be called in the twentieth century 'conditioning': 'Custom is our nature. He who is accustomed to the faith believes it, and cannot do otherwise than fear damnation, and believe nothing else. He who believes that the king is terrible, etc. . . . ' (449). Arguments based on custom were translated into arguments based on habit in the eighteenth century, and were finally, with much greater sophistication, translated into behaviorism. Pascal foresaw the transformation in his own language, i.e., that man generally speaks in his own image, judges by his size, and ultimately falls into the erroneous belief that it was not God that created man, but man that created God. Anticipating Feuerbach and other nineteenth-century German philosophers, Pascal states simply that 'Men . . . judge God by themselves' (450).

Pascal begins his ultimate argument with his favorite antithesis of the infinite opposed to nothingness. 'Le Pari' – 'the Wager' – is not intended as an argument for God's existence, for no argument by logic or experience, deductive or inductive, is valid or is without objections. In spite of the rather grotesque appearance of the notion of betting or wagering that God exists, Pascal's argument should be construed as transcendental, as leaping beyond the limits of both geometrical and empirical reasoning, in the same way that someone truly in love with another must take to the air, take flight. Abject love fears rejection; self-interested love hopes for reward. Love of God fearing rejection, or hoping for reward, is equally abject. Pascal's argument – a term too formal and abstract, and therefore 'plea' or 'entreaty' is more in order – leads to a conclusion both self-interested and not self-interested, both abject and loving. It is difficult for a commentary on Pascal not to be sometimes as paradoxical as the text itself, and so the crucial text should be quoted in full before further commentary.

Infinity – nothing. Our soul is thrown into the body, where it finds number, time, dimensions. It reasons thereon, and calls that nature necessity, and cannot believe otherwise.

One added to infinity does not augment it in the least, any more than a foot added to an infinite measure. The finite annihilates itself in the presence of the infinite and becomes pure nothingness. Thus our spirit before God; thus our justice before divine justice. There is not such a great disproportion between our justice and that of God as between unity and infinity.

God's justice must be enormous, like His mercy. For justice toward the reprobates is less enormous and should shock less than mercy for the elect.

We know that there is an infinity, but are ignorant of its nature. As we know that it is false that numbers are finite, it is therefore true that there is an infinity of numbers. But we do not know what it is: it is false that it is even, it is false that it is odd, for in adding unity its nature is not changed; however, it is a number, and all numbers are even or odd (it is true that that is understood of all finite numbers). Thus, one can well understand that there is a God without knowing what He is.

Is there not a substantial truth, seeing that there are so many true things which are not truth itself?

We are acquainted with the existence and the nature of the finite because we are finite and extended as it is. We are acquainted with the existence of the infinite and are ignorant of its nature because it has extent like ourselves, but not limits like ourselves. But we are not acquainted with either the existence or the nature of God because He has neither extent nor limits.

But by faith we know His existence; by glory we know His nature. For I have already shown that one can quite well know the existence of a thing without knowing its nature.

Let us now speak according to the light of natural intelligence.

If there is a God, He is infinitely incomprehensible since, having neither parts nor limits, He has no relation with us. We are therefore incapable of knowing what He is or whether He is. That being the case, who will dare to undertake to resolve this question? Not we who have no relation with Him.

Who therefore will blame the Christians for not being able to give a reason for their belief when they profess a religion for which they cannot give a reason? They declare in exposing it to the world that it is a folly, a *stultitiam*; and then you complain that they do not prove it! If they proved it, they would break their word: it is in lacking proof that they do not lack sense.

In a passage of dialogue Pascal seizes his interlocutor for a final time, for now the interlocutor must decide, must choose, and must take the leap:

'Yes, that excuses those who offer their religion as such and removes the blame for presenting it without a reason, but that does not excuse those who accept it.

'Let us examine this point and say: "God is or He is not." But toward which side shall we lean? Reason cannot decide anything: there is an infinite chaos that separates us. It is a gamble at the extremity of this infinite distance where it will be heads or tails. What will you bet? By reason you cannot make one or the other; by reason you cannot defend either of the two. Do not blame those who have made a choice for being false, for you know nothing about it.'

'No, but I will blame them for having done it, not for this choice, but for any choice; for both the one who plays at heads and the one who plays at tails commit the same fault. The right thing is not to wager at all.'

'Yes, but you must wager. It is not voluntary, you are embarked. Which then will you take? Let us see. Since one must choose, let us see which interests you the less. You have two things to lose, the true and the good, and two things to enlist, your reason and your will, your knowledge and your beatitude; and your nature has two things to flee from, error and misery. Your reason is not more wounded in choosing the one or the other since it is absolutely necessary to choose. That subject is exhausted. But your beatitude? Let us weigh up the gain and the loss involved in calling heads that God exists. Let us assess the two cases: if you win you win all; if you lose you lose nothing. Wager and He does exist – do not hesitate.'

'That is wonderful. Yes, I must bet, but perhaps I am betting too much.'

'Let us see. Since there is an equal chance of winning or losing, if you stood to win only two lives for one you could still win. But if you stood to win three, you would have to play (since you must necessarily play) and you would be imprudent, since you are obliged to play, not to risk your life to win three lives at a game in which there is an equal chance of losing and winning. But there is an eternity of life and happiness. That being so, even though there were an infinity of chances, of which only one would be in your favor, you would still be right to bet one to win two; and you would be acting wrongly, being obliged to play, in refusing to stake one life against three in a game where out of an infinite number of chances there is one in your favor, if there were an infinity of infinitely happy life to be won. But here there is an infinity of infinitely happy life to be won, one chance of winning against a finite number of chances of losing, and what you are staking is finite. That settles the matter; wherever there is infinity, and where there are not infinite chances of losing against that of winning, there is nothing to weigh up – you must give all. And thus, since you must play, you must be abjuring your reason if you keep your life rather than risk it for an infinite gain, just as likely to come as a loss amounting to nothing.

'For there is no point in saying that it is uncertain whether you will win, that it is certain that you are taking a chance, and that the infinite distance between the *certainty* of what you are risking and the uncertainty of what you might win makes the finite good you are certainly risking equal to the infinite good that you are not certain to gain. This is not the case. Every gambler takes a certain risk for an uncertain gain; nevertheless he is taking a certain finite risk for an uncertain gain without sinning against reason. There is no infinite distance between the certain risk and the uncertain gain: that is false. There is, in truth, an infinity between the certainty of winning and the certainty of losing. But the relation between the uncertainty of winning and the certainty of what is being risked is in proportion to the chances of winning or losing. And from that it follows that if there are as many chances on one side as on the other you are playing for odds. And in that case the certainty of what you are risking is equal to the uncertainty of what you may win; by no means is it infinitely distant from it. Thus, our proposition has infinite force, when the stakes are finite in a game where there are equal chances of winning or losing and something of infinite worth to win. This is conclusive, and if people are capable of any truth, this is it.'

'I confess, I admit it. But isn't there a way of seeing what is at the bottom of the game?'

'Yes, Scripture and the rest, etc.'

'Yes, but my hands are tied and my lips sealed. I am being forced to wager and I am not at liberty. I am being held fast. And I am made in such a way that I cannot believe. What do you want me to do then?'

'It is true. But at least learn that your inability to believe is because of your passions, since reason impels you to believe and you cannot do so. Work not on convincing yourself by argumentation and proofs of God's existence, but on diminishing your passions. You want to find faith, yet you do not know the route. You want to be cured of unbelief and you ask for the remedies: learn from those who were bound like yourself and who now wager all their goods. These are persons who know the road that you want to follow, and who are healed of the evil of which you want to be cured. Follow the way by which they began: it is doing everything as if they believed, taking holy water, having masses said, etc. That will make you believe naturally and will tame you.'

'But that is what I fear.'

'But why? What have you to lose? Only to show you that this is the way, the thing is that it diminishes the passions, which are your great obstacles.'

'*End of this discourse*. What harm will come to you for taking this course? You will be faithful, humble, grateful, full of good works, a sincere and true friend. It is true that you will not be having vile pleasures, glory, delights, but won't you have others? I tell you that you will win in this life, and that at every step you take along this road you will see so much certainty of winning and so much certainty that you are risking nothing, that you will know at the end that you have wagered on something certain and infinite for which you have paid nothing.'

'This discourse transports me, overwhelms me . . .'

'If this discourse pleases and convinces you, know that it was made by a man who went down on his knees before and after to pray to this infinite and indivisible Being, to whom he submits his own being, that he might bring your being also to submit to Him for your own good and for His glory, and that thus strength may be reconciled with lowliness.'

Pascal proposed, then, to treat the question of believing in God's existence as a matter of rational decision. If we choose not to believe in God, then we may feel entitled to lead the life of a libertine with impunity. However, if He does not exist, we shall be held accountable for our actions and be punished for them in the afterlife. On the other hand, if He does exist after all, we have neither lost nor gained anything by not believing in Him. If we choose to believe in God, our conduct must be far more circumspect; but if He does exist, the gain of Paradise is infinitely to be preferred to any earthly pleasures. Yet even if we are mistaken and He does not exist, being mistaken is better than choosing atheism if He does exist. Consequently, so long as there is at least some probability that God exists, however small, theism is a more prudent course than atheism. The well-advised will therefore wager that God exists.

How convincing is Pascal's position? Pascal is aware that belief is a posture of the mind, often simply the result of custom or habit. Belief does not belong in the province of the will: one may *want* to believe, but one cannot *will* oneself to believe. Moreover, many people believe things that they are aware fly in the face of evidence, or for which the evidence is very tenuous. Pascal's position is that the best-advised person will conduct his life under the hypothesis that God exists, in the same way that someone doing research in cancer (though this is not Pascal's example) will work under the hypothesis that cancers are caused by viruses rather than by, let us say, malevolent spirits casting spells from Mars. To take another example, closer to Pascal's own recurrent imagery: if one sets out on a journey one takes along various medicines; one does not *believe* that one will succumb to some malady, but one is prepared if one does come down with something. And so the well-prepared traveller should alter his course in light of the possibility of God's existence. By dint of working under the theistic hypothesis, we imperceptibly begin to modify our own behavior. By acting as Christians, from the formalities of crossing ourselves with holy water to the athletic acts of acting charitably even when we do not feel so inclined, the results of our wager will grow into strong belief. We have prepared the ground for the theological virtue of faith. To take another example, again not Pascal's: suppose we have a great love of music, but do not know whether we have any real talent. It is more prudent to make the audacious assumption that we have considerable if not great talent, and work hard under that hypothesis, than to assume that we have no divine voice or wizardly pianism to be released. Pascal believes that acting under the hypothesis of God's existence is not only more fulfilling and enriching in this dimension, but also in the next dimension.

It must be remembered, however, that Pascal's God is the 'God of

Abraham, of Isaac,' as he states in the 'Mémorial,' the God of Christianity. Pascal is not presenting only two alternatives, atheism and Christianity; in the fragments preceding *'infini–rien'* Pascal tried to dispose of other religions, and to show the inadequacies of the God of the philosophers and of deism. The wager is on a Christian God because only His possible existence synthesizes the two infinities of man – his finiteness and misery, his immortal longings and grandeur. Granted, Pascal's acquaintance with other religions is sketchy; he does not even mention Buddhism. Had he done so, he might have argued that the Buddhist story, involving eternal death and rebirth until one achieves Nirvana, is based on a warped and faulty reading of the human condition. Buddhism ignores the grandeurs of man and concentrates on the miseries; and its postulate of individual birth and rebirth has no explanatory power, unlike the doctrine of original sin. Pascal approaches religions as more or less elaborate systems, and the Christian system is the best on which to wager.

It must be admitted, however, that the argument assumes the possibility that at least some religion with transcendental bearings is true. In that case Pascal's wager has considerable power. If on the other hand we believe that all religions with otherworldly dimensions are false and impossible, and that some are merely less flagrantly impossible than others, the argument becomes jejune. If one believes that the existence of all the Greek mythological beings is equally impossible, it would be odd to be asked to wager on the possibility of the existence of Pallas Athena over Medusa because the former is wise in the industries of peace and the arts of war, and the latter is only a ghastly Gorgon who enjoys turning handsome young heroes into stone if they look at her. If one believes that the Christian God is not an impossibility, then Pascal is advising us to behave in a certain way, e.g., obeying the Ten Commandments, observing the seven sacraments and the precepts of the Church. But if we believe that the Christian God is highly improbable, then the well-advised should not alter their behavior to accommodate Him, any more than the high improbability of being struck by lightning while in your bathtub should keep you from bathing yourself. For a hypothesis, such as the reality of the Christian God, to alter one's behavior, it must be a live hypothesis, one that explains and offers more than any of its rivals.

As Pascal was well aware, the chief rival to his Christian hypothesis is naturalism, the belief that natural phenomena require only natural explanations. The naturalist argues that 'God' is only a euphemism for 'ignorance.' Pascal's reply is twofold. Accepting the powers of science is not incompatible with behaving according to the hypothesis of the Christian God. Indeed, both Pascal's own life and Isaac Newton's are proof of the compatibility. The history of science in no way forces the negation of the hypothesis. Secondly, and this is why 'the wager' must be interpreted within the entire plan of the *Pensées*, Pascal views man as uniquely situated in the realm of being, poised between the macrocosm and the microcosm, between galaxies and tiny particles, or microbes. Man's awareness of his finiteness and his grandeur give a further dimension to his uniqueness in the vastness of being. A unique situation requires a unique hypothesis. It is reasonable, then, to make the wager, and act in light of the hypothesis. The acting is a kind of formalism which over time will become second nature; and the second nature will become interiorized, and with the grace of God firm faith will follow.

It is clear that the extent of the logical possibilities concerning supernatural beings far exceeds the extent of live hypotheses concerning them. Pascal knew enough of polytheism and paganism to know that they had neither fulfilled prophecies nor given acceptable answers to man's condition; moreover, their temples are abandoned and their altars without celebrants. From Descartes Pascal could have taken the notion of a '*génie malin*' – some perverse god whose chief delight is man's torment. But such a deity does not present a live hypothesis, simply because so many things do not go so systematically wrong. From this one logical possibility, any number of other silly hypothetical beings can be conceived – a God who has a companion demonic colleague in whom man must believe if the master god is to give an infinite reward. The wager rises above logic-chopping objections because it concerns the live hypothesis of the existence of one omnipotent, omniscient, and omnibenevolent God, for whom the world is but an imperfect image. His existence is not rendered any less probable by the reality of evil, for as Pascal had already stated (416) nature has both perfections and imperfections, in order to show that nature is the image of God but 'only the image'.

19

THE HEART

Pascal never allows himself to drift into the smugness of self-assurance concerning religion, 'for it is not certain' (452). But he reminds his interlocutor of all the endeavors that man willingly undertakes which are also uncertain, from sea-voyages to battles. But those who demand a totally sufficient reason for doing or believing anything will end up neither believing nor doing anything. 'True Christianity consists in submission and the use of reason' (463). Although Pascal does not use the ancient imagery of the mystical ladder, he often speaks of reason as a means of getting to a certain level and then the necessity of discarding the means. 'There is nothing more in conformity with reason than this disavowal of reason' (465). Reason is most reasonable when it admits that it is weak and that a multitude of things are beyond it. And if natural things surpass it, 'what will one say of supernatural things?' (466). Pascal does not oppose the 'heart' to the 'head' any more than he opposes the Old to the New Testament; both the 'heart' and the New Testament are fulfillments: 'la raison' precedes the true reasonableness of 'le coeur,' just as the law of righteousness announces the message of love. By emphasizing the capital importance of 'le coeur,' Pascal is far from championing the cause of unreason, let alone the violent separation of reason and sentiment that was to become so prevalent in British philosophy in the eighteenth century, especially with Hume.

The relationship between reason and faith, or the intellect and the heart, is complex. Reason can show the necessity of faith and make the heart receptive, but cannot of itself give faith. The heart allows for the passage from the 'order of intelligence' to the 'order of charity.' Pascal holds that the heart alone knows 'first principles' – 'les *premiers principes'* – such as the three-dimensionality of space, the nature of time and movement, and the infinity of number. Reason therefore depends on the heart – or instinct, as Pascal sometimes writes – for its very foundations. Reason best reveals its reasonableness in recognizing its limitations; yet it is an unreasonable move to reject the possibility of any knowledge, as do the Pyrrhonians. God is known through the heart, not through reason.

It is important to recognize that Pascal is far from surrendering the powers of reason to the heart or sentiment. Nature has consigned only a few objects of knowledge to the heart; the bulk of what we know can only be acquired by reasoning and experimentation. 'And it is as useless and ridiculous for reason to ask the heart for proofs of its first principles before admitting them, as it would be for the heart to demand from reason a feeling for all demonstrated propositions before accepting them' (479).

Pascal compares the infinite distance between the physical and the mental to the even greater infinity between the order of intelligence and the order of charity. The physical, or corporeal, is the lowest of the 'three orders' because it cannot be self-reflective or self-aware. 'All bodies taken together, and all minds taken together with all their products, are not worth the least movement of charity, for it is an order infinitely higher' (829).

Research into the functions of the brain had barely begun in Pascal's time, and was limited to such primitive conjectures as Descartes's theory that the mind and body interact through the pineal gland, located in the center of the brain. But distinctly modern questions can be traced to Pascal's meditations on the roles of intelligence and 'the heart.' For example, can genuine intelligence be embodied in something other than the mental – in the organic or electronic? Do the heart or emotions and intelligence have different 'seats' in the brain? Pascal never referred to his calculator as a 'thinking machine,' in spite of the fact that it could out-think or calculate more speedily than the ordinary run of mankind. But could machines have 'heart' or feelings, or be able to deceive human beings or other machines? The capacity to lie, negate, and deceive is as innate in man as his capacity to learn a language or use tools. But could a machine deceive, as opposed to simply making a mistake? What emerges from Pascal's meditations on *'le coeur'* is that what is distinctively human is not intelligence but 'God being sensible to the heart' – '*Dieu sensible au coeur*' (481): 'Faith is a gift of God. Do not believe that we are saying that it is a gift of reasoning. Other religions do not say that of their faith; they give only reasoning to attain to it, which nevertheless will not lead there' (480).

As a further strategy in his apologetics, Pascal states that there are three ways of arriving at belief: reason, custom or habit, and inspiration. Unique to Christianity is that, although both reason and custom play important roles, inspiration is essential. 'The grandeurs and miseries of man are so visible that the true religion must necessarily teach us both that there is some grand principle of the grandeur of man and a grand principle for his misery. It is also necessary that the true religion should make sense of these astonishing contrarieties' (483). The oxymoron of man's condition can only be resolved by the numinous, by what Pascal calls '*l'incompréhensibilité*' (483), and '*la Sagesse de Dieu*' – 'God's Wisdom' (483). Making use of the figure of prosopopeia, or personification, Pascal makes '*la Sagesse de Dieu*' speak, warning man to expect 'neither truth nor consolation from men. I am what formed you, and I alone can teach you who you are. But you are no longer in the state in which I formed you. I created man holy, innocent, perfect. I filled him with light and intelligence; I communicated my glory and marvels to him. Then the eye of man saw the majesty of God. Then he was not in the shadows that blinded him, nor in the mortality and misery that afflicted him. But he was unable to bear so much glory without falling into presumption. He wanted to make himself the center of himself, independent of my help' (483). The tirade of 'God's Wisdom' continues, describing the present fallen and miserable state of man. The numinous or presiding spirit reveals that the fall of man from his glory is the principle that explains the contrarieties of man's condition.

The voice of 'God's Wisdom' becomes more vehement: 'How many contradictions could be found in a simple subject? – Incomprehensible. – Not all that is incomprehensible ceases to exist. Infinite number. An infinite space equal to a finite' (483). In these notes, which Pascal jotted down for his presentation at Port-Royal the next day, there is evidence that he was 'inspired' in the sense that 'his heart' comprehended the nature of the created universe: it is finite and infinite. It is a mistake to ask what lies beyond its edges, for the universe has no edges. Yet it is finite, having been made by God in space and time.

What Pascal calls 'The Ultimate Problem' – '*L'ultime Problème*' – concerns whether man has been raised to a supranatural state. Indeed, all the arguments of the *Pensées* hinge on the reality and the necessity of the supranatural. 'Man is not worthy of God, but he is not incapable of being made worthy. It is unworthy of God to join Himself to miserable man, but it is not unworthy of God to pull him out of his misery' (484).

Pascal believed that it makes sense to ask whether life has a purpose, whether man's being in the universe has a meaning. Considering nature as if it were a great book to be interpreted and deciphered is an ancient tradition; it has three major roots: rabbinical, classical exegesis – especially of Homer and Virgil – and the early Church Fathers. The shared assumption is that nature, like a major literary work, must be approached like a palimpsest. The literal layer of meaning, though of unquestionable importance, is the first to strike the reader's eye, but also the most superficial. Behind it lies the ethical meaning which, when peeled away by hermeneutics, gives way to the allegorical meaning. The ultimate meaning is the mystical. Pascal would argue that the sciences are excellent tools for arriving at the literal layer, but useless for interpreting the 'deeper meanings.'

Certain literary texts require such an approach in order to be understood, for example Dante's *Divine Comedy*. To give an example from the Prologue: exegetes have long debated the meaning of the three wild beasts that Dante encounters in the '*selva oscura*' – the 'dark wood.' Literally they are described as being a leopard, a lion, and a wolf, but clearly their significance does not stop there. The next layer of meaning comes from Jeremiah 5:6: 'Wherefore a lion out of the forest shall slay them, and a wolf of the evenings shall spoil them, a leopard shall watch over their cities: every one that goeth out thence shall be torn to pieces.' But the animals also appear to stand for Dante's vicious habits, which caused him to be lost in the dark wood. Some commentators have argued that the animals stand respectively for luxury, pride, and avarice. Others have argued that since the sins of Hell are arranged under three heads – Incontinence, Violence, and Fraud – the ravenous wolf is Incontinence, the raging lion is Violence, and the stealthy leopard is Fraud. It might also be argued that the three beasts stand respectively for the three great oppressive powers of Dante's personal experience – France, Florence, and the papacy. No attempt will be made here to offer the correct interpretation, in part because the 'Prologue' is only being used as an example of arriving at literary meanings, and in part, perhaps, because there never is '*the* correct meaning' in exegesis. But that point leads on to a larger issue: is Pascal's attempt to find a deeper meaning for man and his place in the universe feasible? Clearly he believed that it was. He also believed that one can give a very strong case for *the* correct mystical meaning.

Unlike Dante's great poem, other literary works might invite exegesis but hardly require it. Early Christian commentators, in their desperate attempts to recycle the ancient world into Christian culture, purported to find mystical meanings and foreshadowings of the Virgin Mary and of Christ in the ostensibly earthy *Georgics* of Virgil. Many of Shakespeare's works, though fraught with meanings within the text, have no extra-textual meanings – 'full of sound and fury, signifying nothing.' And it is at least a plausible view that man and his history are just that: events in history have various meanings, but history itself is not the unfolding of some deeper meaning, let alone 'an ultimate meaning.' Clearly Pascal did not share that view; to advance his argument he turns to the person of Jesus Christ. Pascal held that Christ is the central figure in human history, imbuing Him with four layers of meaning: literal, ethical, allegorical, and mystical. These layers comprise 'the mystery of Jesus.'

20

THE MYSTERY OF JESUS

The explicitly apologetic passages of the *Pensées* do not appear until Pascal undertakes an examination of the 'Proofs of Jesus Christ,' which he bases on the Scriptures. The Old Testament foreshadows *'son attente'* – 'the wait for Him'; the New Testament presents *'son modèle'* – 'His model'; and both Testaments construed together take Christ as *'leur centre'* – 'their center.'

Although the brief text entitled 'Le Mystère de Jésus' – 'The Mystery of Jesus' – has been included in the *Pensées* since the first edition of 1670, there is reason to believe that Pascal conceived of it as an independent statement, an integral text that would stand alone. The text has the same intense fervor as the 'Mémorial.' Many critics have cited 'Le Mystère' as the most poignant and beautiful of all Pascal's works. The meaning and significance of 'Le Mystère' fits precisely into the architechtonic of the *Pensées*. Before turning to the text, we shall reconstruct Pascal's thinking in order to understand why he believes Jesus to be the absolutely central figure in history and the only explication of man's profound ambiguity.

Pascal holds that the history of the people of Israel, and their sacred texts, support the necessity of believing in a Messiah. He argues that at the time Jesus came into the world, the Jews were divided into two opposing camps: those who embraced Him as the Messiah, and those who rejected Him but served as witnesses. The first camp contained 'the spiritual' – *'les spirituels'* – and the second 'the crude' – *'les grossiers.'* If all the Jews had accepted Jesus as the Christ, then we would be left with only suspicious witnesses. On the other hand, if all the Jews had been exterminated, there would have been no witnesses at all. Pascal sets up his argument for the 'Proof of Jesus Christ' –

'Preuves de Jésus-Christ' – in a characteristically antithetical manner. The history of Jesus has to unfold exactly as it did; for, by putting Jesus to death, the Jews gave Him the last mark of the Messiah. By refusing to recognize Him, they remained unassailable witnesses. Unwittingly they were fulfilling the words of the prophets: the Messiah would be reviled, despised, and forsaken.

Let us closely examine Pascal's logic at this point in his apology. Behind the argument lies an assumption that has some validity: human beings generally have divided stances on major commitments, as almost any election to public office will show. If we construed the issue of whether Jesus was indeed the Messiah as such a major commitment, then we would expect a divided constituency. As we know, historically the Jews were divided in their stance. This division does not, however constitute, the 'proof' that Pascal is attempting to forge. Interpreting the historical events and the Scriptures in this light reveals that one is already a believer. Pascal is chargeable with the same mistaken tactic for which he himself had reproached other Christian apologists, which is that of failing to place himself in the position of the unbeliever. There is no evidence as such for anything: evidence must be interpreted, and intepretation is necessarily a story, a construct placed upon the evidence. Looking at the same historical events, and reading the same texts, the atheist would find the whole notion of a Messiah a folly; and the ancient Israelite, like the High Priest of the Temple, would say that 'the evidence' was irrelevant or even blasphemous. It is, however, true that at this point in Pascal's apology his interlocutor is already converted. Convinced by the miseries and the grandeurs of the human condition, the former skeptic or free-thinker – the *'libertin'*[3] – now has faith, and is willing to humble himself by accepting the formalities of the Church. But the argument based on the division of the Jews regarding Jesus is convincing only for those who are already convinced.

For Pascal the prophecies constitute another 'proof' that Jesus was the true Messiah, for they reveal a divine order that Jesus fulfilled. Pascal sketches what would have been a detailed examination of all the prophecies of the ancient Hebrews, and how either Jesus's miraculous acts or His statements precisely fulfilled them. He was the redeemer not only of the Jews, but of the whole human race. Continuing to guide mankind by His teachings Jesus is present in time through the Eucharist and through divine grace.

It is essential that the Scriptures have two senses, according to Pascal, so that the New Testament is the sole fulfillment of the Old Testament. He is careful, however, not to base this contention on belief in the divinity of Jesus, but on the rabbinical tradition itself. 'Proof of the two testaments at the same time. – To prove the two immediately, it is necessary only to see whether the prophecies of the one are fulfilled in the other. In order to examine the prophecies, one must understand them. For, if one believes that they have only one sense, it is certain that the Messiah would not have come; but if they have two senses, it is certain that he came in Jesus Christ' (541). Pascal offers some six 'proofs' which doubtless he would have developed in great detail in the completed *Apology*. (1) By an examination of the Scriptures themselves, their double sense is revealed in figures, tropes, and symbolic foreshadowings. This would have amounted to a hermeneutical analysis of the Scriptures on Pascal's part, interpreting the stories of Adam, of Noah, for example, as symbolic precursors of events described in the New Testament. (2) Pascal argues that the rabbis themselves held that the Scriptures have two senses, and that they must be given a symbolic or spiritual interpretation. (3) The Cabala also supports the dual interpretation of the Scriptures through its system of theosophical and mystical readings. (4) 'Proof by the mystical interpretation that the rabbis themselves give to the Scriptures' (541). (5) 'Proof by the principles of the rabbis, that there are two senses, that there are two comings of the Messiah, glorious or abject, according to their merit, that the prophets have prophesied nothing but the Messiah – the law is not eternal, but must adapt to the Messiah – that then one will no longer remember the Red Sea, that the Jews and the Gentiles will be mingled' (541). (6) Finally, in a cryptic, incomplete sentence Pascal states: 'Proof by the key that Jesus Christ and the apostles give us' (541). Apparently Pascal was referring to the Church and its ancient exegetical traditions. Many parts of these final sections of the *Pensées* are notes that Pascal made to himself, such as his reminder that he must explain the nature of the figurative use of discourse in his chapter on the 'Foundations of the Christian Religion' (571).

In the fragments introduced by the word '*figures*,' which may be translated as 'types,' Pascal argues that it is just as erroneous to take everything in the Scriptures literally as it is to take everything spiritually. The prophets used types such as 'girdle,' 'beard,' 'sword,' or 'shield.' 'The letter kills. Everything happened in types. Here is the cipher that St Paul gives us. Christ must suffer. A humiliated God. Circumcision of the heart, true fasting, true sacrifice, a true temple. The prophets have shown that all these must be spiritual. – Not the meat which perishes, but that which does not perish. – "You shall be free indeed." Therefore the other freedom was only a type of freedom. – "I am the true bread from Heaven" ' (569).

In the few fragments in which Pascal gives some hints of his method of exegesis, or hermeneutics, he begins with his habitual penchant for harmonizing antitheses. In a passage introduced by the word 'contradiction' Pascal writes:

> One can only give a good physiognomy by reconciling all contrary qualities, and it is not enough to keep up a series of harmonious qualities, without reconciling contradictory ones. To understand the meaning of an author, we must make all contradictory passages agree.
>
> Thus, to understand Scripture, we must have a meaning in which all the contrary passage are reconciled. It is not enough to have one which suits many concurring passages, but it must also be one which reconciles even the contradictory passages.
>
> Every author has a meaning in which all the contradictory passages agree, or he has no meaning at all. We cannot affirm the latter of Scripture and the prophets; they are undoubtedly full of good sense. We must then seek for a meaning which reconciles all discrepancies – The true meaning then is not that of the Jews; but in Jesus Christ all the contradictions are reconciled.– The Jews could not reconcile the cessation of the royalty and principality, foretold by Hosea, with the prophecy of Jacob.
>
> If we take the law, the sacrifices, and the kingdom as realities, we cannot reconcile all the passages. They must then necessarily be only types. We cannot even reconcile passages of the same author, nor of the same book, nor sometimes of the same chapter, which abundantly manifests the author's intent. As when Ezekiel, chapter 20, says that man will not live by the commandments of God and will live by them. (558)

Fortified by his examination of scriptural typology, reassured by his analysis of the prophecies and miracles, Pascal begins what would have been the most magisterial section of his apology with the statement: 'From that, I reject all other religions. By that, I find an answer to all objections. It is right that a God so pure should only reveal Himself to those whose hearts are purified. Hence this religion is lovable to me, and I find it now sufficiently justified by so divine a morality. But I find more in it' (600).

'I find it convincing that, since the memory of man has lasted, it was constantly announced to men that they were universally corrupt, but that a Redeemer would come; that it was not one man who said it, but innumerable men, and a whole nation expressly made for this purpose, and prophesying for four thousand years . . . ' (600).

It is at this point that Pascal's meditation on 'Jesus Christ. Man-God. Center of All' (600), is finally introduced, in the 'Mystery of Jesus.' The image of the eternal become temporal, the divine transfigured into the human, and the supremely innocent reduced to suffering, becomes the ultimate oxymoron, the ultimately redemptive contradiction in Pascal's apology for the Christian religion.

What makes 'Le Mystère de Jésus' so noticeably Jansenist in its undertones is the virtual neglect of the major themes of God the Creator and of the Trinity, and the overwhelming emphasis on the Redemption. Throughout all of Pascal's writings on theological subjects, his sole interest in the Old Testament is the prophecy and the expectation of the Messiah. The 'Mystery' must also be interpreted through the veil of Pascal's characteristically extreme way of putting things, i.e., that it is impossible to know God without Jesus Christ. Even such early extremists as Origen or Tertullian would have found this view bizarre. Pascal's version of Christianity is radically Christocentric. The search for certainties outside ecclesiastical authority was widespread in his time – certainties in mathematics, physics, optics, and even subjects that remain most uncertain in the twentieth century, such as ethics and psychology. But philosophers as diverse as La Rochefoucauld, Spinoza, Malebranche, and Descartes believed that they had got to the bottom of such enquiries. Pascal felt compelled to compose a brief meditation on what he was certain was the only certainty of which man is capable. As a mathematician, Pascal abhorred any hint of relativistic or suppositious 'personal' certainty, for truth is either universalizable or it is simply opinion. Pascal conceived of the 'Mystery' as transcending every social convention, every empirically tested hypothesis, every so-called axiom of physics or mathematics. Its uniqueness places the 'Mystery' even outside the possibility of classification. Because 'Le Mystère de Jésus' is the final resolution, the consummation of

Pascal's thinking and feeling, the text must be presented in its
entirety:

Jesus suffers in His passion the torments inflicted upon Him by men,
but in His agony He suffers the torments which He inflicts on Himself.
'He was troubled' ('*turbare semetipsum*').[4] This punishment is inflicted
by no human, but by an almighty hand, and only He that is almighty
can bear it.

Jesus seeks some comfort at least from His three dearest friends, and
they sleep; He asks them to bear with Him a while, and they abandon
Him with complete indifference, and with so little pity that it did not
keep them awake even for a single moment. And so Jesus was abandoned to face the wrath of God alone.

Jesus is alone on earth, not merely with no one to feel and share His
agony, but with no one even to know of it. Heaven and He are the only
ones to know.

Jesus is in the garden, not of delight, like the first Adam, who there
fell and took with him all mankind, but of agony, where He has saved
himself and all mankind.

He suffers this anguish and abandonment in the horror of the night.

I believe that this is the only occasion on which Jesus ever complained. But then He complained as though He could no longer contain
his overflowing grief: 'My soul is sorrowful, even unto death.'[5]

Jesus seeks companionship and solace from men. It seems to me that
this is unique in His whole life, but He finds none, for His disciples are
asleep.

Jesus will be in agony until the end of the world. There must be no
sleeping during that time.

Jesus, totally abandoned, even by the friends He had chosen to watch
with him, is vexed when he finds them asleep because of the dangers to
which they were exposing not Him but themselves, and He warns them
for their own safety and their own good, with warm affection in the face
of their ingratitude, and warns them that the spirit is willing but the
flesh is weak.[6]

Jesus, finding them asleep again, undeterred by consideration either
for Himself or for themselves, is kind enough not to wake them up and
lets them take their rest.

Jesus prays, uncertain of the will of the Father, and is afraid of death.
But once He knows what it is, He goes to meet it and offer Himself up.
'Let us be going. He went forth' (*Eamus. Processit*').[7]

Jesus asked of men and was not heard.

Jesus brought about the salvation of His disciples while they slept.

He has done this for each of the righteous while they slept, in nothingness before their birth and in their sins after their birth.

He prays only once that the cup might pass from Him, even then submitting Himself to God's will, and twice that it should come if it must be so.

Jesus weary at heart.

Jesus, seeing all His friends asleep and all His enemies watchful, commends Himself utterly to His Father.

Jesus disregards the enmity of Judas, and only sees in him God's will, which He loves; so much so that He calls him friend.

Jesus tears Himself away from his disciples to enter upon His agony: we must tear ourselves away from those who are nearest and dearest to us in order to imitate Him.

Jesus being in agony, and in the greatest distress, let us pray longer.

We implore God's mercy, not so that He shall leave us in peace with our vices, but so that He may deliver us from them.

If God gave us masters with His own hand, how gladly we ought to obey them! Necessity and events are infallibly such.

'Take comfort; you would not seek me if you had not found me.'

'I thought of you in my agony: I shed these drops of blood for you.'

'It is tempting me rather than testing yourself to wonder if you would do right in the absence of this or that. I will do it in you if it happens.'

'Let yourself be guided by my rules; see how well I guided the Virgin and the saints who let me work in them.'

'The Father loves all I do.'

'Do you want it always to cost me the blood of my humanity while you do not even shed a tear?'

'My concern is for your conversion; do not be afraid, and pray with confidence as though for me.'

'I am present with you through my word in Scripture, my spirit in the Church, through inspiration, my power in my priests, my prayer among the faithful.

'Physicians will not heal you, for you will die in the end, but it is I who will heal you and make your body immortal.

'Endure the chains and bondage of the body. For the present I am delivering you only from spiritual bondage.

'I am a better friend to you than this man or that, for I have done more for you than they, and they would never endure what I have endured from you, and they would never die for you, while you were being faithless and cruel, as I did, and as I am ready to do, and still do in my elect, and in the Blessed Sacrament.

'If you knew your sins, you would lose heart.' – 'In that case I shall lose heart, Lord, for I believe in their wickedness on the strength of your assurance.' – 'No, for I who tell you this can heal you, and the fact that I tell you is a sign that I want to heal you. As you expiate them you will come to know them, and you will be told: *Behold, your sins are forgiven you.* Repent then of your hidden sins and the secret evil of those you know.'

'Lord, I give you all.'

'I love you more ardently than you have loved your foulness. *As an unclean beast for the mire ('Ut immundus pro luto').*[8]

'May mine be the glory, not thine, worm and clay.

'Acknowledge to your director that in my very words you find an occasion for sin, and for vanity or curiosity.'

' – I see the depth of my pride, curiosity, concupiscence. There is no rapport between me and God or Jesus Christ the righteous. But He was made sin for me; all your scourges fell upon Him. He is more abominable than I, and, far from loathing me, feels honored that I go to Him and help Him. But He healed Himself and will heal me all the more surely. I must add my wounds to His, and join myself to Him and He will save me in saving Himself. But none must be added for the future.

' "You shall be as gods, knowing good from evil."[9] We all act like God in passing judgments: "This is good or evil" and in being too distressed or too delighted by events.

'Do small things as if they were great, because of the majesty of Christ, who does them in us and lives our life, and great things as if they were small and easy, because of His almighty power.'[10]

'Do not compare yourself with others, but with me. If you do not find me in those with whom you compare yourself, you compare yourself to someone abominable. If you do find me there, compare yourself to Him. But whom will you compare yourself to? Will it be yourself, or myself in yourself? If it is yourself, it is someone abominable. If it is I, then you compare yourself to me. For I am God and all in all.

'I speak to you and counsel you often because your leader cannot speak to you; for I do not want you to lack a leader. And perhaps I do it by his prayers, and thus he leads you without your being aware.

'You would not be searching for me if you did not possess me. Therefore do not trouble yourself' (737).

21

LIFE IN THE CHURCH

As Pascal's asceticism deepened, he began to conceive of life in the Church as an intricate and closed system of discipline. Sacraments, feast days and days of obligation, rituals, litanies and prayers were so many methods of subduing desires of the flesh and of humbling the natural arrogance of reason. In face of the unfathomableness of being in the world, the Church offered a system of practices which to the skeptic appear obsessive and unproductive, but to the believer gain meaning and comfort within the basic postulates of the system.

The Church rests upon apostolic succession; the idea that the twelve apostles were impostures is 'absurd.' It is counter to human nature, Pascal argues, to imagine the apostles meeting after the death of Christ to hatch a plot that He was resurrected from the dead. Human nature is given to fickleness and change; but in spite of torture, imprisonment, and even death, the apostles and their successors never wavered from their conviction that Christ had risen from the dead and had reappeared at Epiphany.

Pascal finds an additional proof of the truthfulness and authenticity of the apostles in the style of the Four Gospels. First, the evangelists never allow themselves any invectives against the enemies of Jesus; nor do they write anything untoward against Judas, Pontius Pilate, or the Jews. Their style is uniformly disinterested, dispassionate, almost cold. Such an objective and matter-of-fact style could not be affected, for affectations betray themselves sooner or later. For example, one of the apostles could have put calumny into the mouth of one of the personages in the narrative; none of the apostles uses the device of deflected invective. Second, Christ's recorded statements are remarkable in their simultaneous profundity and simplicity.

'Jesus Christ said great things so simply that it seems as if He had not thought them, and nonetheless so distinctly that one readily sees what He thought. This clarity joined with this näiveté is remarkable' (744).

For Pascal miracles and grace are the twin supports of the Church; both are supernatural, but miracles constitute the exterior foundation, and grace the interior. Well aware of those, like Montaigne, who doubt the occurrence of miracles, Pascal admits that the Church is 'without proof' if the doubters are right. There must necessarily be ways of distinguishing true from spurious miracles; otherwise, the most trivial stroke of good fortune could be interpreted by the credulous as a miracle. Pascal offers as a criterion for at least excluding spurious miracles the following: 'One must see whether the miracle denies God, Christ, or the Church' (752). Pascal warns that the Antichrist will speak against all three. Still, the criterion is too broad; Pascal tightens it by pointing out the reciprocity of doctrine and miracle: doctrines foretell events that miracles fulfill. Pascal proposes a fairly stringent definition of 'miracle': 'It is an effect that exceeds the natural force of the means involved; a non-miracle is an effect that does not exceed the natural force of the means involved. Thus, those who heal by invoking the devil do not perform a miracle, for it does not exceed the natural force of the devil. But . . . ' (755). Unfortunately Pascal left his readers with the ellipsis; nonetheless, the way in which he would have expanded his discussion concerning miracles can reasonably be inferred from a brief work entitled 'Questions sur les Miracles' – twelve questions by Pascal to the Abbé de Saint-Cyran.

Unique among Pascal's writings, the 'Questions Concerning Miracles' follows the scholastic method of presentation. A question is posed; the response, based both on the Scriptures and on the major theologians or philosophers, is given. The first question expands on the definition of 'miracle' in the Pensées: 'Whether for an effect to be miraculous it is necessary that it should be above the force of man, of demons, of angels, and of all created nature' (1069). Pascal's response argues for the affirmative. The second question foreshadows the passage already referred to in the Pensées: what the devil does, or what those do who invoke him, is therefore not miraculous. The third question shows that St Thomas is in accord with the definition that Pascal has presented; and the fourth question settles the matter –

heretics cannot confirm their errors by means of a miracle. Even so, heretics can confirm a truth by means of a miracle (questions 5 and 6). However, neither covert nor overt heretics can confirm anything contrary to the Church by means of a miracle (question 7). Question 8 reinforces the position that miracles are marks of the true Church. The further questions are contained in the treatment of miracles in the *Pensées*.

Pascal asks brusquely: 'Foundation of religion. It is miracles. What then? Does God speak against miracles, against the foundation of the faith that we have in Him?' (760). Pascal replies in a grandly hypothetical way: 'If there is a God, it must be that there is faith in Him on earth. For Christ's miracles are not predicted by the Antichrist, but rather the miracles of the Antichrist by Jesus Christ. Thus, if Jesus Christ were not the Messiah, He would have led into error; but the Antichrist cannot lead into error. When Jesus Christ predicted the miracles of the Antichrist, did he believe he was destroying faith in His own miracles?' (760).

The synagogue was the prefiguration of the church and therefore contained truth; but being only a prefiguration, it is now superannuated. What sets Christianity apart from all other religions, for Pascal, is its continuity, its prefigurations in Judaism, and its miracles. 'And thus the two worlds. The creation of a new heaven and a new earth (2 Peter 3:13), new life, new death. All things doubled, and the same names remain' (788). 'The source of all the heresies lies in not comprehending the agreement of the two opposing truths and believing that they are incompatible' (788). Heresy is the result of not being able to comprehend the synthesis of two antithetical or oxymoronic positions. Pascal gives a number of examples. The first naturally centers upon Christ, both God and man. The Arian heresy affirms only the humanity of Christ, and denies His divinity. Thus the Arians have part of the truth, but having only part, fall into heresy. Again, in an allusion to Luther, Pascal describes those who construe the Blessed Sacrament as solely figurative as failing to see the truth of the equally valid position that the Sacrament contains the real presence of Christ.

As for papal infallibility Pascal attempts to find a delicate balance between the Church as a whole and the pope as its head, a balance between plurality and unity. 'Plurality which is not reduced to unity is confusion; unity which does not depend on plurality is tyranny'

(809). It is as erroneous to affirm only the democracy of the Church as to affirm only its monarchy: both must be brought into a higher synthesis to understand the true nature of the Church. 'The Church teaches, and God inspires, both infallibly. The work of the Church is of use only as a preparation for grace or condemnation. What it does is enough for condemnation, not for inspiration' (817).

The ultimate synthesis for Pascal is 'the folly of the Cross.' 'Our religion is both wise and foolish: wise, because it is the most learned and the most solidly founded on miracles, prophecies, etc.; foolish, because it is not those reasons that make one a member of it . . . What makes one believe is the Cross' (828). The Cross is therefore the culmination of the third order = the order of charity. 'The infinite distance from the corporeal to the intellectual characterizes the infinitely more infinite distance from the intellectual to charity; for charity is supernatural' (829). The 'three orders' are generically distinct and separate. The first order, matter, is the realm of things, from atoms to stars; matter has no self-awareness. The second order, the realm of the mental or intellectual, is self-aware and can be aware of the realm of the material realm. The third, the infinitely highest realm, is that of charity. 'From all the corporeal and the intellectual realms one could not draw out a movement of true charity; that is impossible, of another order, supranatural' (829). Pascal concludes with 'The Mystery of Divine Love': 'God inclines the heart of those whom He loves' (840).

CONCLUSION

The feeling of belonging to 'two worlds' can hardly be alien to modern sensibility. Conflicts between Church and State, one's ethnic origins and present homeland, one's wishes of what ought to be rather than one's realization of what is: all these are conflicts in which a reflective person might find himself. Pascal had to experience the torture of being extremely reflective, and of possessing consummate intelligence. His poignancy of argument will therefore strike some readers today just as much as in his own time – as exaggerated, even repugnant. To give an antidote to this reaction, it may be helpful to quote from a twentieth-century English writer, Christopher Dawson, who drew from the same religious and philosophic sources as Pascal:

> The Western mind has turned away from the contemplation of the absolute and eternal to the knowledge of the particular and the contingent. It has made man the measure of all things and has sought to emancipate human life from its dependence on the supernatural. Instead of the whole intellectual and social order being subordinated to spiritual principles, every activity has declared its independence, and we see politics, economics, science and art organizing themselves as autonomous kingdoms which owe no allegiance to any higher power.[1]

Whatever consolations the new physics of the seventeenth century afforded the intellectuals of the time, thinkers such as Pascal felt themselves robbed of their feelimg of being 'at home' in nature. The world of matter was soundless, colorless, unfeeling, and infinite in space and time. All that was human – sensation, feeling, suffering, and thinking – the realm of the mind – seemed alien to the vast mechanical system of nature. Characteristically Pascal found himself caught between the opposing realms of matter and mind. His solution was to turn to God, in the belief that He transcends and somehow unifies both realms through His grace.

Rationalism and the experimental method had opened new routes of challenge to ecclesiastical authority, with the result that skepticism became not only intellectually respectable but fashionable. Many of Pascal's early friends flaunted their skepticism, sometimes going so far as to argue that atheism was philosophically more compatible with the new physics than deism, not to mention the old-fashioned theism presented by Christianity. In France, however, more than in most other European countries, the power of the Counter-Reformation was still strong, in religious tracts and in political strategies. Lutheranism had required secular support from its inception, mainly because it was not a hierarchical or international organization. The Peace of Westphalia had meant that Calvinism commanded no super-national loyalty, and was therefore doomed to insularism. Rome, however, in spite of the many challenges to its authority, maintained immense international influence. Catholicism was strengthened by its ancient mendicant orders, the papal nuncios, and the recently founded (1534) Society of Jesus, the Jesuits. The popular aversion to the Jesuits was clear evidence of their strength.

Pascal realized that he could not base his defense of Christianity on what was seen as the outmoded scholastic method. Why did he reject scholasticism without even knowing, as he frankly admitted, much scholastic philosophy? The answer can be found in examining how scholastic thought appeared to the mind of the seventeenth century.

Metaphysical in its approach, scholasticism avoided empirical experimentation as such, as well as mathematical investigation. The scholastic mind asked questions about being and essence, cause and purpose. Appropriating the doctrine of the 'Four Causes' from Aristotle, the scholastic would typically attempt to explain some object or event by asking: (1) What is its material cause? i.e., What is it made of? (2) What is its formal cause?. i.e., What is its structure or essence? (3) What is its efficient cause? i.e., Who, or what, made it or brought it about? and finally (4) What is its final cause? i.e., What is its purpose?

Scholasticism was a synthesis of the two traditions that supported the Middle Ages: on the one hand the pagan philosophers, notably Plato and Aristotle, and on the other, the tenets of Christianity as interpreted by the Church Fathers and the Councils. Its purpose was to bring about harmony between reason and faith, metaphysics and revelation. Theology emerged as the supreme enquiry because it purported to be a science of God. In scholasticism a branch of knowledge gained its prestige from the importance of its subject matter; to the medieval mind no 'subject' was so important as the Supreme Being. This Being responded perfectly to all of Aristotle's 'Four Causes.' The soul was held to be the 'image of God,' in some way made from divine substance. The tripartite soul – memory, reason, and will – corresponded to the Trinity. God was believed to be the Creator of the soul, and He was hoped to be the purpose, in the Beatific Vision, of each individual soul.

Although the new scientific spirit of the seventeenth century did not regard such theological theses as nonsense – as would positivists in the next two centuries to follow – thinkers, both Catholic and Protestants, wanted to avoid pitting questions of faith against the dynamically more interesting issues of science. Central ideas of the scholastics were simply being redescribed, rather than rejected. It is a curious phenomenon that throughout the Christian nations of the seventeenth-century world from Europe to the New World, the most uneducated peasant would give his word 'in the name of God', and philosophers as august as Descartes would find it necessary to found their philosophical systems on God's sustaining presence. With his scientific training, and mathematical genius, Pascal wanted to describe his relationship to God in a unique way, but not contrary to the spirit of the two greatest scholastic philosophers, St Albertus Magnus (c. 1193–1280) and St Thomas Aquinas (1225–74). Both thinkers conceived of reality as arranged in a strict hierarchical order, proceeding from the *'infimae species'* – the 'lowest forms of matter' – to the *'ens realissimum'* – God. When asked why God had gone to such trouble to communicate Himself to His created world, given that He was perfect in every way, the standard scholastic answer was basically the same that Pascal gave in his discussion of the Incarnation in 'Le Mystère de Jesus' – love. The scholastic belief was that God created, sustains, and governs the world through love. Pascal was to translate the same philosophic tenet into a personal and intimate description of the role of Jesus in human history, a role that the scholastic thinkers had preferred to render in a more abstract vein.

Scholasticism was premised on the belief that all created things have a specificity that cannot be changed. Although God loved His created world, He ruled by natural law. Man was conceived as unique in that he was both corporeal and spiritual; he is a free agent who may therefore believe what he wants to believe, love whom he chooses, and sin as he wants to sin.

The scholastic mind attempted to encompass all reality and to form an architectural synthesis of thought. The mind of the Renaissance developed the abstractive, tightly contained attitude of the sciences. The scholastic reliance upon 'received knowledge,' authority, and revered texts was repugnant to the scientific temper of the seventeenth century. But not only were the modes of scholastic explanation deemed useless, but particular explanations were often considered irrelevant. The rejection of the scholastic theory of motion is a prime example of the dramatic change in the approach to the natural sciences. Following Aristotle, St Thomas Aquinas discussed motion as a metaphysical question. He used the set terms 'act' and 'potency,' and concluded that motion occurs because everything in a state of potentiality strives to actualize itself, or seeks a place proper to it. In his treatment of motion, Galileo wasted no time in refuting Aquinas, but simply ignored him. Galileo realized that his own mode of explanation was generically different from that of the scholastics. He dropped weights from a tower, or down inclined planes, to observe the results. He was interested in explaining motion in a mathematical not metaphysical manner. With the telescope that he had perfected, he could observe phenomena that Aristotle had only speculated about, such as generation and corruption: 'We have in our age new accidents and observations, and such that I question not in the least, but if Aristotle were now alive, they would make him change his opinion.'[2]

Pascal was profoundly affected by the new scientific temper of his epoch, but was never totally 'converted' to the scientific method, unlike Descartes. Pascal believed that the mathematical method was valid, but only for a certain range of explanation; similarly, the experimental method worked well with some phenomena, but was irrelevant to others. He found it impossible to decide between the Ptolemaic, the Copernican, and the Tychonic descriptions of the solar system, because all three satisfactorily describe the visible celestial phenomena. 'Who, then, without danger of error, can support any one of these theories to the detriment of the others?'

Pascal was haunted by the infinite magnitude of the cosmos, more so than any other thinker in Western philosophy. Some philosophers, such as St Bonaventure and Giordano Bruno, have derived a religious exultation, a feeling of aesthetic rapture, from contemplating the magnitude of the world. Pascal found the '*infini créé*' – the 'created infinite' – both terrifying and oppressive. The infinity of the cosmos was for Pascal an argument, a testimony to the insignificance of man. But denigrating man's self-esteem was only part of Pascal's homiletic project: he also wanted to raise man's sense of self-respect:

> If he boasts about himself, I shall denigrate him; if he is self-deprecating, I shall boast about him; and I shall contradict him always, until he realizes that he is an incomprehensible monster.[3]

In this striking passage, Pascal reveals the fundamental characteristic of his thought and style, the oxymoron, which has provided the leitmotif or thesis of this introduction to Pascal. As we have seen, the oxymoron is a rhetorical figure in which contradictory attributes are brought together. In Pascal's thought there is a sense of recurrent vertigo, for no sooner does he argue for man's superiority to matter because man can know matter, than he complains about man's fragility and the extreme limitation of his rational powers.

Pascal ascribed to a theory of truth, sometimes referred to as the Coherence Theory of Truth, according to which statements can be known to be true only if they are construed in the total system of truths. To know the meaning of a part entails knowing the meaning of the whole, and conversely. The difficulty, according to Pascal, is that the individual parts can be divided *ad infinitum*, and the whole continues infinitely. Man is caught in the middle, unable to grasp the whole and drawn into the whirlpool of minutiae. Our knowledge of first principles is therefore ultimately non-rational. Apart from habit, faith, or revelation, our assurance of first principles is that we feel comfortable with them. Yet a natural feeling is hardly a guarantee of truth. For Pascal, only faith assures us that we were made by a benevolent, omniscient, and omnipotent God. Reason can give equally compelling arguments that man was made by an evil demon, or is simply the result of chance events in the cosmos. Ironically, one cannot even become a complete skeptic, for radical skepticism implies that one at least knows that knowledge is impossible.

For Pascal, the notion of infinite number or infinite magnitude staggers the mind and carries us into endless and terrifying vistas. The infinity of the cosmos (although this is not Pascal's comparison) is like a recurrent, obsessive nightmare in which one is a prisoner in an endless structure, in which one goes from room to room, opening one door after another, going everywhere and nowhere. If mathematics is premised on the infinite, Pascal argues, people should not be surprised to find religion, and especially the true religion, centered upon a Being infinitely incomprehensible and vast, a Being whom we know only through supernatural means.

Pascal thought that the infinity of the world, of the cosmos, was a possible route to understanding the possibility of the supernatural, and God. However, he never entertained the idea that at least some of the other worlds might have a humanoid, or some other form of intelligent population. Thinkers such as Kepler and Giordano Bruno entertained the possibility of life on other planets, and sometimes argued that there must be other intelligent life 'out there.' Looking out on the immense universe, some thinkers did not feel alone, but were only annoyed that communication with 'the others' was not yet possible. The Italian humanists of the Renaissance had a much more fecund imagination than did Pascal, were much less bound by religious dogmas, and had a far more cheerful attitude towards the infinity of nature. A number of speculative works on the possibility of other worlds appeared in the seventeenth century, culminating with the work already mentioned, Fontenelle's *Entretiens sur la pluralité des mondes*. Pascal, however, was not drawn to such speculations, because of his religious convictions and his belief in a supernatural revelation through the ancient Hebrews and through Christianity. He would have had to pose such questions as: Are these other rational beings subject to original sin? Are they also in need of redemption? If so, then the same structural story of the Fall of Man must permeate the universe. On the other hand, if the other rational beings are not tainted by original sin, then the necessity of religion seems to be peculiar to the planet earth. The corollary of that implication might be that the 'true religion' is no more than superstition. Pascal's incapacity for, or perhaps conscious rejection of, such fanciful speculations greatly simplified his projected defense of the Christian religion.

Leibniz, in his 'Double Infinite chez Pascal et monade' – 'The Double Infinity in Pascal and Monad'[4] – rejects Pascal's view of man as a point situated between the infinities of God and matter:

> What Monsieur Pascal says about the twofold infinity which environs
> us in regard to increase and decrease, when he speaks in his *Pensées*
> about our general knowledge of man, is but one entry in my system . . .
> [My monad or primitive subject of life and action is] a micro-divinity, a
> universe of matter eminently contained; God in ectype and this same
> universe in prototype; imitating God and imitated by the universe in
> respect to its distinct thoughts; like God through its distinct thoughts,
> like matter through its confused ones.

Leibniz must have been referring to the section in the *Pensées*
entitled 'The Place of Man in Nature: the Two Infinities' (no. 84):

> For after all, what is man in nature? A nothingness in respect to the
> infinite, everything in respect to nothingness, a middle term between
> nothing and everything. Infinitely distanced from understanding the
> extremes, the purpose of things and their origin are completely hidden
> from him in an impenetrable secret; man is equally incapable of seeing
> the nothingness from which he is drawn out, or the infinity into which
> he is sunk . . . Having failed to contemplate these infinities, men have
> boldly gone in search of nature, as if they had some commonality with
> her . . . I hold that it is impossible to know the parts without knowing
> the whole, and similarly, we cannot know the whole without a detailed
> knowledge of the parts.[5]

Both mathematicians of the first order, Pascal and Leibniz emerge
with totally different attitudes after contemplating the infinities of
God and matter. Pascal is humbled, and turns to a fideistic skepticism; Leibniz is jubilant, and argues for an optimism based on
mathematics.

Ultimately, Pascal must be understood as a positivist in religion, an
empiricist in physics, and a mystic in matters of piety. His genius, or
personal tenacity, held that none of these categories should exclude
the other. Many of the tenets of Catholicism resembled the pre-
scripts of the codes of justice: they were the law. Canon law under the
ancien régime closely paralleled civil law. Tradition ruled, and rightly
so, in Pascal's mind, simply because neither mathematical nor empirical discoveries could rightly dominate the realm of Christian orthodoxy. There was never a split in Pascal's mind between science and

religion. It was his mysticism that prevailed. Just as pride is the first of sins, so is its scientific parallel – the vanity that science is or can ever be the measure of God – the road to materialism and destruction. Whilst living in an age of violent conflict between rationalism and religious belief, Pascal foresaw the age of secularism.

Pascal's life and works may be described as a long and painful effort to reconcile the opposing claims of science and faith, of Cartesian rationalism and religious discourse, of State and Church, and of reason and faith. Although Pascal, one of the most self-effacing and humble men of genius who has ever lived, does not cite St Matthew for his motto, it is appropriate to do so:

> Blessed are the peacemakers: for they shall be called the children of God.[6]

CHRONOLOGY OF THE LIFE OF PASCAL

1602   Angélique Arnauld, at the age of eleven, becomes the abbess of the convent of Port-Royal des Champs.

1609   25 September. Mère Angélique introduces important reforms at Port-Royal, including increased prayer and solitude, absolute sequestration, and strict examination of conscience.

1616   Etienne Pascal marries Antoinette Bégon. (Etienne Pascal, a high-ranking officer in the fiscal bureaucracy of the region of Clermont-Ferrand, was born in 1588. His father was Martin Pascal, a counsellor of the king, a treasurer of France, and in charge of the finances of the general region surrounding Clermont-Ferrand, in Riom. His mother was Marguerite Pascal de Mons, a member of the lesser nobility. Antoinette Bégon, born in 1596, was the daughter of Victor Bégon, a merchant, and Antoinette de Fontfreyde.)

1620   Gilberte Pascal is born.

1623   19 June. Blaise Pascal is born in Clermont-Ferrand, rue des Grads.

1624   Blaise falls victim to *'langueur'* after a witch put the 'evil eye' on him.

1625   Jacqueline Pascal is born.

        Port Royal is transferred to Paris.

1626   Blaise Pascal's mother, Antoinette, dies.

1630   Mère Agnès succeeds Mère Angélique as abbess of Port-Royal.

1632   Etienne Pascal moves to Paris with his three children, though maintaining his position until 1634 as president of the fiscal court of

Clermont-Ferrand. The family take up residence in the rue de la Tisseranderie, close to the Marais, then moves to the neighborhood of the Luxembourg Palace, across from the town residence of the Prince de Condé. The family finally move to the rue Brisemiche, near the church of Saint-Médéric or Saint-Merry. A governess named Louise Delfault is in charge of the house. Etienne Pascal refuses to have private tutors or to send his son to college, which would most likely have been a Jesuit college. Instead the father takes charge of the education of his children, believing that he is following the precepts of Montaigne. At the same time Etienne Pascal frequents the former mistress of Vincent Voiture and the sister of the poet D'Alibray, who belonged to a group of free-thinkers, or 'libertins.' After meeting the mathematician Le Pailleur, Etienne Pascal has access to many of the best scientific and mathematical minds, such as Father Mersenne, Desargues, and Roberval.

1634   Saint-Cyran becomes spiritual director of Port-Royal.

1636–7 In a lively debate Etienne Pascal and Personier de Roberval engage in criticism of Descartes's *Discours de la Méthode*. They side with Pierre de Fermat in a scientific controversy against Descartes.

1638   Etienne Pascal protests against the fiscal measures imposed by the city of Paris, under the order of the Chancelier de Séguier. Etienne Pascal flees to Auvergne to escape imprisonment in the Bastille.

1639   February. Jacqueline, who had shown precocious literary talents, is invited to the château of Saint-Germain-en-Laye to recite her sonnet (written in 1638) 'Sur le sujet de la grossesse de la Reine' – 'On the Pregnancy of the Queen,' Anne of Austria. Invited to Cardinal Richelieu's palace, Jacqueline recites an elaborate compliment in verse, thereby winning the Cardinal's favor. Madame de L'Aiguillon, her sponsor, speaks in favor of Etienne Pascal, and urges the Cardinal to grant him some special favor. She also mentions that the father has a son, barely fifteen years of age, who has shown great talent in mathematics. Etienne Pascal is subsequently sent (in November) to Rouen as the king's deputy commissioner for the raising and levying of taxes.

1640   January. Under the orders of Séguier a riot triggered by harsh taxation in Rouen is ruthlessly suppressed. Etienne Pascal witnesses it. Blaise publishes his first work, 'Traité des Coniques,' based on the theorem of the mystical hexagram, discovered through the works of Girard Desargues, a mathematician from Lyons.

The pivotal work in the Jansenist controversy, *Augustinus*, by Cornelius Jansen (Jansenius), bishop of Ypres, is published posthumously.

1641   13 April. Gilberte Pascal marries her cousin, Florian Périer.

1642   To help his father perform his duties, Blaise tries to construct an automatic calculator.

1643   Saint-Cyran dies and the influence of Antoine Arnauld, brother of Agnès and Angélique, increases at Port-Royal.

Under the influence of Jean Guillebert, pastor of Rouville, a town near Rouen, a new movement of spirituality, inspired by Saint-Cyran and Arnauld, gains a foothold in Normandy. Some friends of Pascal belong to the movement.

1645   Pascal publishes a dedicatory letter to the Chancelier de Séguier entitled 'Sur le sujet de la nouvelle machine inventée par le sieur Blaise Pascal.' This was the first of the five models of his mathematical calculator that Pascal worked on. The patent would not be granted until 1649; the final model of the *'Pascaline'* would not be finished until 1652.

1646   January. Etienne Pascal slips on the ice and breaks his hip. Two lay brothers, Deschamps des Landes and Deschamps de La Boutellerie, who had been swashbuckling duellists but were now converted to the views of Saint-Cyran, are engaged to treat Etienne Pascal's broken hip. Living with the Pascals for three months, they gain the devotion of Blaise, and soon the entire family. The brothers Deschamps relate their readings of Saint-Cyran, and Arnauld's *De la fréquente communion* – 'On Frequent Communion' – published in 1643. Blaise Pascal experiences his so-called 'first conversion,' but does not renounce his scientific and mathematical research.

August–November. Pascal and his father repeat at Rouen Torricelli's experiment on the vacuum left in a tube by the descent of a column of mercury. They are assisted by the mathematician Pierre Petit, who is a friend of Gassendi. A verbal account of the experiments is extant.

1647   February. Jacques Forton, called Frère Saint-Ange, a former Capuchin, gives a few lectures in Rouen. Forton reveals a strong penchant for rationalism in his theological disputations. Pascal and two of his young friends attend the lectures, disagree with his position, and demand that he retract certain propositions. When Forton refuses, Pascal and his friends go to his superior, Jean-Pierre Camus. Not satisfied with the strength of Camus's censure, Pascal and his friends go to the archbishop of Rouen, François de Harlay, who forces Frère Saint-Agne to retract certain propositions. Pascal's career as indefatigible defender of the faith is launched.

23–24 September. Pascal again succumbs to various illnesses. Living with his sister Jacqueline and their father in Paris, Pascal has two meetings with Descartes, the first of which takes place in the presence of Personier de Roberval. Descartes was curious to meet the young mathematician who had already become known to the scientific world. Descartes and Pascal failed to resonate to each other. Later, their opposing views on the nature of the vacuum or void would set them further apart.

4 October. Pascal publishes his 'Expériences nouvelles touchant le vide' – 'New Experiments on the Vacuum.' He re-edits his 'Preface for a Treatise on the Vacuum.' Pascal has his first debate with a Jesuit, the Reverend Father Noël, who was rector of the Collège de Clermont in Paris. To vindicate his views Pascal publishes 'A Response to Father Noël' – 'Réponse au très bon R. P. Noël' – in October 1647, and in February of the following year the 'Lettre à Monsieur Le Pailleur.' Both Noël and Le Pailleur held to the established view that 'Nature abhors a vacuum.' Pascal disagreed. Pascal writes to his brother-in-law, Florian Périer, inviting him to take part in some experiments at the Puy-de-Dôme to verify the hypothesis of Torricelli. The experiments took place on 19 September 1648. Pascal repeats the experiments in Paris at the Tour de Saint-Jacques de la Boucherie. Pascal confidently concludes that 'La Nature n'a aucune répugnance pour le vide' – 'Nature has no dislike for the void.'

1648–9 The 'Fronde parlementaire' – the first phase of the civil war.

1648   Some of the nuns move back from Port-Royal de Paris to Port-Royal des Champs.

        March. Pascal writes an essay in Latin concerning the nature of conic sections, which is no longer extant. Leibniz made use of a copy of the manuscript.

July. Etienne Pascal returns to live in Paris, in the Marais. Etienne Pascal discovers that his children have entered into relations with Port-Royal, where they hear the sermons of Antoine Singlin and have talks with Antoine de Rebours. Jacqueline has come to know Mère Angélique and Mère Agnès, and expresses her intention of entering the monastery. Her father and brother oppose her intentions.

October. Pascal publishes the 'Récit de la grande expérience de l'équilibre des liqueurs.'

1649 May. The Fronde breaks out for the second time; the 'Jeune Fronde,' or the 'Fronde des princes,' lasts from 1649 to 1653. Etienne Pascal leaves Paris with his children for Clermont-Ferrand. Pascal works on his mathematical calculator.

1650 November. The Pascal family returns to Paris.

1651 July to August. Pascal publishes two 'Lettres à Monsieur de Ribeyre' to vindicate his claim to the original research on the vacuum. The 'Letters' are filled with asperity. Pascal begins work on a treatise concerning the void, which he will never finish. Fragments will be published after his death.

24 September. Etienne Pascal dies. Jacqueline gives up her part of the inheritance to Blaise; he sets up an allowance for her. For several months Blaise attempts to convince Jacqueline not to enter the convent of Port-Royal.

1652 4 January. Jacqueline Pascal secretly enters Port-Royal. Blaise, sad and lonely, begins his life in society.

April. Pascal demonstrates his mechanical computer – the 'machine arithmétique' – and explains his theory of the vacuum in the salon of Madame d'Aiguillon, one of the influential 'précieuses' of the period. In June Pascal has a copy of the machine sent to Queen Christina of Sweden with an accompanying letter.

October. Pascal travels to Clermont-Ferrand.

1653 May. Pascal returns to Paris. Together with his sister Gilberte he opposes Jacqueline's wish to give her worldly goods to the convent of Port-Royal. The superior, Mère Angélique, is ready to accept the young novice without a dowry, when Pascal suddenly decides upon a compromise. Although generous, Pascal will bear a grudge against Port-Royal for some time to come. Jacqueline takes her vows on 5 June.

Pascal writes 'Sur la Conversion du pécheur' – 'On the Conversion of the Sinner.'

31 May. Pope Innocent X condemns the 'five propositions' believed to be found in Jansen's book *Augustinus* in a bull, thereby initiating the controversy with the Jansenists.

Pascal writes two treatises, 'De l'équilibre des liqueurs' and 'De la pesanteur de la masse d'air,' published posthumously in 1663.

Autumn. Pascal travels through Poitou – Poitiers, Oiron, Fontenay-le-Comte – with the duc de Roannez, the chevalier de Méré, and Damien Mitton, his closest friends, but also self-avowed religious skeptics. Gilberte records later in her biography that her brother at this time took on the airs and graces of the Court so perfectly that one would have thought that 'he had been nourished there all his life.' Pascal makes some lucrative business deals. His so-called 'worldly period' does not last long.

1654   Pascal writes the 'Traité du triangle arithmétique,' published posthumously in 1665, and 'L'Adresse à l'Académie parisienne de mathématiques.' Thanks to Leibniz a copy of this address was preserved. In the 'Address to the Parisian Academy of Mathematicians' Pascal exuberantly announced the imminent invention of a '*géométrie de hasard*' – 'a geometry of probability.'

September. Pascal is overtaken by a great distaste for society and the worldly life. He confides his feelings to his younger sister, Jacqueline. He moves from the Beaubourg to live in the Faubourg Saint-Michel.

23 November. Pascal has a mystical experience which he records in his 'Mémorial.'

1655   7–21 January. Pascal makes a retreat at Port-Royal des Champs. He has a conversation with Monsieur de Saci, one of the spiritual directors. Pascal still remains in society; he converts his closest friend, the duc de Roannez, to the rationality of belief in the Christian God.

1656   23 January. The first of the *Provincial Letters* appears. The other letters appear every fortnight or every month until January 1657, then from 24 March to 1 June 1657. On 6 September the *Provincial*

Letters are placed on the *Index Librorum*, the index of forbidden books.

24 March. The miracle of the Holy Thorn occurs at Port-Royal in Paris. The recipient of the miracle is Pascal's own niece.

August to September. Pascal writes a series of spiritual letters to Charlotte de Roannez, his friend's sister. He is working on his *Apology for the Christian Religion*, the notes for which will subsequently be published as the *Pensées*.

1657   Pascal helps edit the *Factums des Curés de Paris* (December 1657–July 1658) – an exposé of the moral practices of the Parisian clergy. The work heightens the conflict between the Jesuits and the Jansenists, and results in the condemnation of the *Apologie pour les casuistes* – 'Apology for the casuists' – in which Father Picot had attempted to defend the practices of the Jesuits and other casuists. Pascal writes his 'Ecrits sur la grâce,' which will not be published until 1779, and the 'Eléments de géométrie,' which was intended for the pupils of Port-Royal; the latter work is no longer extant.

1658   June to July. 'Première lettre circulaire relative à la cycloïde.' Pascal defies the mathematicians of Europe to give a solution to the problem of the cycloid. Carcavy, Sluse, Wallis, Huyghens, and Father Lalouère enter the competition. Pascal writes 'De l'esprit géométrique et de l'art de persuader.' Sometime during October or November Pascal presents his plan for the *Apology* at Port-Royal des Champs.

1659   February. Carcavy writes to Huyghens that the illness from which Pascal has long been suffering has become even more serious. The letter recounts that Pascal has fallen into a state of total prostration. Witnesses recount that Pascal has almost totally given up his work.

1660   May to September. Pascal stays with his sister Gilberte at Bien-Assis, near Clermont-Ferrand. His life in Auvergne is as austere as it was in Paris. He shows great concern for the poor. It is probable that he writes the 'Prayer to Ask God for the Right Use of Sickness' during this period, and three 'Discourses on the Condition of the High Nobility.'

1661   1 February. The Assembly of the Clergy demand that all priests and religions sign the oath of March 1657 condemning Cornelius Jansen, bishop of Ypres, and by implication Jansenism and the religious currents of Port-Royal. The Counsel of State confirms the condemnation under the direct order of Louis XIV. The teaching capacities of Port-Royal are laid under interdiction and dismantled. The convent is forbidden to admit any new novices. Father Arnauld and his colleagues succeed in obtaining on 8 June a mandate from the vicar-general that allows for the distinction *de juris* and *de facto* in regard to the 'five propositions' held to be found in Jansen's work *Augustinus*. The 'five propositions' are held to be heretical, but are not to be found in the work. The mandate is annulled in July.

4 October. Jacqueline Pascal dies. The division between claims of conscience and the oath of obedience to her religious superiors had greatly affected her.

31 October. A new mandate is obtained which makes it obligatory to sign the oath without any distinction between *de juris* and *de facto*. Mère Angélique signs, but others refuse. Pascal writes 'Ecrit de la signature' – 'Concerning Signing the Oath.' Port-Royal opposes Pascal's views. Pascal totally withdraws from the controversy. Mère Angélique dies shortly after signing the oath.

1662   January. Pascal obtains a patent for his *'carrosses à cinq sous,'* his idea for setting up a vehicle for public transport. The first Parisian omnibus is inaugurated on 18 March.

29 June. Pascal has himself moved to his sister Gilberte's house in the parish of Saint-Etienne-du-Mont. On 4 July he makes his confession to the parish priest, Father Beurrier, and see several times the confessor of Port-Royal, Sainte-Marthe, who is living in seclusion. On 3 August Pascal makes his last will and testament and receives Extreme Unction on 17 August.

19 August. At one in the morning, Pascal dies.

1664   Persecution of Jansenism until the Church grants a *Pax Ecclesiae* in 1668.

1709   Under orders of Louis XIV – 'I shall run the plough through Port-Royal!' – the convent, church, and other buildings of Port-Royal (excepting the dovecot) are totally destroyed and the building materials are sold and removed. Even the nuns' cemetery is dug up and their remains exhumed.

NOTES

Introduction

1 Jacques Chevalier, *Pascal*, p. 14.
2 Emile Bréhier, *Histoire de la Philosophie*, tome III, 1ère partie, p. 129.
3 James Collins, *Interpreting Modern Philosophy*, Princeton University Press, 1972, pp. 242–3.
4 *A King's Lessons in Statecraft: Louis XIV. Letters to his Heirs*, ed. J. Longnon, trans. Herbert Wilson. London, 1924, 149.
5 Louis XIV's best-remembered confessor was Father LaChaise.
6 Cf. *Pensées*, 'Sur le pape.'
7 '*Libertin*' in seventeenth-century French meant simply a 'free-thinker.' The term did not acquire the connotations of lasciviousness or moral turpitude until the eighteenth century.
8 'Il a des vices qui ne tiennent à nous que par d'autres, et qui, en ôtant le tronc, s'emportent comme des branches' (140).
9 'L'homme n'est qu'un roseau, le plus faible de la nature; mais c'est un roseau pensant' (264).
10 'On croit toucher des orgues ordinaires, en touchant l'homme. Ce sont des orgues, à la vérité, mais bizarres, changeantes, variables, [dont les tuyaux ne se suivent pas par degrés conjoints.] Ceux qui ne savent toucher que les ordinaires ne feraient pas d'accords sur celles-là. If faut savoir où sont les [touches.]'
11 'Car il ne faut pas se méconnaître: nous sommes automate sautant qu'esprit; et de là vient que l'instrument par lequel la persuasion se fait n'est pas la seule démonstration. Combien y a-t-il peu de choses démontrées. Les preuves ne convainquent que l'esprit' (470).
12 'Prorsus credibile est, quia ineptum est.'
13 'Certum est, quia impossible est.'
14 Aristotle, *Rhetoric*, book 2, chap. 23, sec. 22.
15 *Ibid.*
16 Pascal's *Pensées*, Everyman's Library, ed. by Ernest Rhys. London, Dent; New York, Dutton, 1931.

17 'Quelle chimère est-ce donc que l'homme? Quelle nouveauté, quel
monstre, quel chaos, quel sujet de contradiction, quel prodige! Juge de
toutes choses, imbécile ver de terre; dépositaire du vrai, cloaque d'incer-
titude et d'erreur; gloire et rebut de l'univers.'
'Qui démêlera cet embrouillement?' (258).

Part One

1 One can date Pascal's emphasis upon the role of the Virgin from this date,
an emphasis that he would later underline in 'L'Abrégé de la vie de Jésus'
and in 'Le Mystère de Jésus.'

Part Two, Section I

1 *De Rerum Natura*, book I, 1. 101.
2 Book I, c. xv.

Part Two, Section II

1 1548–1617.
2 *Regulae ad directionem ingenii.*
3 On *'libertin'* see no 7, p.214 above.
4 John 11:33. Reflexive in Vulgate Latin.
5 Matthew 26:38.
6 Matthew 26:41.
7 Matthew 26:46.
8 Horace, *Ep.*, I, 2. V. 26.
9 'Eritis sicut dii scientes bonum et malum,' Genesis 3:5.
10 All preceding, 736.

Conclusion

1 Christopher Dawson, 'Christianity and the New Age,' in *Essays in
Order*, 1931, p. 66.
2 Galileo, *Mathematical Collections and Translations*, trans. Thomas
Salusbury, 1661, 37.
3 Letter to Père Noël, cited by Brunschvicg in his edition of the *Pensées*, II,
131.
4 *Textes inédits*, ed. G. Grua, II, 553–5.
5 *Pensées*, 420.
6 The Sermon on the Mount, Matthew 5:4–10.

BIBLIOGRAPHY

Baird, Alexander William Stewart. *Studies in Pascal's Ethics.* The Hague: M. Nijhoff, 1975.

Béguin, Albert. *Pascal par lui-même.* Paris: Editions du Seuil, 1952.

Berliet, Julie. *Les Amis oubliés de Port-Royal.* Paris: Dorbon-Ainé, 1921.

Bishop, Morris. *Pascal, the Life of Genius.* London: Bell, 1937.

Boutroux, Emile. *Pascal.* Paris: Hachette, 1912.

Brunschvicg, Léon. *Descartes et Pascal, lecteurs de Montaigne.* New York: Brentano's, 1944; reprinted, Neuchatel: Baconniere, 1945.

Cailliet, Emile. *The Clue to Pascal.* London: SCM Press, 1944.

Carré, Jean Raoul. *Réflexions sur l'anti-Pascal de Voltaire.* Paris: Librairie Félix Alcan, 1935.

Chamaillard, Edmond. *Pascal, mondaine et amoureux.* Paris: Presses Universitaires de France, 1923.

Chevalier, Jacques. *Pascal.* Paris: Plon-Nourrit, 1922.

Clark, William Robinson. *Pascal and the Port Royalists.* New York: Scribner's, 1902.

Collet, François. *Fait inédit de la vie de Pascal.* Paris: Joubert, 1848.

Cousin, Victor. *Jacqueline Pascal.* Premières études sur les femmes illustres et la société du XVII e siècle. Paris: Didier, 1862.

Daniel-Rops, Henry. *Pascal et notre coeur.* Strasbourg: F. X. Le Roux, 1949.

Davidson, Hugh McCullough. *The Origins of Certainty: Means and Meaning in Pascal's Pensées.* Chicago: University of Chicago Press, 1979.

Delacour, André. *Pascal et notre temps.* Paris: Messein, 1933.

Demorest, Jean Jacques. *Dans Pascal: essai en partant de son style.* Paris: Editions de Minuit, 1953.

Dieux, Marie-André. *Pascal mis au service de ceux qui cherchent.* Paris: Librairie Bloud et Gay, 1927.

Dorival, Bernard. *Album Pascal.* Paris: Gallimard, Bibliothèque de la Pléiade. 1978.

Duclaux, Mme Agnes Mary Frances. *Portrait of Pascal.* New York: Harper, 1927.

Eastwood, Dorothy Margaret. *The Revival of Pascal: A Study of His*

Relation to Modern French Thought. Oxford: Clarendon Press, 1936.

Filleau de La Chaise, Jean. *Discours sur les Pensées de Monsieur Pascal*. Paris: Chez Guillaume Desprez, 1672; reprinted Editions Bossard, 1922.

Finch David. *La Critique philosophique de Pascal au XVIII ͤ siècle*. Philadelphia: University of Pennsylvania Press, 1940.

Flottes, Jean Baptiste Marcel. *Etudes sur Pascal*. Montpellier: F. Séguin, 1846.

Gazier, Cécile. *Histoire du Monastère de Port-Royal*. Paris, Perrin, 1929.

Gazier, Cécile. *Port-Royal des Champs. Notice historique à l'usage des visiteurs*. Paris: Typographie Plon-Nourrit, 1920.

Giraud, Victor. *La Vie héroique de Blaise Pascal*. Paris: Crès, 1923.

Hallays, André. *Le Pèlerinage de Port-Royal*. Paris: Perrin, 1923.

Hallays, André. *Les Solitaires de Port-Royal*. Paris: Plon, 1927.

Harrington, Thomas More. *Pascal philosophe: une étude unitaire de la pensée de Pascal*. Paris: Société d'édition d'enseignement supérieur, 1982.

Harrington, Thomas More. *Vérité et méthode dans les 'Pensées' de Pascal*. Paris: J. Vrin, 1972.

Humbert, Pierre. *Cert effrayant génie . . . l'oeuvre scientifique de Blaise Pascal*. Paris: Michel, 1947.

LaFuma, Louis. *Recherches pascaliennes*. Paris: Delmar, 1949.

LaFuma, Louis. *Trois pensées inédites de Pascal*. Paris: Editions litteraires de France, 1945.

Le Guern, Michel. *L'Image dans l'oeuvre de Pascal*. Paris: A. Colin, 1969.

Lhermet, Jean. *Pascal et la Bible*. Paris: Librairie Philosophique J. Vrin, 1931.

Madelin, Louis. *La Fronde*. Conférences prononcées à la Societé des Conférences en 1931. Paris: Plon, 1931.

Maire, Albert. *Bibliographie générale des oeuvres de Blaise Pascal*. Paris: Giraud-Badin, 1925–7.

Mauriac, François. *Blaise Pascal et sa soeur Jacqueline*. Paris: Hachette, 1931.

Mesnard, Jean. *Pascal, l'homme et l'oeuvre*. Paris: Boivin, 1951.

Molinard, Patrice. *Port-Royal des Champs*. Paris: Editions Sun, 1949.

Pascal, Blaise. *Blaise Pascal. Pensées*. Ed. Zacharie Tourneur. Paris: Editions de Cluny, 1938.

Pascal, Blaise. *Greater Shorter Works of Pascal*. Trans. Emile Cailliet and John C. Blankenagel. Philadelphia: Westminster Press, 1948.

Pascal, Blaise. *Les Lettres de Blaise Pascal*. Paris: G. Grès, 1922.

Pascal, Blaise. *Les Pages immortelles de Pascal*. Ed. François Mauriac. New York: Editions de la Maison Française, 1941.

Pascal, Blaise. *Les Provinciales, ou Les Lettres écrit par Louis de Montalte*. Cologne: Chez Pierre de la Vallée, 1657.

Pascal Blaise. *Les Provinciales, or, the mysterie of Jesuitisme discovered in certaine Letters, Written upon occasion of the present differences of Sorbonne, between the Jansenists and the Molinists from January 1657 to March 1657 . . .* London: J. G., 1657, reprinted 1658.

Pascal, Blaise. *The Living Thoughts of Pascal.* Ed. François Mauriac. New York: Longmans, 1940.

Pascal, Blaise. *L'Oeuvre de Pascal.* Ed. Jacques Chevalier. Paris: Editions de la Nouvelle Revue Française, 1950.

Pascal, Blaise. *The Miscellaneous Writings of Pascal.* Trans. M. P. Faugère. Ed. George Pearce. London: Brown, Green, and Longmans, 1849.

Pascal, Blaise. *Monsaieur Pascall's Thoughts, Meditations, and Prayers, Touching Matters Moral and Divine, as they were found in his papers after his death.* Trans. Joseph Walker. London: Judge's Head, 1688.

Pascal, Blaise. *Oeuvres de Blaise Pascal.* Ed. Léon Brunschvicg and Pierre Boutroux. 10th edn. Paris: Hachette, 1908–23.

Pascal, Blaise. *Oeuvres Complètes.* Paris: Gallimard, Bibliothèque de la Pléiade, 1978.

Pascal, Blaise. *Original des Pensées de Pascal.* Ed. Léon Brunschvicg. Paris: Hachette, 1905.

Pascal, Blaise. *Pascal.* Ed. Marcel Arland. Paris: Editions à L'Enfant Poète, 1946.

Pascal, Blaise. *Pascal. Pensées.* Ed. Victor Giraud. Paris: Rombaldi, 1935.

Pascal, Blaise. *Pascal. Pensées.* Introduction by Robert Garric. Paris: Hachette, 1950.

Pascal, Blaise. *Pensées.* London: Dent; New York: Dutton, 1931.

Pascal, Blaise. *Pensées.* Trans. W. F. Trotter. *The Provincial Letters.* Trans. Thomas M'Crie. New York; Modern Library, 1941.

Pascal, Blaise. *Pensées de Monsieur Pascal sur la religion et sur quelques autres sujects.* Paris: Chez Guillaume Desprez, 1670, reprinted, 1702; Amsterdam: Chez Henri Wetstein, 1709; Par La Compagnie, 1766; Paris: Garnier Frères, 1918.

Pascal, Blaise. *Pensées de Pascal.* Ed. Ernest Havet. Paris: Delagrave, 1918.

Pascal, Blaise. *Pensées de Pascal.* Ed. Henri Massis. Paris: Grasset, 1935.

Pascal, Blaise. *Pensées, fragments et lettres de Blaise Pascal.* Ed. Prosper Faugère. Paris: Andrieux, 1844.

Pascal, Blaise. *Pensées sur la religion, et sur quelques autres sujets.* Paris: Editions du Luxembourg, 1952.

Pascal, Blaise. *The Physical Treatises of Pascal: the Equilibrium of Liquids and the Weights of the Mass and the Air.* Trans. I. H. B. and A. G. H. Spiers. New York: Columbia University Press, 1937.

Pascal, Blaise. *The Provincial Letters.* Trans. with an introduction by A. J. Krailsheimer. Baltimore: Penguin, 1967.

Pascal, Blaise. *The Thoughts, Letters and Opuscules of Blaise Pascal.* Trans.

O. W. Wight. New York: Hurd and Houghton, 1859.

Racine, Jean Baptiste. *Abrégé de l'histoire de Port-Royal*. Paris: Le Musée du Livre, 1926.

Raymond, Georges-Marie. *Eloge de Blaise Pascal, accompagné aux Notes historiques et critiques*. Lyon: M. P. Rusand, 1816.

Sainte-Beuve, Charles Augustin. *Port-Royal*. Paris: Hachette, 1922.

St Cyres, Viscount. *Pascal*. London: John Murray, 1909.

Soreau, Edmond. *Pascal*. Paris: Société Française d'Editions Littéraires et Techniques, 1934.

Steinmaan, Jean. *Pascal*. Paris: Editions du Cerf, 1954.

Stewart, Hugh Fraser. *The Secret of Pascal*. Cambridge: Cambridge University Press, 1941.

Strowski, Fortunat Joseph. *Histoire du sentiment religieux en France au XVIIe siècle: Pascal et son temps*. Paris: Plon, 1921–2.

Suarès, André. *Puissances de Pascal*. Paris: Chez Emile-Paul Frères, 1923.

Truc, Gonzague. *Pascal, son temps et le nôtre*. Paris: Michel, 1949.

Vinet, Alexandre Rodolphe. *Etudes sur Blaise Pascal*. Lausanne: Payot, 1936.

Wednesday Afternoon Club, New York. *The Wednesday Afternoon Club*. New York: Knickerbocker Press, 1927.

INDEX

INDEX

INDEX

Condorcet, Antoine, marquis de, 19, 146
Constantine, 7
Copernicus, 12, 165
Corneille, Pierre, 14
Cornet, Nicolas, 101
Counter-Reformation, 199
Cournon, 27
Cousin, Victor, 63
Crusades, 27
cycloid, 20, 41, 42, 83, 130

Dante, 141, 184f
Dawson, Christopher, 198
Democritus, 39
Descartes, René, 1, 10, 12, 14, 19, 26, 29, 52, 75, 80, 145, 147, 150, 153f, 159, 162, 167f, 180, 182, 200f
Dettonville, Amos, 42
Dionysius the Areopagite, see Pseudo-Areopagite
Diderot, Denis, 146
Donatism, 95f
Ducas, A., 64
Duvergier de Hauronne, Jean, see Saint-Cyran

Eliot, T.S., 15, 17, 159; Four Quartets, 15
enthymene, 16
epanalepsis, 13
epanastrophe, 13
Epictetus, 68–70
Epicureans, 39
L'Ermite, Pierre, 27
Escobar, Antonio y Mendoza, SJ, 115–22 passim
Euclid, 25, 31, 32, 39

Fermat, Pierre de, 83
'Five Propositions,' 82, 102ff
Fontenelle, Bernard, 11, 12, 203
'Formulaire,' 82, 84
Forton, Jacques, 35
Four Articles, 8
France, 5, 6, 96, 184, 199
Franciscans, 7
Fronde, 6, 9, 19, 61, 97

Galileo Galilei, 12, 128, 201
Gallicanism, 7
Gazier, Augustin, 63
Gibbon, Edward, 132
Giraud, Victor, 64
Gomberville, 131
Granges, 10
Grotius, Hugo, 145

Habert, Bishop Isaac, 102
Hals, Franz, 26
'heart, the,' 4, 21, 38, 61, 181–5
Helvétius, 146
Henry III, 27
Henry IV, 9, 97f
Henry of Navarre, see Henry IV
heresies, 4, 8, 16
Hobbes, Thomas, 12, 157, 161
Holy Thorn, 20, 39, 50, 77, 82, 137
Homer, 184
'honnête homme,' 87, 112
Huguenots, 8, 85, 97
Hume, David, 132
Huyghens, Christian, 83

Immaculate Conception, 52
Incarnation, 16–17
Innocent X, Pope, 7, 8, 78, 82, 84, 104, 117
Inquisition, 82
Isaac, 179
Isaiah, 2

Jansen, Cornelius (Jansenius), 9, 36, 56, 88, 97ff; Augustinus, 56
Jansenism, Jansenist, 5, 8, 9, 10, 18, 20, 35, 36, 56, 57, 59, 82, 96ff, 190f
Jansenius, see Jansen, Cornelius
Jesuits, see Society of Jesus
Jesus Christ, 16, 35, 55, 57, 79, 84, 87, 106–33 passim, 185, 186–93, 194ff
Judaism, 168f
justice, 86ff
Justin Martyr, 143

Kant, Immanuel, 2, 44, 45

La Fontaine, Jean de, 111